Harsh Punishment

HARSH PUNISHMENT

International Experiences of
Women's Imprisonment

EDITED BY

Sandy Cook and Susanne Davies

Northeastern University Press
BOSTON

Northeastern University Press

Library of Congress Cataloging-in-Publication Data
Harsh punishment : international experiences of women's imprisonment /
edited by Sandy Cook and Susanne Davies.
p.   cm. — (The Northeastern series on gender, crime, and law)
Includes bibliographical references and index.
ISBN 1-55553-412-0 (cloth : alk. paper). — ISBN 1-55553-411-2 (pbk. : alk. paper)
1. Reformatories for women.   2. Women prisoners.   I. Cook, Sandy.
II. Davies, Susanne, 1962- .   III. Series.
HV8738.H37   2000
365'.43—dc21   99-31173

Designed and composed by inari in Bloomington, Indiana.

Printed and bound by Maple Press in York, Pennsylvania. The paper is Sebago Antique Cream,
an acid-free sheet.

Manufactured in the United States of America

03 02 01 00 99   5 4 3 2 1

This book is dedicated
to the memory of those women
who have died shortly after
leaving prisons in Victoria, Australia.

CONTENTS

Current Issues in Women's Imprisonment

ACKNOWLEDGMENTS

There are a number of people who have contributed to the production of this volume to whom we owe our thanks. In particular, we are grateful to Mignon Turpin and Jean Crowther for their encouragement and tireless efforts in providing technical and administrative assistance. We are also thankful to Cherry Grimwade who provided research assistance in the earliest stages of the project and to John Albanis who undertook essential library work toward its conclusion.

We are indebted also to the members of Somebody's Daughter Theatre Company who, through their performances, motivated us to commence this project. Community workers from various agencies have offered their support and generously shared their knowledge of women's imprisonment with us. In recognition of their contribution, all royalties from the sale of this book are being donated to Flat Out, a Melbourne-based accommodation agency that offers support to women prisoners post-release.

We would like to acknowledge the support of the School of Law and Legal Studies at La Trobe University, where we work, and, in particular, the efforts of Professor Margaret Thornton, who has constantly encouraged us and provided invaluable professional advice.

Special thanks to Claire Renzetti for her helpful suggestions and for encouraging us to pursue this project. Finally, we owe much to the publication team at Northeastern University Press, especially William Frohlich, and Emily McKeigue. Their professionalism, the support they have provided to us as editors, and their commitment to this project have been quite remarkable.

Harsh Punishment

Will Anyone Ever Listen?
An Introductory Note

Sandy Cook and Susanne Davies

THIS IS AN EXTRACT OF A LETTER we received recently from an international funding body. It was written in response to a request we had made for financial assistance to continue a large-scale research project investigating the post-release mortality of women prisoners in Victoria and, more broadly, the health and welfare needs of women both during and after imprisonment.

> Thank you for your letter. . . . We were interested to learn about your research project, "Women, Health and Imprisonment: Pre and Post Release Issues." I regret to inform you, however, that [our agency] is unable to support this effort with a grant. Program focus, limited budget, and an increasing number of requests make it impossible for us to respond positively to all of the worthy requests we receive. . . . Please understand that our inability to provide support is not a reflection on the merits of your work but rather on our specific criteria. We receive proposals at the rate of six a day, and our limited budget necessitates that we make some very difficult decisions.[1]

Over the past year, we have received many such letters. Although being awarded an initial grant from a state government health promotion agency to commence this research,[2] our subsequent attempts to secure financial support had—until very recently—proven unsuccessful. For more than eighteen months, we applied to academic funding bodies in Australia and to local and international agencies, both public and private. Despite general expressions of support for the project and favorable assessors' reports, we were consistently informed that the weight of applications received by agencies, together with their limited resources, meant that the research could not be funded.

For those with an interest in women's imprisonment, our experiences will come as no surprise. It has always been difficult to secure support for projects concerning women prisoners, and today, amid cutbacks in funding and ever increasing requests, the situation has only become worse. This is despite the fact that now more women than ever before are being criminalized and imprisoned.

The difficulty involved in securing funding for such research might also point to deeper, nonmaterial issues of concern however. It is important to note, for example, that historically, in both academic circles and in public debate, very little specific attention has been paid to the particular circumstances and experiences of women who transgress the law and are formally punished for it. In the discipline of criminology, for instance, only feminist criminologists have recognized that consideration of gender is crucial if we are to develop meaningful understandings of crime and criminal justice processes. Since criminology's disciplinary emergence over a century ago, its spotlight has remained tightly focused on male offenders, their experiences, and their treatment. In the field of penology, which is dedicated to the study of legal punishments, women have similarly remained hidden in the shadows. With the exception of feminist contributions to this area, women's imprisonment has rarely been recognized as a subject deserving study in its right. Even the radical theorizations of punishment that have emerged in recent decades have failed to acknowledge the significance of gender. As Adrian Howe has commented:

> [F]or all the advances made, the new critical perspectives on punishment remain deeply flawed in a significant, but as yet barely acknowledged way—they are, with very few exceptions, profoundly masculinist. The problem is not simply that the new theorizations of punishment ignore women or treat them as footnotes to the main

event—the punishment of men; they also overlook the question of gender, or better still, the deeply sexed nature of punishment regimes and, by extension, their own analytical frameworks.[3]

Inattention to women and to the broader dynamics of gender have also traditionally characterized correctional systems. The fact that women have always been vastly outnumbered by men in prison populations has resulted in women prisoners being neglected and denied many of the facilities and opportunities afforded to their male counterparts. Moreover, within and beyond correctional systems, the continued dominance of conventional notions concerning women and women's criminality have operated to ensure that women prisoners remain subject to a unique and highly punitive form of condemnation. In the eyes of many, women prisoners are not only guilty of transgressing man-made laws; they are also guilty of transgressing the laws of nature that supposedly constitute women as passive, nurturing beings. In criminological textbooks, as in the mass media, women offenders and prisoners are commonly portrayed as more dangerous, wayward, and irreclaimable than their male counterparts, and therefore as best forgotten.

Out of sight, out of mind thus aptly describes the position of the increasing numbers of women who are imprisoned throughout the world today. Physically locked away from the societies to which they belong, they are subject to harsh punishment. They are rarely thought of and, more rarely still, are they allowed to speak or be heard. The voices of prisoners, especially women prisoners, are notably absent from public and academic discourses about imprisonment, even though it is they who know best what it means to be imprisoned. One of our aims in producing this book has been to try to at least partly redress this absence by creating a space for women to write of their experiences of criminalization and imprisonment. That is why this book begins with the personal accounts of women who either have been or are currently imprisoned. The contributions of Lauren Shanahan, Marcia Bunney, Elizabeth Morgan, and Helen Barnacle shed light on women's imprisonment in the United States and Australia. Each of their accounts is unique; no woman's experience of imprisonment is ever identical to another's. Yet collectively their stories point to a range of issues that, to varying extents, touch the lives of most women in prison. These include the impact of the "war on drugs" on women, the violence of criminal justice processes and of the prison environment, the effects of separation from family and friends and in particular from children, and the daily struggle for dignity and survival that women wage in prison. Their accounts offer us insights into the many ways in which women's experiences of imprisonment differ from those of men.

As these accounts reveal, women who offend and are imprisoned are not demons in disguise. Why then, we might ask, are they subject to such condemnation, punishment, and neglect? In the chapter entitled "The Sex of Crime and Punishment" we seek to locate women's criminalization and imprisonment in broader historical and social contexts. We argue in this chapter that inequitable social relations between the sexes are mirrored in the production of knowledge about women and their offending, and that each of these inextricably relates to practices, understandings, and experiences of crime and punishment.

In recent decades, the relationship between social inequality, crime, and punishment has manifested itself in the "law-and-order" agendas adopted by the governments of most Western nations. In the third section of this book, the implications of this for women are explored through an examination of current trends in women's imprisonment in the United States, Canada, England, and New Zealand. The contributions of Barbara Owen, Karlene Faith, Pat Carlen, and Allison Morris and Venezia Kingi point to what, in most countries, has been an alarming increase in the rate of women's imprisonment. While the numbers of women imprisoned in Western countries have dramatically increased, the conditions that they endure while in prison have remained unchanged and, in some cases, have deteriorated. The specific female prisoner populations described in these chapters also illustrate the fact that it is those women who are most socially and economically marginalized who constitute the overwhelming majority of imprisoned women.

We had hoped to include in this book more essays on recent developments in other parts of the world, in particular Asia, Eastern Europe, South America, and Africa. Unfortunately, we have not been able to achieve this goal. As we searched for contributors, it became clear to us that while there are few researchers concerned with women's imprisonment in Western nations, there are even fewer in non-Western countries. Those researchers and activists who do pursue such work are also often stretched to the limit; they are forced to address a myriad of urgent concerns with few resources and sometimes in overtly hostile political environments. Gaining contributions from women imprisoned in non-Western countries, we also soon realized, would be near impossible and potentially dangerous for any woman able or willing to speak out. It is difficult enough in Western nations for women prisoners and ex-prisoners to do so.

Nevertheless, we have been able to include contributions concerning recent developments in women's imprisonment in Poland and Thailand. They raise some issues that are similar to those previously identified as noteworthy in Western countries; however, they also raise quite different issues. Monika Platek's contribution, for example, highlights the way in which the number of women in Polish prisons has constantly fluctuated according to changes in political regime. She argues that women have always been the first prisoners to be subjected to experiments in correctional policy, but that despite this, they have remained largely neglected and invisible; their treatment and status mirror the position of women in Polish society generally.

In contrast, Carol Ransley discusses the detention of Burmese women in Thailand as an example of the way in which women who transgress national borders are punished. She highlights how changing economic and political circumstances in Burma have led to increasing numbers of women crossing into Thailand where, if they are discovered, they are detained as illegal immigrants. Their detention, she argues, has largely been ignored by Western commentators but deserves to be understood and theorized as a form of women's imprisonment.

The final section of this book deals with current issues in women's imprisonment. The contributions of Amanda George, Stephanie Bush-Baskette, Evelyn Gilbert, Margaret Shaw, Cherry Grimwade, and ourselves canvass a range of issues, some of which are newly arising and others that are depressingly persistent. The chapters on the privatization of women's prisons in Australia, the gendered impact of the "war on drugs" in the

United States, and Canadian experiences of the ambiguous uses of technology address issues that have relevance far beyond the borders of any one country. All are pivotal to understanding the nature of women's imprisonment at the start of the twenty-first century.

These recently emerged issues also exist within a broader continuum of concerns. The overrepresentation of African American women within United States prisons is part of a longer history of enslavement and is echoed in other countries where indigenous women remain disproportionately represented among those imprisoned. Similarly, the failure of prisons and post-release services to recognize and meet the needs of women after their release from prison reflects a longer tradition of societal and correctional condemnation and neglect. The fact that such issues have received so little academic or public attention in the past has at least partly been due to the difficulties involved in undertaking research into women's imprisonment. In the final chapter of this volume, these difficulties are canvassed. The cutting and channeling of research funds, the privatization of prisons, and the threat of legal action against researchers, are a few of the many factors identified as threatening the possibility of conducting research into women's imprisonment in the future. If this possibility is lost, then it is certain that women prisoners will slip even further from our view.

We hope that this book will foster concern, reflection, and debate, not merely among those who are familiar with women's imprisonment and all it entails, but more importantly, among those who have never contemplated or cared about what it really means. We would like to thank all of those who have contributed to this book. Many of the authors have long experience in raising awareness about women's imprisonment and we are grateful for their efforts and patience. Our special thanks are extended to those prisoners, ex-prisoners, and community workers who have taught us so much about what women's imprisonment means.

NOTES

1. Professional correspondence to the authors dated 28 December 1998. For obvious reasons, we do not wish to identify the funding body concerned.

2. A large VicHealth grant, together with small research grants made by the School of Law and Legal Studies at La Trobe University where we are employed, have allowed us to complete the first two stages of this five-stage project. The William Buckland Foundation, a local philanthropic trust, has recently awarded a grant to enable the completion of the project.

3. Adrian Howe, *Punish and Critique: Towards a Feminist Analysis of Penality* (London: Routledge, 1994), 2.

REFERENCE

Howe, Adrian. *Punish and Critique: Towards a Feminist Analysis of Penalty.* London: Routledge, 1996.

Speaking Out:
Personal Accounts of
Women's
Imprisonment

No Winners Here

Lauren Shanahan

MY EDUCATION in prison protocol and standards came from a man with whom I'd been in a relationship with for a number of years. He had spent many years in the notorious H Division of Pentridge and my views were colored by his experiences. The lessons were fairly succinct and unquestionable: "All screws are maggots," "You never lag on anyone," "Never let anyone stand over you," "Never lay down," "Watch your back." These lessons and more, part of the "prison code," helped to support the "us and them" mentality that was prevalent. These were the thoughts that were foremost in my mind on the prison van journey from the police cells to begin my first "laggin" at the women's prison. These were the things that I repeated to myself as I was escorted into the reception area. This became my reality as I was taken through the procedure of being strip-searched, weighed, measured, having my scars and tattoos listed, photos taken, details noted, and handed my collection of prison issue clothing and bedding that I would use over the next eight months. This was how I walked into the mainstream compound, wary and insolent.

This was the facade that I presented to my new world, proud and not to be fucked with. A bit like the characters portrayed by Gene Wilder and Richard Prior in the movie *Stir Crazy*. A bravado that was false and uncalled for. It didn't take me too long to realize my error. I learnt quickly, by my own observation and the wise advice of a friend, that if you look like you've got a chip on your shoulder you can back it in that there is someone else who has a bigger chip on theirs and is only too happy to remove yours for you. I was fortunate in that the bravado kept others questioning for a number of hours before being "worded up" by my friend that it was deemed more appropriate and certainly a hell of a lot safer to keep your mouth shut, your eyes open and observe, observe, observe. A lesson I was never to forget. Certainly, I was to find myself involved in some minor altercations, where some of the original advice and lessons came into play, but on the whole, I managed to survive my time by keeping to my own crew and doing my own jail.

There are particular cliques between maybe only two to four people, perhaps with six to eight additional women who form a peripheral crowd that comes and goes according to the potential and usefulness of individual members. These crews usually look out for their own and defend each other if attacked or slighted, be it real or imagined. They share what they have with each other and the motto is "all for one and one for all." I'd encountered violence in my own life but the reality of violence perpetrated by women upon other women was a new and often very ugly experience. Even though you may learn to accept it as part of the daily life of an unreal and insular community, I could never come to terms with the ferocity and brutality of some of it.

There was never much physical brutality handed out by the prison officers during my time; theirs was the more subtle and not-so-subtle game of power, mind, and emotions. Many of the women suffered the consequences of these games when children were used as pawns in order to make a woman comply with a particular wish or "order." Visits or phone calls with children, family, or loved ones were often used as a form of threat by officers and administration staff. Certainly, when a woman broke one of the rules or was "under investigation" for an infraction that woman could and would be removed from the mainstream, forcefully, and escorted to solitary confinement. There, away from the watchful eyes of the other women, she could and would be subjected to physical assault by prison officers. Many stories of such events eventually filtered back to the mainstream prison population.

There have been times when I've witnessed a riot or demonstration by the women, usually in response to an unseemly decision or procedure handed down from either an officer or management. Such events have ended with the prison riot squad entering the prison to regain order. These fellows are dressed in padded riot gear, wielding batons and leading German shepherd dogs. The melee that follows is not a pretty sight. I know of many women who still bear the scars, emotionally and physically, of these assaults, including three women who were gassed by prison authorities for refusing to exit a van upon being removed to isolation after a demonstration. Violence is a part of prison culture; however, I believe the approach by prison management and prison officers toward women held in prisons certainly plays a major role in whether that violence escalates and becomes an ongoing part of the culture. The education of prison officers and management toward understanding the reality of these women's emotional and physical histories, and their level of well-being, is an integral part of the changes that need to occur in order for the women to gain insight into their own behaviors and beliefs so they can modify or change them.

One Life in Prison
Perception, Reflection, and Empowerment

Marcia Bunney

> *The art of life is not controlling what happens to us, but* using
> *what happens to us.*
> —Revolution from Within: A Book of Self-Esteem, Gloria Steinem

I AM A PRISONER of the state of California, which currently operates the largest and most costly prison system in the United States, incarcerating more people as a percentage of the general population than any nation in the world.[1] The prison in which I am presently housed, Central California Women's Facility (CCWF), is distinguished as the largest institution in the world to confine female offenders exclusively.

Like hundreds of other women in California's immense prison system (157,529 state prisoners as of May 1, 1998),[2] I am one of 18,165 lifers; individuals sentenced to terms of "x" years to life.[3] Also like many other such women, the underlying dynamic in my commitment offense was domestic violence: I am a battered woman convicted of killing my abuser.

Much has been written regarding the importance of fostering self-esteem in prisoners as part of an effort to correct negative behavior and reduce recidivism. How true this is for women; however, I doubt that experts fully appreciate the difficulty experienced by women prisoners in their attempts to develop a sense of self-worth. This is particularly so for those of us who have lived through the uniquely hellish experience of killing an abusive spouse or lover.

My personal experience of prison may well be singular—not necessarily in the sense of specific things I have seen and felt and done, but in my perception of prison as an alien environment that combined with the need to cope affirmatively within a negative environment and produced an impetus for growth.

The distinguishing feature that separates human beings from all other existing forms of life is the ability to reflect. Education is not the acquisition of information; rather, education is the avenue to the acquisition of the skills needed for reflection.

Once confined in prison, the close proximity of many different personalities challenged my own perceptions, habits, and lifestyle and shook me loose from what was dysfunctional; specifically, the interactive patterns developed and entrenched over my lifetime. Reflective by nature, I found education to be the key to the myriad dilemmas of my life, including the path that led to my incarceration. The education I was able to obtain in prison prompted meaningful insight and gave me a voice that my previous life had denied me: I had felt that I did not have a right to speak and be heard and that any thoughts or feelings I had were not worth voicing at all.

My experience of prison is best defined as a journey through a maze; the evolution of a battered woman from victim to healed individual to peer counselor/activist/journalist. Mine is a story of the critical role of women as a cohesive support entity in adverse circumstances; of finding the courage to take small, determined steps into self-esteem and empowerment; of learning to trust, to allow oneself to be guided and mentored—and of coming full circle to do the same for other women in turn. Above all, it is a story of invaluable lessons in the art of doing time as a constructive and affirmative course of survival.

At the time of my arrest and trial in 1981-1982, the legal community in the United States was quite inconsistent in its handling of criminal cases rooted in domestic violence. The attorney who represented me at trial failed to act on information that should have led him to suspect abuse as a component of my personal history. Given the standard of available knowledge at that time, I should have been evaluated by a professional with expertise in the field of domestic violence. Traumatized as I was by years of abuse and the circumstances of my offense, I was unable to independently articulate the underlying nature of my suffering when questioned by my attorney. This literally sealed my fate.

The psychologists with whom my attorney consulted did examine me, but no one discerned the truth of my situation. I went to trial with a fragmented defense, was convicted of first-degree (premeditated) murder, and sentenced to a term of twenty-five years to life in prison. Each of the psychologists prepared a report for my sentencing hearing; these were unanimous in their grim prediction that my outlook for survival in prison was poor. Indeed, the most encouraging prospect, voiced by one doctor, was that the inescapable and noxious reality of prison life might provide a focal point of sorts, a foundation for "this gravely disturbed and unhappy woman," as he described me, to build upon in order to heal.

I was furnished with copies of all the reports, the contents of which naturally shocked and dismayed me. It would have been equally natural to allow myself to be completely disheartened by such a collection of grim prognoses: The words did not merely sting, they slashed, and deeply. Yet, despite the creeping numbness that was beginning to shadow my days, and would hover for the next three years, I realized that the clinical cruelty of those all-but-hopeless reports did not have to become my destiny. Despite the waves of fear and emotional distress that oddly partnered the numbness, I dimly realized that I had survived an array of horrific circumstances and that if I had been able to endure all that and come away alive then I could survive prison, too.

Thus it was that I entered the California Institution for Women (CIW) in 1982 with no clear understanding of what had occurred or why. I had never broken the law before; I had no criminal record, no history of violent behavior.

The prospect of facing the unknown world of prison would have been daunting enough had I possessed full understanding. In retrospect, it is striking that, lacking any fundamental clue, it nevertheless became my responsibility to find answers to the hows and whys of behavior that was not only uncharacteristic and unlikely but so incomprehensible as to be senseless, given the conduct of my lifetime prior to the offense.

The hows and whys were a mystery but it was evident to me that my life was severely dysfunctional. It remains unclear to me today exactly how I came to the conclusion that the only way for me to salvage the wreck that was my life was to take an objective and honest look at myself, assess the areas in need of change, and somehow effect improvements. All that made sense to me at the time was that I was solely responsible for implementing the nebulous positive changes I envisioned.

In retrospect, it is clear that the very presence of the ability to make such a choice at that early stage was a singularly hopeful sign. At the time, however, I viewed it as the only option I could live with. The idea of allowing myself to fall into the limbo produced by psychotropic medication was repugnant. Equally unsavory was the prospect of yielding to the mindless treadmill of prison mentality and routine, as I saw other women do, and take no steps to better my situation or myself.

It would take six long years for me to recognize and validate the fact and the extent of the abuse I had suffered and begin a conscious course of specific healing. The task would be rendered all the more difficult by the inherently hostile, demeaning, and abusive nature of prison life.

There is much to be said on the subject of confining victimized women in the brutal environment of prison. At the beginning of my incarceration, I was too debilitated to do more than exist, suffering from the physical and emotional effects of jail confinement, in conjunction with the terrible grief and disorientation resulting from the commission of a violent act against the man I loved. The prison system offered no overt help. I was screened, put to work at a menial job, and left to find my own way to cope. The combination of my own emotions and memories, amplified by the bizarre and menacing atmosphere of prison, produced a feeling that I can only describe as "weighted." Thus I functioned, reporting to my job in the garment factory and doing what was expected of me.

The prison routine, which was actually quite simple, puzzled me. Mealtimes were traumatic because I had somehow acquired the notion that prisoners were assigned to specific eating areas and that using the wrong door to the cafeteria would be cause for a disciplinary report. This fear caused me to avoid most meals for my first few days in the main population until I became acquainted with a woman on my housing unit who recognized my plight. She literally led me by the hand to the cafeteria, as one would a small child. For years afterward, we often went to meals together, sometimes hand in hand as a reminder of the way our friendship had begun. From a reflective standpoint, I can see humor as well as pathos in contrasting the meek, apprehensive person I was against the confident and assertive woman I have become. In fact, I use the story when I conduct domestic violence workshops in the prison's substance abuse classes to illustrate the crippling effects wrought by years of abuse.

I have found that women prisoners have widely varied concepts of empowerment. The need to exert some degree of power and control over one's own life, however small, is fundamental to human nature. Making decisions in prison is considered a luxury,[4] and choices that seem trivial to the outsider are important to a prisoner.

For example, during my first year or so in prison it made little sense to me that the cafeteria menu for the week was posted on the bulletin board in the housing unit. Breakfast, lunch, and dinner would be served daily and there was no choice of entrée, so why the concern? Gradually, however, as I made my way through the early stages of adjustment and learned to prepare satisfying meals with items purchased from the canteen, I also began to refer to the menu and base my mealtime activities on my own preferences. I avoided meals I disliked, or stayed in to savor the peace and quiet of a virtually empty building during the all-too-brief interlude when everyone went to eat.

In the same vein, it took some time for me to understand the strata of prison subculture related to food. It amazed me to learn that one of my neighbors on the unit, a lifer with nearly ten years in the system, almost never went to the cafeteria for meals. Instead, she paid another prisoner, a culinary worker, to bring her food at mealtimes; cigarettes and other canteen items served as currency. At first this seemed odd: Why pay someone to bring food, when one could simply walk over to the cafeteria and eat? As I continued to observe, however, I saw that my neighbor was not eating the typical prison meals: Her "food girl" cooked special dishes for her, brought fresh fruits and vegetables, and obtained a steady supply of little luxuries such as butter, ham, and seasonings.

Eventually, my own concept of what constituted an appropriate meal regimen was dramatically altered. As the prison population increased and the facility became desperately overcrowded, the press of people in the dining area became unbearable. The quality of food preparation and service deteriorated noticeably. The crowding and noise made me extremely anxious to the extent that I had trouble keeping my food down; frequently upon returning to the housing unit after a meal I would vomit. Digestive disturbances became more common among the women, and there were documented instances of food poisoning. I acquired the services of a food girl, and combined kitchen supplies with my canteen purchases to create dishes that were tastier, more nourishing, and certainly prepared in a more sanitary fashion than those available en masse. So great did my distaste for group meals become that I literally did not enter the cafeteria building for five years. Even now, I seldom take my meals in the dining area, subsisting on canteen purchases and limited food items obtained in packages from home, primarily nuts and dried fruit.

Many women choose to seize some small degree of power and control by taking food from the dining room at mealtimes. The rule is that only certain items—usually whole fruits or packaged cookies—may be taken out. The irony in the situation is that if the food is not eaten then or allowed to be removed for later consumption on the housing unit, it will be discarded. This makes no sense to women who are hungry, both for the food itself and for the fleeting sense of power they derive from the act of thwarting authority.

Similar acts of self-assertion may be seen in every aspect of prison life. Women who shoplift, deal drugs, or forge checks on the outside often do so for the sheer thrill of committing acts that are defined by society, through the penal code, as wrong. Although my own level of powerlessness upon entering prison was extreme, the idea of theft or other misconduct as a means to feel somehow better about myself has consistently lacked any logical appeal whatsoever.

One of my earliest distinguishable steps to self-esteem was initiated by the concern of another prisoner, my section's lead worker in the sewing factory. She told me one day that she had been watching me, that she knew I had a long sentence, and that I would probably "nut up" (go insane) if I didn't find something constructive and interesting to do. She then offered to teach me to crochet, a skill I had attempted to learn years before without success. My initial impulse, wary of the potential for frustration, humiliation, and failure, was to refuse. The genuine kindness of her suggestion, coupled with my abiding interest in the craft, overcame my lack of self-confidence.

We lived on the same housing unit, and the relaxed attitude of our guards allowed me to visit her living quarters often for crocheting lessons. My early efforts, in retrospect, reveal much about my state of mind. I was so tense and nervous that the foundational row of stitches was too tight to allow reinsertion of the hook, rendering it impossible to construct anything. I ripped out untold thousands of stitches before I learned to relax enough to produce an acceptable length of chain stitches. Over time, the act of controlling the size of my stitches became a way to induce relaxation, much like meditation.

Progress was slow, beginning projects very simple. Gradually, I began to laugh rather than cry or become frustrated by my mistakes. I found that it wasn't humiliating, after all, to redo my work—just pull out the stitches and start anew. I began to realize that I was appreciating the process itself, rather than focusing primarily on the end result. Years later, I came to understand that what had taken place was a form of occupational therapy—which I, too, would use in efforts to ease the adjustment of other women to prison life.

As my skill level grew, so did my confidence and self-esteem—and my ambition. Eager to try new things, I sent away for pattern books, stitch encyclopedias, and new types of yarn. I began to make gifts to send home to my family, slippers and other homely items. The hobby shop manager praised my work and expressed an interest in placing certain items in the prison's crafts showcases to be offered for sale. This small income, along with my earnings from the factory, enabled me to be financially independent, another critical element in the development of self-esteem.

The items I made as gifts acquired a special significance when a member of my family was expecting her first child. It is common among women prisoners to experience strong feelings of guilt connected to our abandonment of our loved ones through the commission of criminal acts and the imposition of isolation via incarceration as punishment. Unable to be with my family during this important time, the only meaningful thing I could think of to do was create an abundant collection of garments and blankets for the new baby.

At this time, another woman on the unit stepped in as a mentor. She had tried for some time to instruct me in knitting and had even persuaded me to purchase knitting needles. I was convinced that my success with crochet was merely luck, that knitting was much too complicated, that I could never manage to control two needles at once—my array of excuses was impressive, but she persisted. When I mentioned that I was crocheting baby clothes for a relative, she told me, "That's it! No more excuses! There's no better reason to learn to knit than a new baby in the family. Go and get those needles and some yarn—we will start right now."

My friend was right, of course. She coached me carefully, and when I was comfortable with the basics, we embarked upon simple projects. This time, I took more risks in trying new techniques, and had fun doing so. My first baby sweater was a laughable thing, meant as an experiment only—but my family insisted that I send it along with everything else. Much to my delight, the baby wore it often until it was finally outgrown, and it is now carefully packed away with the rest of her little clothes, an amusing heirloom.

I continued to make sweaters and such for several years, until my circumstances changed and it was no longer practical for me to indulge in what had become a virtual obsession for needlework. Fortunately, I had had the foresight to make some items to be put away for future use, and these were only recently outgrown. Every stitch—how many millions, I wonder?—has forged a very special bond.

Haunted by the pervasive negativity of prison, it was difficult for me to independently identify any positive qualities I possessed. The initial breakthrough with needlework was therefore typical of the steps involved in my course of healing. The concern shown by other women, who were people of kindness, intelligence, and hard-won wisdom, began to make inroads in the perceptions and attitudes that had crippled and nearly destroyed my ability to function. Through their efforts, I was shepherded to others, including prison staff, who were committed to making a difference in the lives of women prisoners.

So it was that three years into my sentence, through the encouragement of peer mentors, I found myself applying for a position in the office of the head of the education department. I possessed strong clerical skills, which I had used to support myself prior to incarceration, and I welcomed the opportunity to use them. What my mentors did not tell me was that the work was not particularly demanding and I would have the time—and the support of my new supervisor—to participate in college courses.

Difficult experiences at school during my childhood and adolescence had left me with memories of loathing conventional education and everything connected with it. I was skeptical of the idea of returning to school, certain that college was beyond my ability, ready to give up before I had given myself a chance to start. Fortunately, my supervisor was wise and knew exactly how to deal with me: College classes, he informed me, were part of my job, and I had a reputation as an excellent worker.

I can still feel the fear and its physical manifestations as I experienced them the afternoon I walked into my first class, a course in women's studies. My hands shook, I felt nauseated; the urge to run away was nearly overpowering.

Many of the students were people I knew. Aware of my nervousness, a friend beckoned me to a seat next to hers. The professor, a pleasant young man, commenced the lecture with a disarming statement about the novelty of being male and designing a course in "The History of Women in America" for presentation to a class comprised of thirty women prisoners. He expressed his concern that all of us feel at ease and made his feminist perspective absolutely clear. This was a novel experience for me: a man who obviously liked and respected women and was willing to be quite open about it.

When texts for the course were issued, I felt overwhelmed—four or five books for one course!—and fought panic as I tried to imagine assimilating all the information they contained. The verbal abuse I had suffered in relationships played and replayed in my mind, like a continuous tape: "You're never going to get through all that. This class is too advanced for you." I gritted my teeth, opened the books, reviewed my lecture notes, and began to study effectively for the first time in nearly twenty years. The course was designated upper division, normally not within the range of classes open to a new student such as I. The college program coordinator was known to make exceptions when warranted by circumstances, however, and her suggestion that I enroll in that particular course was based upon her assessment of my ability, combined with her appreciation of the effectiveness of academic success as a therapeutic tool.

The semester passed and I lived in dread of examinations. I can easily recall the cold terror of sitting for the first one, the sinking feeling of waiting until the following week to learn my grade—and the joy of passing with top scores, a joy so great that I wept at my desk, not caring who noticed my tears.

Academic success proved to be virtually addictive. I enrolled in two or three classes each term, depending on my anticipated workload in the office. Much of the coursework, and a large proportion of exam questions, required extensive written input; the essay was a favored format. Fortunately, I was already comfortable with written expression, having maintained extensive and regular correspondence with family members and friends. I was articulate in the sense that I demonstrated facile use of descriptive and narrative approaches, which for the most part appeared to satisfy the recipients of my letters.

Composition in conjunction with my coursework was different. My professors challenged me, shaping my ability to analyze and organize information, influencing my style in the process. Courses in English and history were my favorites, and I took great interest in the degree of overlap between the two disciplines. I began to realize that I was not merely acquiring information: I was learning how to think. I remember making an entry to this effect in one of my English course journals; it was a rather wistful observation that if only someone had bothered to explain to me when grade school was such an unpleasant puzzle that my thought processes were being developed, it would have made such a difference in my view, my attitude—and very likely, the course of my life.

I thought relatively little of writing, as such, until we began to produce literary critiques as exercises in an English course. We worked with short stories, selections from our textbook. As I skimmed the various choices for an assignment, one story drew my attention and prompted me to produce an essay that not only earned an excellent grade but also changed my perception of my commitment offense in a way that would have far-reaching consequences. The story, "A Jury of Her Peers," was a tale of a woman driven by verbal and emotional cruelty, and the strangling of her beloved pet canary, to kill her abusive husband.

I spent three years in the college program on a part-time basis, ultimately earning my associate in arts degree. Beyond the specific components of the curriculum, I learned many valuable lessons, the greatest of which was that I was *capable*. After a lifetime of seeing myself as a failure and as inferior, this represented a complete reversal, one that admittedly required effort to accept and absorb.

Other opportunities for personal development and growth followed, enabling me to draw on newfound confidence and strength to move forward.

In 1988 I was approached by another prisoner who asked for my assistance in starting a self-help support group for battered women prisoners. By this time I had gleaned enough information through college courses, independent study, and peer interaction to understand that abuse was the pivotal factor in the dysfunctional patterns of my life. I realized that I had been viciously and relentlessly abused for most of my life prior to my incarceration, and that the offense for which I was tried and convicted very likely had its basis in the battered woman syndrome. I agreed to join the group, sensing that my real healing was about to begin. One of the prison administrators learned of the effort to start the group, and her interest and support were key elements in its implementation. Our proposal was approved by the prison administration, the records of prospective participants were screened, and with thirteen charter members the group held its initial meeting.

As it was with college classes, the battered women's group encouraged awareness and reflection that extended beyond the core curriculum. Once I had begun to understand the mechanics of domestic violence, particularly the role of verbal and emotional abuse, much of what had long puzzled, irritated, distressed, or frightened me in prison began to make sense as well.

In particular, I learned to recognize—and resist—the efforts of others to manipulate and control me. In prison, this is often done through the imposition of labels and role expectations, by staff as well as by other prisoners. This results in a tightly focused microcosm in which each person occupies a behavioral niche. The unwritten and unpardonable sin, in the eyes of those to whom such things matter, is to place oneself outside the boundaries of those expectations, appearing not only to reject the norm but to refuse to accept the fact that one is a prisoner at all. This phenomenon has been addressed in research that posits, among other theories, that the rejection demonstrated by withdrawal from other prisoners and their activities necessarily reflects denial of one's status as a prisoner.[5]

In my own experience, a reflective nature combined with ample privacy during my formative years served to encourage a lifetime habit of solitary pursuits. Faced with the unfamiliar and often bizarre elements of prison life, it was quite natural for me to eschew various activities in favor of those that were familiar to me. To behave *otherwise* was deviant, in the sense of being untrue to my nature; allowing myself to be pressured into leaving my cell, because another person with different habits, values, and preferences deemed it abnormal to spend so much time alone, constituted unnatural behavior.

Recognition and validation of the role of abuse in my life was but a beginning, in more ways than I anticipated. In response to a newspaper article about a domestic violence case, I was moved to submit a letter to the editor. The letter was printed, and I received an award. It occurred to me then that writing could play an important part in my future.

It became obvious to me that refusal to tolerate abuse by prison officials was a central component in my agenda of personal healing and growth. I learned to use the prison grievance system and became skilled enough that other women sought my assistance. Eventually, despite the illegality of such treatment, official retaliation for my use of this skill was a factor in my involuntary transfer to another, reputedly harsher, prison: CCWF.

Ironically, the transfer, instead of breaking my will as intended, provided unanticipated opportunities for outreach and growth. It also strengthened my determination to overcome the system's obstacles and enhance my ability to advocate for positive changes from within.

I obtained a position as an office assistant in the prison library, where I was required to use a computer as part of my duties. It had been more than a decade since I had used a computer, and the technology had advanced tremendously. I was apprehensive, but my supervisors offered encouragement. I focused on the habit of success I had acquired in other endeavors, and gave myself the freedom to experiment.

Working in the library placed me in close proximity to the law collection, which I began to regard with increasing fascination. Women who had known me at CIW, and were aware of my facility with the grievance procedure, began to approach me to ask questions about the law. Untrained and unaware, I usually had to say "I don't know"—and so I decided to learn.

I made the choice to abandon my needlework and commit my time and energy to learning the law, empowering myself and others by virtue of that knowledge. Eventually I was hired to work in the law library. My tenure there fostered additional growth through various projects, including the publication of several articles. I joined the National Lawyers Guild through the organization's Prison Law Project, and in 1994 was elected as one of five prisoner representatives to the project's National Steering Committee. Other work has included the establishment of a group for battered women at CCWF, as well as ongoing domestic violence workshops in the prison's education department as an auxiliary function of the group.

The deplorable quality of medical care in women's prisons has long provided a focal point for my desire to implement positive changes. During the years I spent at CIW many women died of ailments that were readily treatable, such as asthma. Like countless other women, at CIW I endured long lapses in the provision of prescribed medication, experienced difficulty in obtaining timely access to a physician, and resisted surgery for fear of ineptitude and/or the lack of appropriate aftercare.

Upon arriving at CCWF, it was immediately apparent to me that the standard of care was dismal, decidedly inferior to that at CIW. The supply of prescribed medication I had brought with me from CIW, which was processed on my transfer papers and held separately from my boxed personal belongings to facilitate ready access, was summarily confiscated by nonmedical personnel. Weeks elapsed before I could see a doctor in order to initiate a local prescription, weeks during which I suffered excruciating pain and extensive sleep deprivation.

Within a month following my transfer, I initiated contact with an attorney known to have an interest in prison-conditions litigation. Soon I was organizing the active acquisition of information to support claims of systemically inferior medical care, including the names and particulars of prisoners willing to come forward to be interviewed. Word spread rapidly among the women of CCWF that someone on the outside cared, was interested, and wanted to help. The flood of names and medical horror stories grew, and the original attorney enlisted the aid of other professionals to conduct prisoner interviews. With the support of the attorneys involved, I used my involvement in the process to gain knowledge regarding civil litigation. My strong composition skills were an asset, and I grew adept at drafting clear, concise declarations as a means of documenting the serious medical problems of many women, including several who proceeded to file individual actions for damages.

It was fascinating to watch as the collection of statements continued to grow. The women were elated when counsel determined that we had a case that merited litigation as a class action suit. Other attorneys joined as counsel of record, and two large law firms made sizable contributions in terms of pro bono hours. The American Civil Liberties Union agreed to oversee the litigation and provided the services of lead counsel. It was determined that medical care at CIW warranted litigation as well, and attorneys commenced a series of interviews there.

In April 1995, *Shumate v. Wilson,* the class action lawsuit alleging the provision of substandard medical care at both CCWF and CIW, was filed in United States District Court. Within weeks after the filing I was removed from my position in the law library, an action recognized as retaliation, generating strong peer support. I have continued to support the litigation, referring women for interviews. More than six years following initial outreach to counsel, *Shumate* is currently in an assessment phase, pursuant to a settlement agreement signed in late 1997. It is anticipated that the case may go to trial in 1999.

There is, of course, a price to be paid for activism. In addition to the loss of my position in the law library, I have been threatened with transfer and other retribution by prison staff seeking to curb my efforts and retaliate against me for joining the *Shumate* litigation as a named plaintiff. I have even been approached by officers concerned for my well-being, people who have told me that I should stop, that my legal activities will cost me any chance of obtaining a parole date. I have been told that I will never leave prison if I continue to fight the system. My answer is that one must be alive in order to leave prison, and our current standard of medical care is tantamount to a death sentence. Therefore, I have no choice but to continue.

It is difficult for a woman who has suffered abuse to achieve a meaningful degree of insight and healing in the prison environment. Conditions within the institution continually reinvoke memories of violence and oppression, often with devastating results. Unlike other incarcerated battered women who have come forward to reveal their impressions of prison, I do not feel "safer" here because "the abuse has stopped." *It has not stopped.* It has shifted shape and paced itself differently, but it is as insidious and pervasive in prison as ever it was in the world I knew outside these fences. What has ceased is my ignorance of the facts concerning abuse—and my willingness to tolerate it in silence.

The profusion of alarming statistics concerning the prevalence of abuse in the background of female prisoners calls for access to effective therapeutic and educational programs.[6] Incarcerated battered women who are able to participate in comprehensive educational, self-help, and therapeutic programs certainly maximize their ability to overcome the devastating effects of abuse. Additional benefits to be derived from such program opportunities include minimizing negative interaction with other prisoners and enhancing the ability to effect successful reintegration into the community upon release. Ultimately, the provision of comprehensive assistance to women victims of violence should be a priority component of the mission and philosophy statement of every prison system in which women are confined.[7]

NOTES

1. See Mark Koetting and Vincent Schiraldi, *Singapore West: The Incarceration of 200,000 Californians* (San Francisco: Center on Juvenile and Criminal Justice, 1994), 2.

2. Pro-Family Advocates, *Newsletter,* June 1998, 6.

3. Ibid.

4. See Christina Jose-Kampfner, "Coming to Terms with Existential Death: An Analysis of Women's Adaptation to Life in Prison," *Social Justice* 17, no. 2 (1990): 110–25.

5. See Jose-Kampfner, "Coming to Terms," 113–14.

6. Russ Immarigeon and Meda Chesney-Lind, "Women's Prisons: Overcrowded and Overused," (San Francisco: National Council on Crime and Delinquency, 1992), 6, 9.

7. United Nations, *Report of the World Conference on Women,* 1985, paragraph 258 (Quoted in Jane Roberts Chapman, "Violence Against Women as a Violation of Human Rights," *Social Justice* 17, no.2 [1990]: 54–65).

REFERENCES

Immarigeon, Russ, and Meda Chesney-Lind. *Women's Prisons: Overcrowded and Overused.* San Francisco: National Council on Crime and Delinquency, 1992.

Jose-Kampfner, C. "Coming to Terms with Existential Death: An Analysis of Women's Adaptation to Life in Prison." *Social Justice* 17, no. 2 (1990): 110–25.

Koetting, Mark, and Vincent Schiraldi. *Singapore West: The Incarceration of 200,000 Californians.* San Francisco: Center on Juvenile and Criminal Justice, 1994.

Pro-Family Advocates. *Newsletter.* June 1998.

Roberts, Jane Chapman. "Violence Against Women as a Violation of Human Rights." *Social Justice* 17, no. 2 (1990): 54–65.

Steinem, Gloria. *Revolution From Within: A Book of Self-Esteem.* Boston: Little, Brown and Company, 1993.

The Violence of Women's Imprisonment
A View from the Inside

Elizabeth Morgan

Introduction

> *For in thee I shall discomfit an host of men: and with the help
> of my God, I shall leap over the wall.*[1]

THESE WORDS could be the prayer of the incarcerated woman—a search for
God, a yearning for freedom, a terror of men. I write with confidence, having been incarcerated three times, the third time for twenty-five months.
Although jailed, I was never accused of a crime; I was detained indefinitely
for protecting my child from incest. Immediately, the reader may doubt my
credibility. Let me deal with that first.

I am a licensed physician and board-certified plastic and reconstructive surgeon with a number of professional publications. I have a B.A.
magna cum laude in biology from Harvard University; have twice done
research at Oxford University; have an M.D. from Yale University; and for
ten years had a successful solo practice in plastic surgery. I have written scientific and popular articles and books, one of them a best seller. Before
becoming a surgeon I worked as a psychological assistant for my parents,
who were clinical psychologists.

Those who have been incarcerated, as I was, must deal with the
assumption of others that they are ipso facto dishonest, self-serving, and

manipulative. Furthermore, those who have been involved in public litiga-tion, as I have been, have allegations made against them there to which they need to respond.

Background to Imprisonment

My charge was civil disobedience (also known as civil contempt), which is one's refusal to obey a judge's order. It is not a crime but in most U.S. states a judge can jail a noncriminal contemnor indefinitely with none of the rights accorded to criminals, such as a trial, an impartial judge, and a sen-tence. This judicial power in the United States to indefinitely incarcerate the noncriminal derives from that of the British monarchs with respect to political crimes.[2]

My civil contempt arose from my refusing, after more than two years of compliance, to continue to send my daughter on unsupervised visits with her birth father. My refusal was based on my daughter's credible complaints, beginning at age two, that her father was severely sexually abusing her. It was also based on the findings of the experts in the field of abuse who were involved in either or both my daughter's case or the case of the birth father's older daughter, who also at age two began to complain of his sexual abuse.

The cases of the two girls were handled by different judges, in differ-ent jurisdictions, with different results. The older child's unsupervised visits ended in early 1986 on her judge's order when she was five and my daugh-ter was three. At the same time, our judge ordered my daughter's unsuper-vised visits to continue. My civil contempt began shortly after that and put a stop to the unsupervised visits for a year, but they resumed in 1987.

By August 1987, after six months of further unsupervised visits and further severe abuse of my child, our judge would still not protect her so I decided to act. What made me so sure that our judge was wrong?

First, he had excluded what was, to me, obviously relevant evidence: the evidence about the older child including her description of witnessing my child's abuse and much expert evidence about my child, including the abuse findings of the policeman who interviewed her.

Second, the judge seemed illogical. After months of renewed unsuper-vised visits, he ruled that it was equally likely that abuse had and had not occurred during this time. He thereupon ordered the unsupervised visits to continue on the grounds that conditions such as my ability to telephone my preschool daughter "neutralized" the risk of harm to her. These "neutralizing" conditions were not new, and had not prevented her from being abused by her father on past visits.

Third, the judge seemed to rely unduly on the denials of the birth father, unsupported by any other evidence, that he had not abused my child. The judge ruled that the father's claim that he had not abused my daughter was as convincing as the unanimous testimony of all the experts to the contrary. This evidence relied on physical, psychological, and psychiatric findings. Yet, weighing the word of the accused abuser against all the experts, the judge found the evidence "in equipoise," making it clear that without a confession from the accused abuser the judge would not protect my child. At this point, my own passport having been seized by the court the year before, I sent my daughter abroad with my parents and the judge jailed me indefinitely for civil contempt.

The birth father has sued many people (me three times) for claiming or suggesting that he is an incestuous child molester. He vigorously denies that he is one. His central claim is that I am a liar. I deny this. But my denial is supported by many publicly available documents, such as the four volumes attached to the affidavit of an investigating journalist who was deposed during one of the father's lawsuits against American Broadcasting Companies, Inc. (ABC), in which he claimed that he was libeled by a docudrama about the case. I was not involved in the making of this program. The journalist's research convinced him that thirty of the birth father's important contentions, including that I am a liar, were "false, misleading and/or marred by significant omissions."[3] Dismissing the birth father's lawsuit, the judge wrote that the journalist's information "was verified against court records, newspaper reports and television stories," and that ABC had "no reason to doubt his credibility, his veracity or his talents."[4] This lawsuit is the tenth unsuccessful libel lawsuit filed by the birth father.

I was jailed for twenty-five months. I was not allowed to do any professional work in jail. The judge ordered me to pay the abuser's legal fees, fined me $250,000 for contempt, and tried to sell my home to pay the fine. This was overruled on a technicality but the judge retains the deed to my home and the court of appeals itself never released me from a 1986 trust of $200,000 placed on my home to ensure my appearance in court.

After the Jailing

In 1989, the U.S. Congress passed a bill, introduced by U.S. Representative Frank Wolfe, compelling the Washington, D.C., courts to release me from jail by limiting the time that a judge could jail a civil contemnor in a domestic case.

Soon after my release the birth father found that my daughter was living in New Zealand with my parents and sought temporary custody of her there. Having invoked that country's jurisdiction, he was not granted custody of my daughter. Rather, under pressure from the New Zealand Family Court, our U.S. judge allowed me to travel to join my daughter. In New Zealand I was made her sole custodial parent, as I was in the U.S., and the birth father was not allowed contact with her. Unable to work in New Zealand as a physician, I obtained a Ph.D. in psychology, my 250,000-word jail diary being approved as my source of data. My goal was to understand my experiences in and observations of the jail and the legal system it served.

In 1996, ten years after my first jailing on my daughter's behalf, the U.S. Congress passed further legislation, again introduced by U.S. Representative Wolfe, enabling my child to live safely in the United States without the threat of forced visits with her sexual abuser. In 1997 we returned home.

In D.C. Jail

Background

The jail in which I was incarcerated was the District of Columbia Department of Corrections Detention Center, or "the D.C. jail." It was and is the only correctional institution in the city, which is the capital of the United States and a federal jurisdiction. The jail is a maximum security detention center for men and women that holds all federal and local detainees arrested in the city as well as various convicted federal and local criminals.

The D.C. jail has sixteen cellblocks; each block houses about 120 inmates in eighty cells. In 1986, only half a cellblock was needed to house women, but by 1987 the rise in the number of women inmates necessitated the use of three cellblocks, and by 1989 four cellblocks were needed and they were overcrowded. Most women were incarcerated for nonviolent crimes, at a time of rising male violence in the city.

My cellblock was South One, the main intake cellblock. Its cells had barred gates, not solid doors. Because everything happened in public, it was comparatively safe. For the first year, because I was not a criminal, I was in a cell by myself. After that, apparently on orders from the judge, I was reclassified as an unsentenced criminal and given roommates. This enabled me to me talk privately with roommates, some of whom knew a great deal about the system.

The System, Its Values, and the Staff

Despite the lip service they gave to values of nonviolence and equality, the jail and the criminal justice system that it served enforced values based on violence and abuse of the weak.

The jail was run by senior administrative staff, headed by a chief administrator. There were three chief administrators during twenty-five months. There was no noticeable difference between their administrations. Their organized degradation of women was blatant. They had loud, sexually aggressive music piped into all cellblocks for eighteen hours a day and they refused repeated requests by nonviolent employees and inmates to stop this practice. They ordered that women inmates be kept confined at virtually all times to their blocks. They allowed the male inmates, most of whom had been jailed for extreme repeated violence, including rape, to roam the jail unsupervised and to go into the entry halls of the female cell blocks unsupervised.

Once in the blocks, these male inmates (and often various senior male employees) watched, shouted obscenities, and threatened us while we showered, dressed, and used the toilet. The male inmates, for instance, stood a few feet away from the female showers, watching us through clear glass walls, hammering on the glass and screaming threats. This was deliberate policy, because the administration specifically refused to allow female blocks to have dark glass around the showers, a privilege accorded only to male blocks. The administration issued women inmates with jumpsuits that had snaps and buttons torn off in the chest and groin and refused to let us repair them. The senior administrators justified these and other similar conditions on the grounds that the male inmates "needed" them.

There was also a systematic cover-up of severe physical abuse of male inmates. I discovered this from a roommate who was a legal professional and was given work in one of the senior administrative areas. She told me that almost daily she heard violent male employees discussing their group beatings of inmates while these same employees were waiting for her to type up their official reports denying that they had used excessive force. At my request she asked a male senior administrator how many inmate complaints of violence were upheld on administrative review. He reported that in his ten years at the jail, there had been only one, and that was the complaint made on behalf of an inmate who suffered permanent severe brain damage after being violently assaulted by male employees.

Heading the hierarchy of power in the jail were the senior administrators, the enabling leaders of this system, who were not themselves known to be physically violent. Next came violent employees, whose violence supported the power position of the senior administrators. Third came the most violent inmates, who were allowed to be violent and aggressive provided they did not target senior administrators and violent employees. Fourth came nonviolent employees, whom violent inmates and violent employees harassed. At the lowest level in the hierarchy were the less violent and nonviolent inmates, who were treated worst by the most violent.

Within this hierarchy, males dominated females at each level. The effect, intended or not, was to put the senior administration, violent employees, and violent inmates in league together, using violence and threats to keep the nonviolent employees and inmates from successfully challenging this abusive system.

To maintain such a system and their own position within it, high-ranking professionals, not just administrators, would have to abuse their power, whether voluntarily or under pressure to do so. Was this the case? I kept records of interactions in order to examine professional conduct.

I started with the various mid- and low-ranking professional employees, from parole supervisors to cellblock supervisors, who interrogated me, apparently on orders of the judge. Their interrogations went like this:

Q: If I ask you where your daughter is, you won't tell me, will you?

A: No.

Q: Where is your daughter?

A: I won't tell you.

Q: That's all I need.

None of these professionals were known to be involved in any professional misconduct. Three higher ranking professionals also interrogated me: the jail psychologist, the jail chaplain (a Protestant), and a police detective. Each of the three presented herself or himself to me as a supportive friend, smiling, leaning toward me, taking my hand and saying with a direct honest gaze that she or he wanted to help me. Their lies were breathtaking. With his hand on the Bible, the chaplain insisted that Christians had no moral duty toward children and that God wanted me to give my child unconditionally to the judge. The chaplain was later credibly reported to have sexually exposed himself to another female inmate.

The psychologist, over coffee and doughnuts, claimed to want to help me keep in touch with my daughter and held out her telephone, insisting at length that it was safe for me to call my child and wrong of me not to do so. I knew from lower-level employees that the judge had ordered all of my phone calls tapped. The psychologist was later credibly reported to run a late-night "group therapy" session in which she allowed male inmates to have sex with female ones.

The policeman, arriving at night and improperly interrogating me without the knowledge of my lawyers, assured me that he cared for kids and would definitely not tell the judge where my daughter was if I would give him her address so that he could visit her. Although I had been polite, even friendly, to all my interrogators so far, at this point I jumped up screaming at the policeman to get out of my sight because I hated people who tried to get my child raped. A lower-level employee, supervising the area, ordered the policeman out of the jail on the grounds that he was not entitled to upset prisoners. I was never interrogated again. The policeman later admitted to a federal prosecutor that he illegally trespassed on distant property in another state, without a search warrant or local police permission, in his search for my daughter.

The conduct of these professionals supported the idea that the system as a whole was based on values that support the abuse of power, with those at the top being the ones who committed the worst power abuses. If that is so, the professional administration of medical care in the prison may well reflect this. In my diary I recorded sixty-eight descriptions of the medical care of other inmates. Of these cases eighty-seven percent (sixty-one instances) were outright refusals of care, abusive treatment, or clearly inadequate care. Furthermore, a medical director did not have his contract renewed after strenuously advocating improvements in care. These examples supported the view of a power-abusing system. In such a system it appeared that dishonesty had to be prevalent at all levels, not just among the criminals.

Dishonesty, denial, and irrationality proved to be closely related and hard to distinguish. For instance, the administration served fruit to inmates at breakfast and then held shakedowns a few hours later to seize the fruit as contraband. The administrative explanation was that contraband was anything not distributed to inmates. Because the fruit clearly had been distributed to inmates and because inmates were allowed to keep other food in their cells, the administration's explanation was irrational. But these administrators were educated men with no other evidence of mental incompetence. Their conduct could more easily be understood as rational but dishonest—the deliberate use, followed by denial, of a program to emotionally abuse inmates to destabilize them and keep them cowed. Some evidence also suggests that at least some senior administrators were involved in drug distribution within the jail and that they used these shakedowns to conceal it. Thus dishonesty, denial, and irrationality were part and parcel of the system.

I reviewed every diary entry that described laughter, smiles, and cheers that I had witnessed and discovered that the majority of such instances arose when a person—or, in one case, a mouse—was being hurt or humiliated. The other instances occurred when people shared safe experiences or were supportive of one another. So "friendly" behavior could be very misleading; truly friendly behavior was only possible in clearly safe situations.

Most "friendly" behavior in the jail was accompanied by danger. For instance, I witnessed an attempted gang rape of a young woman in front of a large crowd. The victim herself was laughing as she struggled violently to escape and cried out for help. The laughter of aggressors, witnesses, and the victim stopped only when I intervened with a shout of protest on her behalf. The aggressors ran off and the victim rose and angrily confronted the crowd, which dispersed silently.

Thus all "friendly" behavior in an unsafe situation appeared to signal an increasing power differential between the abuser and the victim. "Friendly" behavior in unsafe situations seemed to disappear in aggressors, victims and witnesses alike, in the face of effective resistance by, or on behalf of, the victim.

This left my successes over the policeman and the would-be rapists unexplained. In a power-abusing system, how was it that I, clearly the weaker party, had prevailed? I examined instances in my diaries of physical fights; who won and who fled from them. I had recorded sixty-one diary entries describing physically aggressive encounters, including mutual combat, unprovoked attacks, and self-defense. Most were between women inmates; the rest were between inmates and employees or between two employees. It was clear that losers of these encounters always left the area before the winners. In draws, both parties left at the same time.

In a little over half of these episodes the winner prevailed not by superior physical strength but by surprise. This seemed to create confusion in the mind of the other party, who could not mentally interpret the situation and accordingly fled. Thus my successes could be explained as my unwitting use of surprise as a tactic. But in my observations of physical fights, it became apparent that they were verbal as well as physical encounters. This led me to look at words used in such confrontations.

I then looked at physical fights in terms of whether the use of the word "fuck" affected the outcome. I chose the word "fuck" because it was widely used. I found fifty instances of "fuck" being used in physical confrontations. In most it was used by the winner only. It appeared to be a weapon that played a large part in winning a physical fight. I found also that graphic, nonobscene descriptions of the other party's sexual mutilation were even more effective weapons but required exceptional language skill. Further, in looking at all uses of "fuck," I realized that almost every time it was used in conversations, it described aggression against others, or threats of it.

All of this suggested that pervasive and severe abuse of power and aggression, reflecting values based on violence and violation, were characteristic of the correctional and criminal justice systems, as well as the criminals whom they claimed to "correct." If this were true, trauma would be an inevitable outcome of the "correctional" experience.

Many of the women inmates and employees suffered from trauma, and generally it originated in childhood. I had fifty descriptions of childhood experiences from inmates and employees, most describing severe childhood abuse and/or abandonment. When I compared the two groups, it seemed that abused inmates described far more complex and severe childhood traumatic experiences: often lifelong abuse involving multiple abusers, multiple types of abuse, multiple kinds of neglect and abandonment, and disruption of all positive childhood bonds as a result of abuse. Abused inmates also described "protective" interventions by the legal system, all of which led to further abuse that was complicated by the complete destruction of any remaining positive attachments.

In contrast to abused inmates, employees who had been abused described one kind of abuse, generally one abuser, effective protection, shorter periods of abuse, and enduring positive bonds with their birth mothers. No employees described legal intervention in childhood.

Given this, it was not surprising that compared to employees, the inmates displayed more complex and severe post-traumatic dissociative behaviors. The jail and criminal justice system did not cause these original childhood injuries, but their management exacerbated them to the point of re-injury. For one thing, "rehabilitation" was an obvious failure; almost all inmates were recidivists. Further, the sexualized and misogynist conditions in the jail, as set by the administration, triggered post-traumatic behaviors in traumatized inmates and employees.[5]

Given the large number of inmates with complex and challenging post-traumatic disorders, the jail was obviously a de facto mental health institution. The employees, many of them severely traumatized themselves in childhood although less so than inmates, were vulnerable to secondary traumatization by working so closely with inmates.[6] The cumulative traumatic effect on the employees, working with no support or training and under a hostile administration, appeared to easily account for the difficulties of the employees with alcohol and drug abuse, emotional outbursts, and difficulty coming to work. It could also have accounted for much of their violence.

Reflecting on the System

The underlying problem in the criminal justice/correctional system in Washington, D.C., seemed to be that its claim to democratic values was a sham. The men in charge, white and black, were educated, hardworking, and rational, but clearly regarded might as right. People who value power over decency hold the values commonly associated with violent dictatorships. Such power abuse leads to systematic violence, dishonesty, and sexual degradation of the most vulnerable. I call all such systems "power abuse systems." Is it credible to suggest that systematic values of power abuse can explain the problems in the capital's apparently well-intended correctional system?

Validation can be found in lawsuits filed by women inmates and employees of the jail. In 1993, women inmates sued the city and the jail to protest their systematic mistreatment, including unprofessional medical care and extreme sexual "harassment." In December 1994, Federal Judge Green ruled that these women's constitutional rights had been violated and issued an order with thirty-one pages of specific remedies.[7]

In 1995, a federal jury found the city liable in a class action sexual harassment lawsuit in which women employees described being fondled, kissed, and pressured for sex by co-workers and superiors. An $8 million settlement of these claims was reached. And, in 1997, a woman inmate filed suit against the city for being pressured by a woman employee to perform a public striptease on a cellblock.[8]

Not everyone in a system shares its values, and this was obviously the case in the jail. There was a pervasive rebellion against these values by many mid- and lower-level nonviolent employees that explains their overt support for me.

The leaders of such systems would not necessarily admit to their real values because it might endanger their jobs. Nor would such leaders necessarily understand the impact of their values on those far below them. The people at the bottom of such systems are invisible by virtue of the enormous disparity in power between top and bottom. This helps explain the disparity between the administration and the legal system's claims to care for the welfare of women and their reckless disregard for us.

It is easy to say that the city of Washington, D.C., is atypical and is a particularly bad system. Certainly the city administration has been corrupt and chaotic; the federal government recently wrested power from the mayor, a convicted criminal himself.

However, chaos was not the chief problem in the correctional system, despite the city and the chaos of its systems. Although chaos in the jail originated from abusive neglect by the administration, it was also reflected in the ability of nonviolent employees to openly break abusive rules on behalf of many inmates—in a less chaotic system abuse would have been more efficiently delivered.

Rather than finding chaos as the core of the problem, my participant study of the city's correctional system appeared to reveal a deeper truth: The dominant members of the system, chiefly men, accord themselves an unspoken, unwritten right to abuse their power, mainly by using physical violence to subjugate less dominant men and by using sexual violence inflicted by themselves and the men below them to dominate women. But not all dominant men will choose to exercise this right. And in democracies it must be exercised in secret.

At the time of writing this, evidence emerged that President Clinton engaged in a prolonged sexual affair with a young White House intern; such sexually dominating and exploitative behavior appears to be part of a long-standing pattern.[9] When the values of the capitol's criminal justice and correctional systems resemble those of the country's president, the problems of the city's systems seem more likely to be representative than unique.

Indeed, this right to abuse power that characterized the correctional system in Washington, D.C., may account for the nationwide rise in the incarceration of women. In the D.C. jail, this was evident in the need to increase space for women from half a cellblock in 1986 to more than four cellblocks in 1989. Because most women were arrested for nonviolent misdemeanors and the city had an enormous problem with extremely violent male criminals, the "war on crime" may be a euphemism for a war on women. Perhaps this is the predictable response of a legal system challenged by women demanding freedom from rape. This demand, reasonable as it may seem in a democracy, challenges the rights that dominant men have accorded themselves and that the correctional system uses.

Obviously, in a democracy, a power-abusing system cannot easily operate publicly. Simply publishing this chapter may help, by exposing the problems or by leading to further research into the widespread and abusive jailing of severely traumatized and disadvantaged women. This can help to make these women and this mistreatment more visible, and in so doing, lead to their better treatment.[10] There can be a danger in this approach, however.

Unless thought through carefully, paying heed to the plight of the criminal—male or female—plays into the values of the system. Female employees are also a disadvantaged and traumatized group. To study and help only the woman criminal means that the problems within the system can be easily overlooked, perpetuating the distorted values of the system and dooming good faith efforts. Such research and resulting programs must be made with a clear understanding of how power-abusing systems work. Efforts to improve the plight of women criminals without understanding the power relationships in the system are likely to further empower the most abusive men in the system. For instance, while I was in jail, it was decided that women inmates should be allowed to keep their babies in jail. Without fundamental changes in the values of the system this would merely give the sexually abusive men in the jail access to and the right to abuse these infants.

I concluded that in the D.C. jail and in similar systems, unfettered public access to the institution and to programs to benefit all nonviolent members are most likely to bring about changes in the power-abuse values. For instance, employees function as mental health care providers, specializing in severe post-traumatic disorders. If these employees were given the appropriate training and support, and if they understood self-care, they would be far better able to provide the stable, safe environment that inmates need above all else.

As a result of my experiences in jail, I believe that the correctional service system is based on the abuse of power, allowing mistreatment of both inmates and employees, and in particular the sexual mistreatment of women. Such a system may well be representative of a prevailing widespread ethic throughout the country rather than specific to the D.C. jail. For those within the jail, however, it is important to gain a greater understanding of how the current values affect the correctional system and to design programs that will offer genuine assistance rather than perpetuate a system of power abuse.

NOTES

1. Psalms 18:29, in *The Book of Common Prayer of the Church of England,* rev. ed. (Cambridge: Cambridge University Press, 1969), 365.

2. David Harmer, "The History of the Contempt Power." Section in "Limiting Incarceration for Civil Contempt in Child Custody Cases," *Brigham Young University Journal of Public Law* 4, no. 2 (1990): 245–47.

3. *Foretich, E. A. v. American Broadcasting Companies, Inc., Capital Cities/ABC, Inc., ABC Holding Company, Inc. et al., The Landsburg Company, Victor Paddock, Alan Landsburg, Linda Otto, Jane Doe and John Doe (1-100),* Civil Action no. 93-2620; Civil Action no. 94-0037, consolidated. In the United States District Court for the District of Columbia, footnote 1, page 2 in Defendants' Memorandum in Support of Motion to Enforce Settlement Agreement and for the Imposition of Sanctions, and Request for Expedited Consideration, 24 December 1997.

4. *Foretich E. A. v. American Broadcasting Companies, Inc. et al.,* Civil Action no. 93-2620; Civil Action no. 94-0037, Opinion of Harold A. Greene, (17 October 1997): 22.

5. Jean Elizabeth Morgan, "Types of Dissociative Behaviors Observed in an Urban Jail: 25 Months of Participant Observation," *Dissociation* 9, no. 2 (1997): 89–96.

6. John Wilson and Jacob Lindy, *Countertransference in the Treatment of PTSD* (New York: Guildford Press,1994).

7. *Women Prisoners of the District of Columbia Department of Corrections v. District of Columbia,* Civil Action no. 93-2052. United States District Court for the District of Columbia, Order of Judge Greene, 18 December 1994.

8. "Suit Tells of Reluctant Cellblock Striptease," *Washington Post,* 25 December 1997, C:1.

9. "Clinton Accused of Urging Aide to Lie," *Washington Post,* 1 January 1998, 1.

10. See B. E. Richie and C. Johnsen, "Abuse Histories among Newly Incarcerated Women in a New York City Jail," *Journal of American Medical Women's Association* 51, no. 3 (1996): 111–14, 117; N. El-Bassel, L. Gilbert, R. F. Schilling, A. Ivanoff, D. Borne, and S. F. Safyer, "Correlates of Crack Abuse among Drug-using Incarcerated Women: Psychological Trauma, Social Support and Coping Behavior," *American Journal of Drug*

and Alcohol Abuse 22, no. 1 (February 1996): 41–56; M. I. Singer, J. Bussey, L. Y. Song, and L. Lunghofer, "The Psychosocial Issues of Women Serving Time in Jail," *Social Work* 40, no. 1 (January 1995): 103–113; L. A. Teplin, K. M. Abram, and G. M. McClelland, "Mentally Disordered Women in Jail: Who Receives Services," *American Journal of Public Health* 87, no. 4 (1997): 604–609.

REFERENCES

El-Bassel, N., L. Gilbert, R. F. Schilling, A. Ivanoff, D. Borne, and S. F. Safyer. "Correlates of Crack Abuse among Drug-using Incarcerated Women: Psychological Trauma, Social Support and Coping Behavior." *American Journal of Drug and Alcohol Abuse* 22, no. 1 (February 1996): 41–56.

Foretich, E. A. v. American Broadcasting Companies, Inc., Capital Cities/ABC, Inc., ABC Holding Company, Inc. et al., The Landsburg Company, Victor Paddock, Alan Landsburg, Linda Otto, Jane Doe and John Doe (1-100), Civil Action no. 93-2620; Civil Action no. 94-0037, p. 22 of Opinion of Harold A. Greene, 17 October 1997.

Foretich, E. A. v. American Broadcasting Companies, Inc., Capital Cities/ABC, Inc., ABC Holding Company, Inc. et. al., The Landsburg Company, Victor Paddock, Alan Landsburg, Linda Otto, Jane Doe and John Doe (1-100). Civil Action no. 93-2620; Civil Action no. 94-0037, consolidated. In the United States District Court for the District of Columbia. Footnote 1, page 2 in Defendants' Memorandum in Support of Motion to Enforce Settlement Agreement and for the Imposition of Sanctions, and Request for Expedited Consideration, 24 December 1997.

Harmer, David. "The History of the Contempt Power." Section in "Limiting Incarceration for Civil Contempt in Child Custody Cases." *Brigham Young University Journal of Public Law* 4, no. 2 (1990): 245–47.

Morgan, Jean Elizabeth. "Types of Dissociative Behaviors Observed in an Urban Jail: 25 Months of Participant Observation." *Dissociation* 9, no. 2 (1997): 89–96.

Richie, B. E. and Johnsen, C. "Abuse Histories among Newly Incarcerated Women in a New York City Jail." *Journal of American Medical Women's Association* 51, no. 3 (1996): 111–14.

Singer, M. I., J. Bussey, L. Y. Song, and L. Lunghofer. "The Psychosocial Issues of Women Serving Time in Jail." *Social Work* 40, no. 1 (January 1995): 103–13.

Teplin, L. A., K. M. Abram, and G. M. McClelland, "Mentally Disordered Women in Jail: Who Receives Services." *American Journal of Public Health* 87, no. 4 (1997): 604–609.

Wilson, John, and Jacob Lindy. *Countertransference in the Treatment of PTSD.* New York: Guildford Press, 1994.

Women Prisoners of the District of Columbia Department of Corrections v. District of Columbia. D.C. 93-2052.

Washington Post. "Clinton Accused of Urging Aide to Lie." 1 January 1998, 1.

Washington Post. "Suit Tells of Reluctant Cellblock Striptease." 25 December 1997, C:1.

Ali's Visit

Helen Barnacle

I WAS SENTENCED in 1980 to fifteen years with a twelve-year minimum sentence on drug importation and possession charges relating to heroin. I had been a heroin addict since the age of seventeen. In 1980 when I commenced my sentence I was twenty-six years old and had given birth to a baby daughter, Ali, in March of the same year. At the time in Victoria, Australia, you could only keep your baby in prison with you until they turned one year old. After much lobbying and fighting the system, this was changed so I could keep Ali with me indefinitely. She remained in prison with me for four years and we spent four years separated. I was released on a pre-release program after serving eight years. Ali was then eight years old.

The following excerpt is about what it felt like after Ali had left the prison and I could only see her for an all-day visit once a month.

This week she is coming in to visit. The excitement wells up inside me. We will have all day Saturday and I want it to be the best time that it possibly can. I order some potato chips and lollies and chocolates on my canteen. I make some "hedgehog," one of our favorites. I used to make it when Ali lived in here. I smile to myself as I look forward to the coming weekend.

Saturday arrives; I'm called to the gate. Ali's here. My brother has just dropped her off. She's always happy to see me, the bond of those first four years so strong. Even so, I often find myself wondering if she'll remember her time with me . . . if the love will fade during the time of my absence from her life. But every time I see her smiling face, those little legs running eagerly toward me, the doubts are eradicated. I wonder at the strength of love between a mother and daughter. It seems senseless that we now can't live together and that she has to experience such sadness being separated from me.

We talk, we play. Other kids are in to visit, but Ali is more interested in catching up with some of the women she knows from when she lived here. She was loved by so many of them and she loves them in return. It's beautiful to watch.

The day goes well, but time waits for no one and today it seems to be moving extra fast, and so it's soon time for Ali to leave. I dread this moment. I walk to the gate to return her to my brother who takes her away until another Saturday in a month's time. I pass her through to him and turn and walk away from the gate, the gate I'm not allowed through, back to my cell. My heart aches with the emptiness I now feel. I can't talk to anyone, I feel too raw. Sometimes I think I'll die of heartache. I go to my cell, put the headphones on, and turn the music up loud. I lay there, my head pounding, my heart aching, nowhere to put this pain. I feel the lump rise in my throat . . . it's come to be a common experience as I hold back the tears. One day I wish that I'll just let them flow, but right now I'm too frightened. It feels like a volcano inside me and I'm afraid to let the lid off. . . . I feel like I'd just dissolve and evaporate along with my tears.

I've given up using heroin, so I can find no other release from the anguish. The physical ache in my body is unbearable and I know there's nothing that will ease it. I know that in time it will gradually abate and I'll be able to stand up, open my eyes, walk out to the lounge room in the unit and once again mix with the other women that I share this space with, but not yet . . . not for a couple of hours at least. No one bothers me. They respect my need to be left alone. They know there's nothing they could offer me anyway.

When Ali first left the prison at the age of four, I would think about her all day every day, from the moment she would be getting up in the morning to the moment she'd be going to bed. I used to imagine her getting dressed for school without me. I used to see her laughing little face at the school ground. I used to try to imagine her in class with her teacher. I used to imagine her playing in my brother's backyard after school with her friends. I used to imagine someone else reading her a story in bed at night before she went to sleep. I used to imagine someone else getting "Ted" and "blanket" for her. I nearly went mad thinking about her and what she was doing. I had to find another way to cope. I had to find a way of not thinking about her all the time, of not being consumed by her absence. I had to find a way to fill that black, emotional hole. Drugs were no longer the answer. Heroin didn't work for me any more.

Greg, a friend from the Education Centre, helped me. I learned to meditate. I learned tai chi. Greg taught me a meditation where I would send my heart out beyond the concrete walls surrounding the prison to Ali in bed. I'd visualize my heart wrapping itself around her so that she was enclosed in it. Then I'd breathe love in and through my heart so that she would feel the warmth of that love, even though I wasn't physically there. Those moments gave me some peace of mind. I could feel my heart surrounding her. I felt that she could feel it too. It made me feel close to her, a part of her life, when I couldn't be physically with her. It helped fill my heart with love instead of pain and slowly the more I did this exercise, the more I felt love where pain once lived.[1]

I began to feel warmer inside. I began to feel I had something to offer. I began to step outside myself . . . outside pain. I began to understand the meaning of compassion.[2]

NOTES

1. Helen Barnacle, *Don't Let Her See Me Cry* (Sydney, New South Wales: Transworld, forthcoming).

2. Sadly, these day visits that are so important to women are no longer permitted in the new private prison at Deer Park.

Understanding
the Criminalization
and Imprisonment
of Women

The Sex of Crime and Punishment

Susanne Davies and Sandy Cook

THE LATE TWENTIETH CENTURY might aptly be described as the age of the great incarceration.[1] Although prisons have not always existed and little more than two centuries ago were considered by some to be a curious idea unlikely to succeed in practice,[2] today prisons have assumed almost an unquestionable status. Confinement to prison is presented as, and often believed to be, the commonsense response to crime and the proper form that punishment should take. Over the past thirty years the number of people incarcerated throughout the world has escalated dramatically. Women are among those who in recent decades have been imprisoned at increasing rates; however, they continue to represent only a small proportion of prisoner populations. Women in prison—like women who offend—nevertheless remain the objects of particular scrutiny and condemnation. Liable to be characterized as "bad," "mad," and as "worse than any man," their condemnation is inextricably linked to their transgression of the sexed norms that frame everyday life. The aim of this chapter is to explain how women offenders and prisoners have come to occupy such a vilified position and to explore the challenges that feminists and other critical theorists have posed to "commonsense" understandings of women's offending and imprisonment.

"The God Trick"

"The God Trick," so called by feminist theorist Donna Harraway, refers to the pretense of claiming to be able to see "everything from nowhere."[3] Since the period of Western Enlightenment in the sixteenth and seventeenth centuries, this claim has been manifest in calls for the exercise of pure objectivity and has been put into effect in scientific and social scientific methods and practices. Science, as a paradigm of inquiry, has come to constitute the dominant means through which we might know the world and those who occupy it. Its acceptance as the paramount device through which untainted knowledge is acquired has had profound implications for collective and individual understandings of humanity and social organization. The modern scientific idea of two biologically distinct sexes that, based upon their innate constitutions, possess different natures, characteristics, and roles has, for example, been revealed as an invention rather than as a discovery of science.[4] In proposing and striving to prove this biologically essentialist model of women and men, science has paved the way for the condemnation and punishment of those who depart from these normative categories. This is no more evident than in relation to women who commit crimes and are imprisoned.

Legal codes and their administration have of course played an enduring role in defining the boundaries of tolerable behavior and in dispensing punishment to those who have been judged as transgressing them. As French theorist Michel Foucault has argued, however, the nature of legal judgment, like the nature of punishment, has altered significantly over the past 200 years. The ascendancy of science and its convergence with law have led to a fundamental shift in focus from the crime to "the criminal," and from corporeal forms of punishment to imprisonment. As Foucault explains:

> Certainly the crimes and "offences" on which judgement is passed are juridical objects defined by the code, but judgement is [now] also passed on the passions, instincts, anomalies, infirmities, maladjustments, effects of environment or heredity. . . . The question is no longer simply: "Has the act been established and is it punishable?" But also: "What *is* this act . . . Is it a phantasy, a psychotic reaction, a delusional episode, a perverse action?" It is no longer simply: "Who committed it?" But: "How can we assign the causal process that produced it? Where did it originate in the author himself?"[5]

Although here Foucault is oblivious to the significance of sex, the shift that he traces is inextricably related to the construction of normative notions of maleness and femaleness.[6] In the late nineteenth century, in the wake of the publication of Darwin's theory of evolution, "experts" in a range of newly emerging fields of science set about charting what they perceived to be fundamental differences between people. Normative notions concerning sex, race, class, and age were hypothesized and supposedly proven via the painstaking examination of human bodies. Observation, quantification, and categorization, the staples of scientific method, were used to determine the normality, or, more correctly, the inferiority and indeed abnormality of particular peoples. The findings of Gustav Le Bon, for example, a German craniologist who was a founder of social psychology, were unique in their bluntness but nonetheless not unusual among those who attested that the size and anatomy of the brain correlated with abilities and worth:

> All psychologists who have studied the intelligence of women, as well as poets and novelists, recognize today that they represent the most inferior forms of human evolution and that they are closer to children and savages than to an adult, civilized man. They excess in fickleness, inconstancy, absence of thought and logic, and incapacity to reason. Without doubt there exist some distinguished women, very superior to the average man, but they are as exceptional as the birth of any monstrosity, as, for example, of a gorilla with two heads; consequently, we may neglect them entirely.[7]

But women were not so fortunate as to be neglected entirely by the practitioners of the new sciences. By the late 1870s, physical debilitation, mental unfitness, sexual perversion, and criminality had been added to the list of subjects worthy of investigation. Although explorations into such topics routinely commenced with the study of men, the scientific gaze was later almost inevitably extended to women. This was the case in the emerging field of criminal anthropology. In 1876, *Criminal Man* by Cesare Lombroso, the so-called father of criminal anthropology, was first published.[8] This text marked the full-blooded entry of science into what had previously been largely a legal domain. In this text Lombroso used evolutionary theory and quantitative data, derived through the observation and measurement of male lawbreakers, to deduce that criminals were "evolutionary throwbacks." The criminal, he posited, was distinguishable from the noncriminal by virtue of heredity, in particular the possession of an apelike physique and an innate tendency to savagery.[9] According to Lombroso, a combination of biological and pathological anomalies rendered criminals incapable of adapting to the demands of the civilized world; hence the need via indeterminate sentencing to isolate, observe, and contain them, if necessary, forever.[10]

Nineteen years later Lombroso, aided and abetted by his son-in-law William Ferrero, extended his theory to embrace women. In *The Female Offender* they argued that female criminals, like their male counterparts, were biologically distinct from noncriminal women and occupied a lower place on the evolutionary scale. Here Lombroso's allegiance to Darwinism appeared less evident with a distinction being drawn between the "born" female criminal and the "occasional" female criminal. Although some might attribute this distinction to a more discerning grasp of his subject, it is more likely, however, that it was a response to criticisms that the apelike stigmata he had identified as the primary characteristic of the criminal man were not always present. Rather than being evidence of a tempering of Lombroso's evolutionary fervor, the distinction allowed even exceptions to be incorporated into his general theory of criminality. The "occasional" female criminal, according to Lombroso, included "milder sorts of 'born criminal[s]'" through to "normal women in whom circumstances ha[d] developed the fund of immorality which is latent in every female."[11] Although "occasional" criminals were most often guilty of crimes against property, in Lombroso's revised schema, they only differed from the worst of murderous "born" criminals in terms of degree.

Underpinning this classification system and central to defining women's criminality was a normative notion of femaleness. Although the "occasional" female criminal did not display overt physical or psychological anomalies, she nevertheless lacked moral strength. The "born" female criminal, however, was more extreme in her abnormality and was characterized as more like a man than a woman. Muscular and strong, with thick hair and an "essentially virile" face, she was also said to lack the qualities usually associated with the feminine; she was devoid of maternal and religious feelings, masculine in her style of dress, and "excessively erotic."[12] According to Lombroso and Ferrero, the "born" female criminal was rarer but more dangerous than her male counterpart. Because she was an exception among criminals and an exception among women, she was, to use their words, "a monster."[13] Combining masculine strength and forcefulness with the worst of women's qualities—namely vengefulness, cunning, cruelty, and deceitfulness—the "born" female criminal was thus condemned as the ultimate embodiment of wickedness.[14]

In *The Female Offender*, Lombroso and Ferrero expounded the causal process identified by Foucault as central to contemporary determinations relating to crime and punishment. In their schema, every form of women's offending—from murder, assault, infanticide, and child neglect through to theft, prostitution, begging, and obscenity—could be and indeed was attributed to the uniquely perverse female body and temperament. Although their work may appear to be merely a curious relic of a distant past, its fundamental premises have nevertheless lived on.

Throughout the twentieth century, criminologists of various persuasions have continued to use biological essentialism as a framework for studying and explaining women's criminality. Consider, for example, the contribution of the husband and wife team, the Gluecks, who in 1934 concluded that the 500 criminal women they had studied were "on the whole a sorry lot" who were "burdened with feeble-mindedness, psychopathic personality and marked emotional instability." According to the Gluecks, a major problem of this "swarm of defective, diseased, antisocial misfits was their lack of control of the sex impulse."[15] But too much control, it seems, could also be a problem. In *The Criminality of Women*, published in 1950, Otto Pollak argued that women were responsible for as many crimes as men; however, their greater capacity to conceal their criminal acts resulted in most never being recorded. According to Pollak, women were more deceitful than their male counterparts owing to their ability to fake orgasm, whereas men, he lamented, were "not able to hide [their] failure."[16]

In more recent years, the fetish of mainstream criminologists with women's sex and their related constitution, temperament, appearance, and conduct has persisted and has continued to be used to explain women's offending. Cowie, Cowie, and Slater, writing in the 1960s, followed this well-worn path when they described delinquent girls as "oversized, lumpish, uncouth and graceless."[17] Thrasher's explanation of female involvement in gangs, also offered in the 1960s, is similarly familiar:

[T]he girl takes the role of a boy and is accepted on equal terms with the others. Such a girl is probably a tomboy in the neighbourhood. She dares to follow anywhere and she is ill at ease with those of her own sex who have become characteristically feminine.[18]

Thrasher's explanation is indeed not far removed from Freda Adler's assertion more than a decade later that women's liberation and what she considered to be women's newfound equality had resulted in women adopting more masculine behaviors, including law-breaking.[19] While Adler at least sought to contextualize women's offending, albeit in a rather dubious way, others have preferred to remain firmly within a narrow positivist paradigm. McCorkle's 1995 study of men and women's adaptation to prison, for example, took as its starting point the assumption that psychopathology was linked to infractions against prison rules. He found that male prisoners displayed no "disturbed-disruptive" pattern, but that a strong relationship existed between mental illness and the behavior of women prisoners. Moreover, he found that African American women presented more disciplinary problems, and hence psychopathology, than any of their White counterparts. Although noting the sex-specific problems confronted by women in prison, McCorkle failed to consider the possibility that infractions of prison rules might well be an understandable, and indeed rational, response to the harsh disciplinary regimes and difficulties that women encounter in prison.[20]

Although normative notions of women have provided a basis for the condemnation of women who offend, so too have they been used to explain women's lack of offending. Representations of crime as a masculine endeavor involving assertiveness, ambition, resourcefulness, rationality, energy, courage, and individuality have been offered with monotonous regularity since the mid-twentieth century.[21] The flip side of this, of course, is that more often than not women have been characterized as conformist, passive, dependent, emotional, illogical, and sensual or, to sum it up, as slaves to their sex. In accounting for the predominance of boys in gangs in 1955, Albert Cohen noted that "boys collect stamps, girls collect boys."[22] Although today such assumptions and claims are not so overt, and are often hidden within and behind complex theories and methods, they remain pernicious in their effects. Whether explicit or implicit, they operate specifically to demonize women who offend, and generally to reduce all women to just their sex.

"The God Trick" Exposed

Over the past twenty-five years or so, feminist criminological studies have revealed more about women's offending and punishment than has a century of mainstream criminology.[23] Feminist researchers using approaches ranging from empiricism to postmodernism have highlighted numerous ways in which practices and representations of crime and punishment are informed by gender. In some feminist criminology, as in feminist theory generally, gender has increasingly been used to denote not just the social production of sex stereotypes and roles, but also the cultural construction of bodies as "sexed."[24] Because of the ways in which gender informs subjectivity, practice, and social positioning, feminists have argued that men's and women's offending and punishment, together with their experiences of these, are different. Moreover, they have asserted that an acknowledgment of the significance of gender is a crucial starting point for identifying and understanding the different ways in which women and men offend, are criminalized, and are punished.

At its most fundamental level, the feminist challenge to dominant representations of female offenders has constituted a critique of the Enlightenment notions that underpin criminology as a discipline.[25] In feminist critiques of knowledge, the existence of an "objective observer" capable of discovering an absolute "truth" through scientific means has been questioned. The production of knowledge, as Harraway argues, involves historically and culturally embodied actors who, despite claims to the contrary, cannot ever entirely divorce themselves from their own subjectivity or social context. Thus, rather than discovering or providing an absolute truth, all knowledge producers, including criminologists, can only ever provide embodied, located, and partial perspectives. It is the failure to acknowledge the partiality of all perspectives, together with the ready dismissal of alternative understandings as "unscientific," "subjective," and ultimately "untrue" that Harraway identifies as prohibiting the achievement of any meaningful "objectivity."[26]

More than thirty years ago Hermann Mannheim identified the partiality of criminology in respect to women and offered the following explanation:

> [H]itherto female crime has, for all practical purposes, been dealt with almost exclusively by men in their various capacities as legislators, judges and policemen; and . . . the same was true of the theoretical treatment of the subject. . . . This could not fail to create a one-sided picture . . . this centuries-old male predominance in theory and practice.[27]

As a male criminologist, Mannheim was breaking ranks by acknowledging that criminal justice systems and criminology have historically been dominated by members of his sex. His statement illustrates that recognition of this dominance and concern about its effects are not, as is sometimes suggested, dependent upon one's sex. What is more important is a willingness to acknowledge that sex, like other characteristics, has come to frame the production of knowledge and to explore how this has occurred and what its effects are. Feminist scholars who have analyzed the origins and development of criminology, for example, have highlighted how in the late nineteenth century the interrelated processes of industrialization, colonization, and scientification combined to enhance men's superior social position and also to privilege their partial perspective as an all-encompassing truth. In writing about criminality, White, middle-class, heterosexual men were unreflective about the particularity of their social position and perspectives and how they informed their scientific endeavors. As Carol Smart has argued, the normative idea of women's "true" nature or "natural" role, which was used to distinguish "born" and "occasional" female criminals from others of their sex, was arrived at

> through uncritical, experiential perceptions of middle-class women in Europe during the nineteenth century. Consequently they believed that the inferior social position of women, their inactive lives, their apparent lack of genius and socially desirable skills, their concerns with trivia and luxury as well as their petty rivalries, were true reflections of the nature of Woman.[28]

Lombroso, like the other men who were involved in the scientific quests of the late-nineteenth century, assumed the naturalness of the existing status quo and the propriety of the axes of power that differentiated them from others. Assumptions of their own normality, and indeed superiority, framed their investigations and in turn were legitimated through their findings of abnormality and inferiority in others, be these based on conceptions of race, sex, sexuality, class, or age. As Gould has suggested, within the general theory of biological determinism "'inferior groups' [were] interchangeable."[29] Therefore women were likened to children who were likened to savages who were likened to beasts.

The partiality or, more appropriately, the masculinity of the dominant criminological perspective we have described has been identified by feminist scholars as having a number of enduring consequences for women. The first has been the failure of most criminologists to acknowledge women's offending and punishment as a subject worthy of serious consideration. Often entirely absent from discussions, sometimes relegated to footnotes and appendices or included as an afterthought, women, as Morris so cogently put it, "are not really there."[30] Although this neglect has sometimes been rationalized through reference to women's numerical insignificance among criminals,[31] feminist criminologists have more often attributed it to the fascination of male criminologists with, and indeed valorization of, the male offender and his feats.[32] Even those who have made cursory gestures toward acknowledging the significance of sex have exhibited a willful or negligent refusal to grapple with this issue. Consider, for example, Corrigan and Frith's astonishing explanation as to why girls did not feature in their study of delinquency:

> In this piece we have (in common with almost every other writer on youth culture) ignored women. . . . [O]ur very notion of "the working class kid" is a male one. We have no excuse except ignorance. . . . [W]e know very little about the culture of teenage girls.[33]

A second and closely related problem identified by feminist researchers has been the extension of general theories of criminality to include women. As in Lombroso's case, the practice of including women in general theories that have been framed by an unstated male norm has continued and these theories are usually presented as "sexless" or "gender neutral." In this way the existence of men and women as sexed actors is hidden behind such nonspecific terms as "people," "criminals," and "prisoners."[34] The consequence of this is that even though men predominate among perpetrators of crimes, and sex is therefore arguably the most obvious indicator of criminal activity, men "as a sex" have been obscured from view. So too has the particularity of women in respect to crime been disguised. Judith Allen describes "the failure to theorise the basic sex specificities of criminalities as the greatest intellectual flaw in twentieth century criminology."[35]

In making this statement Allen is not calling for a reassertion of the biologically essentialist understandings of men and women that have continued to characterize most criminological endeavors. Indeed, the persistence of biological essentialism is the third problem identified by feminist scholars as arising from the partiality of traditional criminological paradigms. Although men as a sex have largely been obscured from view, the focus upon women in traditional criminology has rendered women captives of their bodies. As Heidensohn explained in 1985:

> What distinguishes writers on female crime is not only that they represent a particular criminological tradition, but that they seek to rationalize and to make acceptable a series of propositions about women and their consequences for criminal behaviour. Women, in this view, are determined by their biology and their physiology. Their hormones, their reproductive role, inexorably determine their emotionality, unreliability, childishness, deviousness, etc. These factors lead to female crime.[36]

As Alison Young points out, however, feminist criminology itself has not remained entirely free of the taint of biological essentialism. As she suggests, "classical biologism lives on in feminism as a (mistaken) tale of femininity."[37] Feminist assertions of the 1980s that women's non–law-breaking should be taken into greater account, for example, colluded with traditional conceptions of women as inherently passive and conforming.[38] Such calls assumed homogeneity among women and thus, like the masculine perspective they sought to avoid, positioned women offenders as a negative exception to their sex. In more recent years feminist theorists such as Young and Smart have called for a reconceptualization of sex within both traditional and feminist criminology. Drawing upon poststructuralist and postmodern theories, they have argued that "women" and "men" must be understood as the products of discursive categories that are historically and culturally constructed. This does not mean that men and women do not exist—far from it. What it does mean is that the subjectivities, actions, experiences, and social positions of women and men are not natural or determined. Rather they are inextricably related to broader frameworks of knowledge and to the normative concepts of sex that frame our lives and that are continually acted out and frequently enforced in social interactions.[39]

Feminist Interpretations of Women's Offending

In both criminological and criminal justice circles, it is well acknowledged that women commit only a small proportion of total crimes committed and that their offenses tend to be less serious and far more rarely involve violence than those perpetrated by men.[40] Over the past century the forms of offending that have been most closely associated with women have included theft, fraud, prostitution, and reproduction-related offenses such as abortion and infanticide. While women's commission of these offenses has traditionally been explained by references to women's unstable, devious, and hedonistic nature, feminists have argued that women's offending, like men's, needs to be contextualized in relation to broader frameworks of knowledge, power, and sexed relations.

Feminist scholars, for example, have pointed to the way in which the framing and enforcement of laws according to the dictates of biological essentialism have led to women being unfairly targeted in relation to particular offenses. In her work on infanticide and abortion in Australia, historian Judith Allen has argued that despite changes in laws, women, especially those who lack material resources and social support, have remained vulnerable to criminal prosecution. In the late-nineteenth century, abortion and infanticide were by far the most common indictable offenses for which women were charged. Although men obviously contributed to conception, and in many instances encouraged, insisted upon, or facilitated abortions or infanticide, their prosecution was rare.[41] Male medical practitioners who performed abortions are largely absent from the criminal record, and it remains an even more curious fact that in some

Australian states up to the present day only, women can be charged with infanticide.[42] That does not mean, however, that all women are equally liable to commit these crimes or to be prosecuted for them.

Although unmarried women bore a small minority of children in late-nineteenth-century Australia, they comprised an overwhelming majority of those women tried for reproduction-related offenses. According to Allen, the typical infanticide defendant worked as a paid domestic servant on rural properties or in country towns or else lived with her parents. Deserted wives and widows who lived in rural areas were also sometimes brought to trial.[43] Abortion cases, in contrast, most often involved single women living in urban areas. The nature of women's offending thus depended upon their individual circumstances and the opportunities available to them. Abortions could be arranged more easily in large cities than in the country; however, the circumstances that necessitated women's resort to infanticide or abortion were shared. Whether pregnancy was the result of consensual sexual relations or of sexual exploitation and rape, it left single women in an almost impossible position. Because they were limited by their economic circumstances, lacked social support, and knew the shame attached to bearing an illegitimate child, it is not surprising that many single women chose to terminate their pregnancies or else to dispose of babies after their birth. The need for women to do this, like their likelihood of being prosecuted, increased in accordance with their economic and social vulnerability.

Today, as a consequence of women's changing social position and an increase in the options and support available to them, infanticide is now far less common. Abortion, although still illegal in some Western jurisdictions, can in many places be lawfully obtained. In Australia an abortion can be lawfully secured if medical assessments indicate that a woman's physical or psychological health is endangered by pregnancy. The imposition of such criteria, however, serves to medicalize and psychologize women and, together with the maintenance of abortion as a crime on the statute books, perpetuates the notion that it is normal for women to bear and raise children. As Allen has suggested, abortion thus remains a "historically important barometer of power negotiations between the sexes."[44]

Allen's observation is equally pertinent to prostitution. Feminist scholars have long pointed to the ad hoc and hypocritical nature of prostitution laws and how their framing and application have actively shaped the composition, location, and structure of local trades. Contrary to popular belief, in most British and British-derived legal systems, the act of selling sexual services has never been illegal. What have been rendered illegal are various prostitution-related activities such as brothel-keeping, procuring, and soliciting in public space.[45]

Underpinning this distinction has been the assumption that prostitution is necessary, or at least inevitable, as a consequence of men's irrepressible sexual drive and, moreover, that the availability of sexual services for men operates to protect those women who are not prostitutes. In effect, this distinction has ensured men's access to women's bodies while at the same time maintaining a facade of official condemnation through the criminalization of those individual women whose work locations and practices constitute them as the most visible participants in the trade. In Victoria, which claims to have the most "progressive" prostitution laws of any Australian state, this distinction has been further formalized through legislation that allows for the establishment and licensing of legal brothels but continues to identify soliciting on the streets as a criminal offense.[46] Although in Victoria, as in Britain, legislative provisions now exist for prosecuting the male customers of streetwalkers, these provisions are rarely invoked.[47] The legal spotlight thus remains firmly upon women, and even though imprisonment has been abolished for prostitution-related offenses, women charged with such offenses continue to be incarcerated for fine default.[48]

The legal sanctioning of women for offenses relating to prostitution maintains an unequal sexual status quo and continues to reinforce a spurious dichotomy between "good" women and "bad" women. The assumption that women who work in the prostitution trade are "evil," "immoral," "lazy," "hedonistic," and "sexually aberrant" has been challenged by feminists who have identified the diversity of women involved in the trade and have also recognized that their involvement in the profession in most cases is a rational response to women's economically disadvantaged position.[49] Indeed in 1991, a select committee investigating prostitution in Australia's capital city, Canberra, recommended changes to welfare provisions in order to make prostitution a "less viable alternative" for women.[50] This statement perhaps inadvertently acknowledges that prostitution often affords women greater economic return, flexibility, and independence than is currently available through other forms of employment yet, as Melbourne sex worker Helen Koureskas has argued, the decision of women to enter this trade for economic or any other reason continues to be delegitimated through the attribution of "immorality" and persistent claims that these women require punishing or "saving."[51]

The structural inequality that feminists have identified as central to contextualizing and understanding crimes of infanticide, abortion, and prostitution has also been emphasized in relation to property crimes. Industrialization, which fostered the development of separate public and private spheres and facilitated a redefinition of male and female roles according to this division, increased women's economic dependence on men and, later, on the state. In the late nineteenth century the diminished economic opportunities available to women, reinforced by the emerging middle-class ideal of women as "angels of the home," conflicted sharply with the realities of many women's lives. It is no accident that, historically, property crimes have been committed primarily by women who lack material resources and that the nature of their offenses reflect the opportunities available to them. In the late nineteenth century, for example, women who worked as domestic servants and thieved from their employers figured prominently among women offenders. In later decades, shoplifting, an offense inextricably related to women's role as consumers, emerged as a significant form of female offending.[52] In more recent times the relationship between women's offending and their economic circumstances has been reflected in women's commission of Social Security and credit fraud.[53] It is important to note, however, that women's overrepresentation among property offenders might partly be explained through differential policing and judicial processes that, in keeping with dominant stereotypes of the sexes, assume that women are the most likely perpetrators of these offenses. In contrast, numerous studies of shoplifting have shown little difference between male and female rates of offending, and some have indeed shown that men steal more items and items that are often of greater value than the food and clothing typically stolen by women.[54]

Since the mid-1980s, across Western nations, there has been a marked increase in the number of women convicted and imprisoned for property-related offenses. This is no doubt partly due to the nexus between property crime and illicit drug use. This is a subject that also warrants sex-specific analysis, given that women's licit drug use has for the most part been a socially acceptable and indeed enthusiastically promoted activity. Even in exploring the nexus between women's property offending and drug use, however, women's economic marginalization remains crucial. Women are rarely involved in the higher, moneymaking echelons of the drug trade, and as users they are less likely to be able to legally afford to maintain their drug use. Some feminists have argued that the upsurge in property offenses committed by women is due to the "feminization of poverty," but when viewed in a broader historical context it becomes clear that women's economic position today is reflective of more persistent and deep-seated inequalities.

Feminist Interpretations of Women's Imprisonment

In redressing the absence of women in traditional accounts of imprisonment, feminist historians and criminologists have also emphasized the analytical importance of situating women's imprisonment within power relations and the broader social structure.[55] Nicole Rafter, for example, has highlighted the significance of sex, race, and class in her account of the nineteenth-century emergence and nature of the women's prison system in the United States. According to Rafter, this system was largely a product of the "reformist" efforts of White, middle-class women who were concerned by what they perceived as the waywardness and immorality of working-class women. Their concerns and assumptions were mirrored in the establishment of a bifurcated system that was composed of prisons that housed women felons, a disproportionate number of whom were Black, and women's reformatories that confined predominantly young, White women who were guilty of minor sex-related offenses. Rafter argues that the reformatories constituted a major development in prison history. By advocating the detaining of women in a "gentler environment" where they could be trained in domestic service and taught femininity through the example of virtuous women, the reformatories departed from the established model of male prisons. Rafter further argues that this development of a feminized disciplinary regime within the reformatories was based upon an increasing rigidity of class and gender divisions. As Rafter puts it:

> Two groups of women — the working-class offenders and the middle-class reformers — met, so to speak, at the gate of the women's reformatory. The struggle between them was economically functional in some ways to the reformers; it helped maintain a pool of cheap domestic labour for women like themselves, and, by keeping women in the surplus labour force, it undergirded the economic system to which they owed their privileged position. But such purely economic explanations do not account adequately for the dedication with which the reformers went about their tasks of rescue and reform. The struggle also involved the definition of gender. Reformers hoped to recast offenders in their own image, to have them embrace the values . . . of the lady.[56]

The development and nature of women's penal institutions in nineteenth-century Britain followed a similar pattern. By the 1930s, however, on both sides of the Atlantic, women's reformatories had largely been displaced, and in many cases had been transformed, into institutions more akin to prisons. Central to this process was the growing influence of criminology and the theories it promulgated in relation to women who offended. As Dobash, Dobash, and Gutteridge argue, the early decades of the twentieth century saw the emergence of a scientific orthodoxy that characterized women offenders as biologically perverse, sexually aberrant, emotionally disturbed, and intellectually deficient. Women were thus posited as being more difficult to deal with than men and as requiring different and more intensive treatment. This perception of the nature and needs of women prisoners, they suggest, was crucial to the aims, ideals, and practices of the New Holloway and Cornton Vale women's prisons that were constructed in Britain during the 1970s.[57]

Cornton Vale, Scotland's only women's prison, was to later provide the location for Pat Carlen's groundbreaking 1983 study, *Women's Imprisonment: A Study in Social Control.* As Carlen explained, this prison differed sharply from the "overcrowded, brutalising institutions" that had previously provoked the outcries of reformers. Providing each prisoner with a "centrally-heated room with hot and cold water [and] . . . access to night-time sanitation," the women confined within Cornton Vale were "neither brutalised by physical violence nor terrorised by psychiatric intervention."[58] Yet Carlen goes on to expose a far more subtle and complex process at work; one that remained embedded in normative notions of women and was inextricably related to the marginalization and, indeed, dismissal of women within the broader society of which Cornton Vale was a part. Carlen's project aimed to provide more than a study of one prison. Rather, her work was intended to explore "the wider meanings of the moment of prison; a moment not to be confined within the interstices of Her Majesty's Institution; meanings not to be contained within the female subject of penology."[59] By adopting a case study approach and locating the life experiences of the women confined in Cornton Vale within a broader social context, Carlen clearly broke with the narrow focus of criminological convention. The result was a study that linked women's imprisonment firmly to "the invisible nature of the social control of women."[60]

At a general level, the profile and life experiences of the twenty-one women who participated in Carlen's study have been identified time and again as being common to the majority of women detained in Western prisons.[61] Although many of the women Carlen interviewed were older than is typical of women prisoners today, their circumstances and experiences were, and remain, far from unusual. All of the women had little education, most were single or effectively so, many had had unstable accommodation, and most had children, although not all of these children had been in the care of their mothers. Many of the women Carlen interviewed had histories of alcoholism, a precursor perhaps to the prevalence of drug addiction among women prisoners today, and the majority had previous experiences of being sexually and/or physically abused. Nearly all of the women, like most women inmates today, were serving short sentences for minor offenses such as prostitution, breaches of the peace, the nonpayment of fines, fraud, shoplifting, and theft. Carlen goes on to argue that the meanings of women's imprisonment in Scotland cannot be explained through reference to crime statistics or conventional understandings of women offenders or prisons. Rather, they are to be found within discursive forms and practices which, conventionally, are considered to be quite unrelated to penology—within, for example, the conventions of the family and the kirk; within traditional forms of public conviviality and ethics of domesticity and masculinity; within some peculiar absences in Scottish social work practice; within the ideological practices of contemporary psychiatry; and within some over-determined presences (e.g. alcohol, unemployment, poverty) within Scottish culture and society.[62]

Women's imprisonment in Cornton Vale is thus identified as being indicative of broader tensions existing within Scottish society. In particular, Carlen focuses upon the contradictory effects of the cult of domesticity for women. On the one hand, the women she interviewed had been expected to conform to dominant ideals of domesticity, and indeed had tried to conform to these ideals. Yet on the other hand, within this domestic sphere as children and later as wives and mothers, they had found themselves socially isolated, economically dependent, frequently impoverished, persistently vulnerable, and often subject to abuse. According to Carlen, the dominant organization of social and economic life in Scotland has operated to control women, and this control has been further made manifest in processes of criminalization and imprisonment. As Carlen puts it, "the majority of these imprisoned women have not merely broken the law. As women, mothers and wives, they have, also, somehow stepped out of place."[63] And it is precisely this failure or inability of women to conform to dominant expectations about women and their place, she suggests, that informs the nature of their imprisonment. In addition to "the repressive organisational features common to men's prisons," Carlen argues, "modes for controlling many Scottish women outside of prison" are incorporated into the women's prison regime, thus producing "a very fine disciplinary web which denies the women both personality and full adult status."[64]

Although Carlen's focus was on a specific prison and its population, there can be little doubt that her analysis has a wider resonance. Indeed, many of the elements identified by Carlen as being central to the prison regime of Cornton Vale have also been noted in other women's prisons. Feminist scholars, for example, have long observed that in contrast to their male counterparts, women prisoners have generally been afforded fewer educational or recreational opportunities. Emphasis has instead been placed upon their acquisition of domestic skills and their attainment of feminine standards of appearance and behavior. Similarly, the notion that women, especially women prisoners, are more emotionally and psychologically unstable than men has resulted in the widespread practice of medicating women prisoners with prescription drugs in order to promote their compliance and hence easy control.[65] Although they have examined women's imprisonment in different places and at different times, feminist scholars have consistently drawn attention to the profoundly gendered nature of women's imprisonment and, more broadly, to the folly of conventional criminology in attempting to understand women's offending, criminalization, and imprisonment without reference to the broader context of sexed social relations.

Standing at the Crossroads

In 1973, having reviewed the existing literature on women's offending, Dorie Klein concluded that "the road from Lombroso to the present [had been] surprisingly straight."[66] Fourteen years later Allison Morris asserted that the claim remained valid.[67] Now as we near the end of the twentieth century, it seems likely that we have come to the crossroads. Twenty-five years of feminist scholarship has pointed to the theoretical inadequacies and pernicious effects of those dominant forms of criminology that persist in ignoring the significance of gender or, even more commonly, continue to reinforce the negative notions of women and women offenders that were so popular among the new scientists of a century ago. Today more women are entering prison than ever before. Imprisonment rates for men are also escalating dramatically. These spiraling imprisonment rates attest to the failure and indeed the inability of conventional criminology to provide meaningful understandings and effective strategies in relation to crime and punishment. Central to this failure has been its refusal to acknowledge the sexed specificity of men's and women's circumstances, experiences, and social positioning and to explore how these factors relate to and inform patterns of offending, criminalization, and punishment. If the significance of sex continues to be ignored and criminology remains focused on supposedly aberrant individuals rather than on broader and inequitable social relations then it is almost certain that the road ahead, for many more people, will simply lead to prison.

NOTES

1. For overviews of recent trends in imprisonment see Vivien Stern, *A Sin Against the Future: Imprisonment in the World* (London: Penguin, 1998) and Nils Christie, *Crime Control as Industry* (London: Routledge, 1994).

2. Mark Finnane, *Punishment in Australian Society* (Melbourne: Oxford University Press, 1997), 27.

3. Donna Harraway, "Situated Knowledges: The Science Question in Feminism and the Privilege of Partial Perspective," *Feminist Studies* 14, no. 3 (1988): 581.

4. Thomas Laqueur, *Making Sex: Body and Gender from the Greeks to Freud* (Cambridge: Harvard University Press, 1990).

5. Michel Foucault, *Discipline and Punish: The Birth of the Prison* (Harmondsworth: Peregrine Books, 1979), 17, 19.

6. Foucault has been strongly criticized by feminists for his failure to acknowledge the significance of sex. Nevertheless his work has proved useful for feminist theorizing, particularly with respect to the gendered dimensions of punishment. For a discussion on this, see Adrian Howe, *Punish and Critique: Towards a Feminist Analysis of Penality* (London: Routledge, 1994), 82–207.

7. Gustav Le Bon, cited in Stephen Jay Gould, *The Mismeasure of Man* (New York: W.W. Norton & Company, 1981), 105.

8. Cesare Lombroso, *L'uomo Delinquente* (Milan: Hoepli, 1876). For a critique of Lombroso's methods, findings, and influence see Gould, *The Mismeasure of Man,* 123–42.

9. Gould, *The Mismeasure of Man,* 124–25.

10. Ibid., 140–42.

11. Cesare Lombroso and William Ferrero, *The Female Offender* (New York: Appleton & Company, 1898 [1895]), 212.

12. Ibid., 95–96, 187.

13. Ibid., 152.

14. Ibid., 149, 151–52, 187–88.

15. Sheldon Glueck and Eleanor Glueck, *Five Hundred Delinquent Women* (New York: Alfred Knopf, 1934), 299, 303, 96.

16. Otto Pollak, *The Criminality of Women* (Philadelphia: University of Pennsylvania Press, 1950), 10.

17. John Cowie, Valerie Cowie, and Eliot Slater, *Delinquency in Girls* (London: Heinemann, 1968), 16.

18. Frederick Thrasher, *The Gang* (Chicago: Phoenix Press, 1963), 157.

19. Freda Adler, *Sisters in Crime: The Rise of the New Female Criminal* (New York: McGraw-Hill, 1975).

20. Richard C. McCorkle, "Gender, Psychopathology, and Institutional Behaviour: A Comparison of Male and Female Mentally Ill Prison Inmates," *Journal of Criminal Justice* 23, no. 1 (1995): 53-61.

21. Frances Heidensohn, *Women and Crime* (London: Macmillan, 1985), 131-34. One of the most celebrated examples of the valorization of male offenders is provided by Jack Katz, *Seductions of Crime: Moral and Sensual Attractions in Doing Evil* (New York: Basic Books, 1988).

22. Albert Cohen, *Delinquent Boys: The Culture of the Gang* (New York: Free Press, 1955), 142.

23. For general overviews of feminist critiques of conventional criminology and feminist analysis of women's offending and punishment, see Heidensohn, *Women and Crime*; Carol Smart, *Women, Crime, and Criminology: A Feminist Critique* (London: Routledge & Kegan Paul, 1976); Allison Morris, *Women, Crime, and Criminal Justice* (Oxford: Basil Blackwell, 1987); Ngaire Naffine, *Female Crime: The Construction of Women in Criminology* (Sydney: Allen & Unwin, 1987).

24. For a discussion of the feminist theorizations of the relationship between sex and gender see Judith Butler, *Gender Trouble: Feminism and the Subversion of Identity* (New York: Routledge, 1990) and *Bodies That Matter: On the Discursive Limits of "Sex"* (New York: Routledge, 1993).

25. For a brief overview of the connection between criminology and Enlightenment notions of knowledge production see Sandra Walklate, *Understanding Criminology: Current Theoretical Debates* (Buckingham: Open University Press, 1998), 3-4. For a more extensive account of the gendered origins and nature of Enlightenment thought see Genevieve Lloyd, *The Man of Reason: "Male" and "Female" in Western Philosophy* (London: Methuen, 1984).

26. Harraway, "Situated Knowledges," 578-83.

27. Hermann Mannheim, *Comparative Criminology*, vol. 2 (London: Routledge & Kegan Paul, 1965), 691.

28. Smart, *Women, Crime, and Criminology*, 35.

29. Gould, *The Mismeasure of Man*, 193.

30. Morris, *Women, Crime, and Criminal Justice*, 12.

31. Ibid., 1.

32. Heidensohn, *Women and Crime*, 128-34.

33. Paul Corrigan and Simon Frith, "The Politics of Youth Culture," in *Resistance Through Rituals*, ed. Stuart Hall and Tony Jefferson (London: Hutchinson, 1976), 239.

34. Morris, *Women, Crime, and Criminal Justice*, 1.

35. Judith Allen, "'The Wild Ones': The Disavowal of *Men* in Criminology," in *Dissenting Opinions: Feminist Explorations in Law and Society*, ed. Regina Graycar (Sydney: Allen & Unwin, 1990), 21.

36. Heidensohn, *Women and Crime*, 112

37. Alison Young, *Imagining Crime: Textual Outlaws and Criminal Conversations* (London: Sage, 1996), 38.

38. Ibid., 46.

39. See Young, *Imagining Crime;* Carol Smart, "Law, Feminism and Sexuality: From Essence to Ethics?" *Canadian Journal of Law and Society* 9, no. 1 (1994): 15-38.

40. Joanne Belknap, *The Invisible Woman: Gender, Crime, and Justice* (Belmont: Wadsworth Publishing Company, 1996), 45.

41. Judith Allen, "The Trials of Abortion in Late Nineteenth and Early Twentieth Century Australia," *Australian Cultural History* no. 12 (1993): 87-95.

42. Regina Graycar and Jenny Morgan, *The Hidden Gender of Law* (New South Wales: Federation Press, 1990), 266-67.

43. Judith Allen, *Sex and Secrets: Crimes Involving Australian Women since 1880* (Melbourne: Oxford University Press, 1990), 30.

44. Allen, "The Trials of Abortion," 94.

45. Marcia Neave, "The Failure of Prostitution Law Reform," *The Australian and New Zealand Journal of Criminology* 21, no. 4 (1988): 202.

46. *Prostitution Control Act* (Vic) 1994.

47. Susan M. Edwards, "Prostitutes: Victims of Law, Social Policy and Organised Crime," in *Gender, Crime and Justice*, ed. Pat Carlen and Anne Worrall (Milton Keynes: Open University Press, 1987), 47.

48. Ibid., 46.

49. Ibid., 52-53.

50. Select Committee on HIV, Illegal Drugs and Prostitution, *Prostitution in the ACT: Interim Report* (Canberra: Legislative Assembly ACT, 1991), 36.

51. Helen Koureskas, "In a Different Voice: The Prostitute's Voice," *Australian Feminist Law Journal* 5 (1995): 99-107.

52. Gail Reekie, *Temptations* (Sydney: Allen & Unwin, 1993), 111-15; Smart, *Women, Crime, and Criminology*, 8-10; Karlene Faith, *Unruly Women: The Politics of Confinement and Resistance* (Vancouver: Press Gang Publishers, 1993), 85.

53. Dee Cook, "Women on Welfare: In Crime or Injustice?" in *Gender, Crime, and Justice*, ed. Pat Carlen and Ann Worrall (Milton Keynes: Open Universtiy Press, 1983), 29-38.

54. Belknap, *The Invisible Woman*, 52; Smart, *Women, Crime, and Criminology*, 8-10.

55. For a general overview of feminist studies of women's imprisonment, see Howe, *Punish and Critique.*

56. Nicole Hahn Rafter, *Partial Justice: Women in State Prisons, 1800-1935* (Boston: Northeastern University Press, 1985), 175.

57. Russell Dobash, R. Emerson Dobash and Sue Gutteridge, *The Imprisonment of Women* (Oxford: Basil Blackwell, 1986), 124-25.

58. Pat Carlen, *Women's Imprisonment: A Study in Social Control* (London: Routledge & Kegan Paul, 1983), 1.

59. Ibid.

60. Ibid., 3.

61. Stern, *A Sin Against the Future,*138-39; Morris, *Women, Crime, and Criminal Justice,* 115-16; Belknap, *The Invisible Woman,* 101-102; Susanne Davies and Sandy Cook, "Women, Imprisonment and Post-Release Mortality," *Just Policy* no. 14 (1998): 16-17.

62. Carlen, *Women's Imprisonment,* 15.

63. Ibid, 59.

64. Ibid, 16.

65. Elaine Genders and Elaine Player, "Women in Prison: The Treatment, the Control and the Experience," in *Gender, Crime, and Justice,* ed. Pat Carlen and Anne Worrall (Milton Keynes: Open University Press, 1987), 161-75; Josie O'Dwyer, Judi Wilson, and Pat Carlen, "Women's Imprisonment in England, Wales and Scotland: Recurring Issues" in *Gender, Crime, and Justice,* ed. Pat Carlen and Anne Worrall (Milton Keynes: Open University Press, 1987), 177-85; Smart, *Women, Crime, and Criminology,* 140-45; Belknap, *The Invisible Woman,* 97-100, 102-111; Morris, *Women, Crime, and Criminal Justice,* 116-25; Faith, *Unruly Women,* 154-58; Carol Major, "Women in Prison: A Cycle of Punishment and Sedation," *Connexions* (May/June 1993): 3-7; Francine Pinnuck, "The Medication of Women Prisoners: A Cause for Concern," *Just Policy* no. 12 (1998): 13-19; Amanda George, "The Big Prison," in *Women and Imprisonment,* ed. Women and Imprisonment Group (Melbourne: Fitzroy Legal Service, 1995).

66. Dorie Klein, "The Etiology of Female Crime: A Review of the Literature," *Issues in Criminology* 8, no. 3 (1973): 7.

67. Morris, *Women, Crime, and Criminal Justice,* 41.

REFERENCES

Adler, Freda. *Sisters in Crime: The Rise of the New Female Criminal.* New York: McGraw-Hill, 1975.

Allen, Judith. *Sex and Secrets: Crimes Involving Australian Women Since 1880.* Melbourne: Oxford University Press, 1990.

———. "'The Wild Ones': The Disavowal of Men in Criminology." In *Dissenting Opinions:*

Feminist Explorations in Law and Society, edited by R. Graycar. Sydney: Allen & Unwin, 1990.

————. "The Trials of Abortion in Late Nineteenth and Early Twentieth Century Australia." *Australian Cultural History* no. 12 (1993).

Belknap, Anne. *The Invisible Woman: Gender, Crime, and Justice.* Belmont: Wadsworth Publishing Company, 1996.

Butler, Judith. *Gender Trouble: Feminism and the Subversion of Identity.* New York: Routledge, 1990.

————. *Bodies That Matter: On the Discursive Limits of "Sex".* New York: Routledge, 1993.

Carlen, Pat. *Women's Imprisonment: A Study in Social Control.* London: Routledge & Kegan Paul, 1983.

Christie, Nils. *Crime Control as Industry.* London: Routledge, 1994.

Cohen, Albert. *Delinquent Boys: The Culture of the Gang.* New York: Free Press, 1955.

Cook, Dee. "Women on Welfare: In Crime or Injustice?" In *Gender, Crime and Justice,* edited by Pat Carlen and Anne Worrall. Milton Keynes: Open University Press, 1987.

Corrigan, Paul, and Simon Frith. "The Politics of Youth Culture." In *Resistance Through Rituals,* edited by Stuart Hall and Tony Jefferson. London: Hutchinson, 1976.

Cowie, John, Valerie Cowie, and Eliot Slater. *Delinquency in Girls.* London: Heinneman, 1968.

Davies, Susanne, and Sandy Cook. "Women, Imprisonment and Post-Release Mortality." *Just Policy* no. 14 (1998).

Dobash, Russell, R. Emerson Dobash, and Sue Gutteridge. *The Imprisonment of Women.* Oxford: Basil Blackwell, 1986.

Edwards, Susan M. "Prostitutes: Victims of Law, Social Policy and Organised Crime." In *Gender, Crime and Justice,* edited by Pat Carlen and Anne Worrall. Milton Keynes: Open University Press, 1987.

Faith, Karlene. *Unruly Women: The Politics of Confinement and Resistance.* Vancouver: Press Gang Publishers, 1993.

Finnane, Mark. *Punishment in Australian Society.* Melbourne: Oxford University Press, 1997.

Foucault, Michel. *Discipline and Punish: The Birth of the Prison.* Harmondsworth: Peregrine Books, 1979.

Genders, Elaine, and Elaine Player. "Women in Prison: The Treatment, the Control and the Experience." In *Gender, Crime and Justice,* edited by Pat Carlen and Anne Worrall. Milton Keynes: Open University Press, 1987.

George, Amanda. "The Big Prison." In *Women and Imprisonment,* ed. Women and Imprisonment Group. Melbourne: Fitzroy Legal Service, 1995.

Glueck, Sheldon, and Eleanor Glueck. *Five Hundred Delinquent Women.* New York: Alfred Knopf, 1934.

Gould, Stephen Jay. *The Mismeasure of Man.* New York: W.W. Norton & Company, 1981.

Graycar, Regina, and Jenny Morgan. *The Hidden Gender of Law.* New South Wales: Federation Press, 1990.

Harraway, Donna. "Situated Knowledges: The Science Question in Feminism and the Privilege of Partial Perspective." *Feminist Studies* 14, no. 3 (1988).

Heidensohn, Frances. *Women and Crime.* London: Macmillan, 1985.

Howe, Adrian. *Punish and Critique: Towards a Feminist Analysis of Penality.* London: Routledge, 1994.

Katz, Jack. *Seductions of Crime: Moral and Sensual Attractions in Doing Evil.* New York: Basic Books, 1988.

Klein, Dorie. "The Etiology of Female Crime: A Review of the Literature." *Issues in Criminology* 8, no. 3 (1973).

Koureskas, Helen. "In a Different Voice: The Prostitute's Voice." *The Australian Feminist Law Journal* 5 (1995).

Laqueur, Thomas. *Making Sex: Body and Gender from the Greeks to Freud.* Cambridge: Harvard University Press, 1990.

Lloyd, Genevieve. *The Man of Reason: "Male" and "Female" in Western Philosophy.* London: Methuen, 1984.

Lombroso, Cesare. *L'uomo Delinquente.* Milan: Hoepli, 1876.

Lombroso, Cesare, and William Ferrero. *The Female Offender.* New York: Appleton & Company, 1898.

Major, Carol. "Women in Prison: A Cycle of Punishment and Sedation." *Connexions* (May/June 1993).

Mannheim, Hermann. *Comparative Criminology.* Vol. 2. London: Routledge & Kegan Paul, 1965.

McCorkle, Richard C. "Gender, Psychopathology, and Institutional Behaviour: A Comparison of Male and Female Mentally Ill Prison Inmates." *Journal of Criminal Justice* 23, no.1 (1995).

Morris, Allison. *Women, Crime, and Criminal Justice.* Oxford: Basil Blackwell, 1987.

Naffine, Ngaire. *Female Crime: The Construction of Women in Criminology.* Sydney: Allen & Unwin, 1987.

Neave, Marcia. "The Failure of Prostitution Law Reform." *The Australian and New Zealand Journal of Criminology* 21, no. 4 (1998).

O'Dwyer, Josie, Judy Wilson, and Pat Carlen. "Women's Imprisonment in England, Wales and Scotland: Recurring Issues." In *Gender, Crime and Justice,* edited by Pat Carlen and Anne Worrall. Milton Keynes: Open University Press, 1987.

Pinnuck, Francine. "The Medication of Women Prisoners: A Cause for Concern." *Just Policy* no. 12 (1998).

Pollak, Otto. *The Criminality of Women.* Philadelphia: University of Pennsylvania Press, 1950.

Rafter, Nicole Hahn. *Partial Justice: Women in State Prisons, 1800-1935.* Boston: Northeastern University Press, 1985.

Reekie, Gail. *Temptations.* Sydney: Allen & Unwin, 1993.

Smart, Carol. "Law, Feminism and Sexuality: From Essence to Ethics?" *Canadian Journal of Law and Society* 9, no. 1 (1994).

————. *Women, Crime and Criminology: A Feminist Critique.* London: Routledge & Kegan Paul, 1976.

Stern, Vivien. *A Sin Against the Future: Imprisonment in the World.* London: Penguin, 1998.

Thrasher, Frederick. *The Gang.* Chicago: Phoenix Press, 1963.

Walklate, Sandra. *Understanding Criminology: Current Theoretical Debates.* Buckingham: Open University Press, 1998.

Young, Alison. *Imagining Crime: Textual Outlaws and Criminal Conversations.* London: Sage, 1996.

Current Trends
in
Women's
Imprisonment

Women and Imprisonment in the United States

The Gendered Consequences of the U.S. Imprisonment Binge

Barbara Owen

IN THE LAST TWENTY-FIVE YEARS the number of women imprisoned in the United States has increased rapidly and the rate of growth of women's imprisonment has far outpaced that of men's imprisonment.[1] As the United States continues its imprisonment binge,[2] the remarkable gender-based difference in the rate of this increase demands explanation. In 1970, just under 6,000 women were incarcerated in state and federal prisons. By 1980, this number had doubled to about 12,000 women, and by 1996 nearly 75,000 women were incarcerated in state and federal prisons; another 52,000 were in local jails. In California alone, the female prison population rose dramatically from 1,316 in 1980 to over 11,000 in 1998. Other states have imprisoned women at equally high numbers; during 1996 Texas incarcerated about 10,000, New York prisons held just under 4,000 and Florida held over 3,000. The "so-called 'war on drugs' and related changes in legislation, law enforcement practices and judicial decision making" has fueled this dramatic increase in the punishment and incarceration of women.[3] As the United States continues to increase criminal penalties through mandatory sentencing and longer sentence lengths, the gendered consequence of the imprisonment binge must be explained.

The "war on drugs" and analysis of actual crimes and arrests do not entirely explain the extraordinary increases in the numbers of women in prison or give a comprehensive picture of the women being imprisoned. Other factors that need to be examined to understand this include the patriarchal structure of the social control system and the decreasing economic opportunities available to women, including changes in the public welfare system. The following sections look at these factors, current research on the profile of imprisoned women, and the pain and deprivation women prisoners experience.

Patriarchy and Women's Imprisonment

The unwillingness of U.S. society to address the real needs of women and girls on the margins of society and the adoption of the "Three Strikes and You're Out" law-and-order philosophy inevitably create an increase in the number of women in prison. As Nancy Kurshan argues, the imprisonment of women, "as well as all other aspects of our lives, takes place against a backdrop of patriarchal relationships."[4] Kurshan defines patriarchy as "the manifestation and institutionalization of male dominance over women and children in the family and the extension of male dominance over women in society in general." She suggests that:

> the imprisonment of women in the US has always been a different phenomenon than that for men: women have traditionally been sent to prison for different reasons, and once in prison, they endure different conditions of incarceration. Women's "crimes" have often had a sexual definition and have been rooted in the patriarchal double standard. Therefore the nature of women's imprisonment reflects the position of women in society.[5]

The study of women in prison must be framed through the lens of patriarchy and its implications for the everyday lives of women. When women's imprisonment itself is examined separately, the rising numbers of women in prison can be seen as a measure of the society's failure to care for the needs of women and children who live outside the middle-class protection afforded by patriarchy. The increased numbers of women in prison reflect the cost of allowing the systematic abuse of women and children, the problem of increased drug use, and a continuing spiral of marginalization from conventional institutions.[6]

The Gendered Implications of "Three Strikes and You're Out"

Current U.S. prison policy is grounded in law-and-order legislative efforts to control crime, such as mandatory minimum prison sentences and increased sentence lengths.[7] Mona Danner describes the ways in which these trends in correctional policy have affected the lives of women, particularly the increasing penalties for drug offenses. She suggests that the consequences for women in this era of expanded punishments have been largely unexplored. In her view, public debate over "Three Strikes" and law-and-order policy ignores the reality of women's lives and the fact that often women are forced to bear the emotional and physical brunt of these misguided policies.[8] She argues that women bear these costs in three ways. First, the enormous cost of the correctional institutions needed to accommodate an increasing number of prisoners has direct implications for other social services. Danner cites a study by the RAND Corporation that predicts that California's "three strikes" law will require cuts in other government services totaling 40 percent over eight years.[9] She predicts that social services for the poor, especially for women and children, will be hardest hit.

Second, Danner argues that the reduction in these services will result in increased unemployment for women working as social service providers; for example, those employed as social workers, case workers, counselors, and support staff within social service agencies. Third, Danner feels that the "three strikes" laws disproportionately affect women as caregivers, both through the imprisonment of men and women's own imprisonment. Because almost 1.5 million children in the United States are children of prisoners, a significant number of children are growing up with at least one parent incarcerated. The financial and social implications for the community as well as for the individual life chances of these children are yet another cost of the "three strikes" bandwagon.[10]

Crime Rates, the Economic Context, and Social Welfare Changes

In analyzing data from the 1970–1995 Uniform Crime Reports, Darrell Steffensmeir and Emilie Allan found that current arrest trends for women are based, in part, on "the sharp increase in the numbers of women arrested for minor property crimes, like larceny, fraud and forgery."[11] Drug offenses, they state, nevertheless have the most significant impact on female arrest rates. Steffensmeir and Allan argue that "it is female inequality and economic vulnerability that shape most female offending patterns."[12] Elliot Currie has examined the connections between crime, work, and welfare, and asserts that unemployment is a steady predictor of criminality and subsequent imprisonment.[13] Currie sees the lack of adequate economic and social supports for women and children in U.S. society as a key feature in the rising crime rates. The poverty of their lives and the lack of educational and economic opportunity makes crime a reasonable choice for some women; subsequent imprisonment is a predictable outcome. Currie argues that material disadvantage and quality of family life are intimately related and may in fact combine to create conditions that foster crime. Currie also presents evidence that unemployment is also tied directly to substance abuse.[14] As mentioned in the previous section, Danner suggests that social services that benefit women and children are likely to be sacrificed in order to expand the criminal justice system.[15] One specific example of social service cuts is in the Welfare Reform Bill of 1996 that imposed a limit on the period poor women may receive Aid to Families with Dependent Children. She ties the costs of the expansion of the prison system directly to the reduction in these benefits.

These findings have direct relevance for explaining the problems of female imprisonment. Most imprisoned women in the United States struggle with both unemployment and substance abuse. The majority of imprisoned women were unemployed prior to their arrest and have experienced problems with chronic substance abuse. Over half the women surveyed by the Bureau of Justice Statistics (BJS) did not work at the time of their arrest.[16] A study of California's women prisoners I co-authored with Barbara Bloom found that over 60 percent of the women interviewed in 1994 reported that they were unemployed prior to imprisonment.[17] Many of these women prisoners indicated that drug and alcohol problems contributed to their inability to work. "Making more money from crime and hustling," child care responsibilities, and lack of training and education were also reported as reasons for unemployment.[18]

Drug problems and violation of the increasingly stringent drug laws bring women into contact with the justice system at ever increasing rates and aggravate existing personal and social problems. The war on drugs and corresponding punitive incarceration policies have resulted in a disproportionate sanction against women[19] and have contributed to their economic marginalization. As I have argued previously, three central issues shape the lives of women prior to imprisonment: multiplicity of abuse in their pre-prison lives; family and personal relationships, particularly those relating to male partners and children; and spiraling economic marginality leading to criminality.[20] To further explain the connection between America's current imprisonment binge and the effect of economic hardship and changes in public welfare systems on women's lives prior to incarceration, in the following section I outline a description of the changing profile of women in U.S. prisons.

Changing Profile of Women in U.S. Prisons

The national surveys conducted by the BJS, the American Correctional Association (ACA), and the Federal Bureau of Prisons provide profiles of women in prison in the United States.[21] These profiles describe a population that is poor, that is disproportionately African American and Hispanic, and that has little education and few job skills. This population is primarily composed of young women who are single heads of households; the majority of those who are imprisoned (80 percent) have at least two children. Most women enter prison with a complex set of health and personal problems that are not addressed by the U.S. prison system. The most current BJS survey, based on 1991 data, found that women in prison were most likely to be Black, unemployed at the time of arrest, and never married. With a median age of thirty-one years in 1991, the female prison population was somewhat older than those imprisoned in 1986.[22] In the federal system, women were more likely to be somewhat older, with an average age of thirty-six years, and more likely to be White than women in state prisons.[23]

Research on the racial makeup of U.S. prison populations and incarceration patterns clearly shows the disproportionate use of imprisonment in the United States. Bloom uses the term "triple jeopardy" to describe the complex interaction of class, race, and gender that contributes to the ever increasing rates of imprisonment.[24] Stephanie Bush-Baskette examines the impact of the war on drugs on Black women prisoners, offering a strong analysis of the relationship between race, gender, and arrests for drug-related offenses.[25] She notes that Black women have been imprisoned for drug offenses at rates of about twice that of Black males and more than three times the rate of White females.[26] Cora Mae Mann makes a similar argument in her study of arrest categories in three states (California, Florida, and New York).[27] Although demographic profiles describe the problem of racial/ethnic overrepresentation in the female prison population, few studies have examined this issue empirically. Sharon McQuaide and John Ehrenreich suggest that "virtually nothing is known about the characteristics of women prisoners across the racial and ethnic groupings."[28] They further state:

> If knowledge of female prisoners as a group is thin, knowledge of the strengths and differences of female prisoners of different racial and ethnic backgrounds, the unique needs of particular groups of female offenders or the interactions between racial or ethnic identity and the prison experience is all but non-existent.[29]

The issue of social and economic class also needs to be taken into account. Most criminologists see that poor people are much more likely to become imprisoned than individuals from the middle, upper, and propertied classes.[30] In one of our California studies, we found that less than one-half of the women were employed at the time of their arrest and only about one-half had completed high school. About one-fifth of the California prisoners said they were on some form of public assistance in the year prior to their arrest.[31] Clearly poor women, particularly those of color, suffer disproportionately under the punitive sentencing structures of the war on drugs and mandatory sentencing policies.

The Pains of Imprisonment

Women in U.S. prisons, like prisoners throughout the world, face specific pains and deprivations arising from their imprisonment. The Women's Institute for Leadership Development for Human Rights (WILDHR) has indeed argued that U.S. prisons violate three basic human rights:

1. The right to bodily integrity, including freedom from physical and sexual abuse

2. The right to health, including adequate and responsive medical care

3. The right to economic security, including the ability to work and to have an adequate standard of living.[32]

Joy Pollock has described the range of pains and deprivations experienced by women prisoners and their consequences. She found that stress shapes the daily life of women inmates and has three primary sources: arbitrary rule enforcement, assaults on self-respect that are endemic to prison life, and the loss of children. Additionally, she states, lack of autonomy and control over decision making and the impact of monotony and routine create problems for women in U.S. prisons.[33] Detailed below are several specific issues that contribute to the pain and deprivation of women prisoners.

Disparate Disciplinary Practices

Although male prisons typically hold a much greater percentage of violent offenders, women tend to receive disciplinary infractions at a greater rate than men. In her comparative study of Texas prisons, Dorothy McClelland found that women prisoners were cited more frequently and punished more severely than males. The infractions committed by the women in McClelland's Texas sample were overwhelmingly petty and, she suggests, perhaps a result of a philosophy that expects rigid and formalistic rule compliance on the part of women but not on the part of the men.[34] The most common infractions among the women were "violation of a written or posted rule" and "refusing to obey an order." McClelland found that women were more likely to be strictly supervised than men and cited for behavior that would be overlooked in an institution for men.[35] The patriarchal patterns of social control that propel women into prison may also be responsible for the differences in rule enforcement between male and female institutions.

Sexual Abuse

In *All Too Familiar: Sexual Abuse of Women in U.S. Prisons,* Human Rights Watch examines the serious problem of sexual abuse.[36] In their careful review of sexual abuse in selected U.S. prisons, the Human Rights Watch investigators identified four specific issues:

1. The inability to escape one's abuser

2. Ineffectual or nonexistent investigative and grievance procedures

3. Lack of employee accountability (either criminally or administratively)

4. Little or no public concern.

They state bluntly that: "Our findings indicate that being a woman in U.S. state prisons can be a terrifying experience."[37] As Barbara Bloom and Meda Chesney-Lind note, the sexual victimization of women prisoners is difficult to uncover due to inadequate protection afforded women who file complaints and an occupational subculture among the staff that discourages complete investigation of these allegations. Additionally, they suggest, the public stereotype of women as "bad girls" compromises the legitimacy of the women's claims.[38]

Separation from Children and Significant Others

Most research on women in prison describes the importance of family, particularly children, in the lives of imprisoned women.[39] National surveys of women prisoners found that three-quarters of women prisoners were mothers; two-thirds had children who were under the age of eighteen years.[40] Bloom and Chesney-Lind discuss the implications of motherhood among U.S. women prisoners. They argue that mothers in prison face multiple problems in maintaining relationships with their children and encounter obstacles created by both the correctional system and child welfare agencies.[41] Bloom and Chesney-Lind state that the distance between the prison and the children's homes, lack of transportation, and limited economic resources compromise a woman prisoner's ability to maintain these relationships. Slightly over one-half of the women responding to Barbara Bloom and David Steinhart's 1993 survey of imprisoned mothers reported never receiving visits from their children.[42]

The limited economic resources of caregivers, too, is an added difficulty for women prisoners who wish to maintain relationships with their children. Susan Phillips and Barbara Bloom analyze the impact of the changing welfare system on relatives caring for children of incarcerated parents.[43] They argue that lack of financial support for these children is grounded in the inflexibility of public assistance programs that were not designed to meet the needs of care-giving relatives.

Inadequate Health Care

As WILDHR notes, the physical and mental health needs of women prisoners are often neglected, if not ignored. Leslie Acoca argues that the enormity of health care issues may in fact eclipse other correctional concerns as the female inmate population continues to grow.[44] The majority of imprisoned women have significant health care problems and few of these needs are met in the nation's prisons. Acoca suggests that the lack of women-specific drug treatment is one of the factors linked to the high incidence of HIV infection among imprisoned women.[45] Nationwide, about 3.3 percent of women prisoners are thought to be HIV-positive, compared to about 2 percent of male prisoners.[46] Women in prison are also at greater risk of contracting other infectious diseases, such as tuberculosis, sexually transmitted diseases, and hepatitis B and C infections. Acoca asserts that inadequate prison health care as well as risky behavior prior to arrest contributes to this problem.[47]

Pregnancy and reproductive health needs are another neglected area of health care. Estimates of the percentage of pregnant women in prisons and jails range from 4 percent to 9 percent. Acoca states that pregnancy during incarceration must be understood as a high-risk situation, both medically and psychologically, for inmate mothers and their children. She notes that deficiencies in the response of prisons to the needs of pregnant inmates include lack of prenatal and postnatal care, including nutrition; inadequate education regarding childbirth and parenting; and inadequate preparation for the mother's separation from the infant after delivery. An opportunity to provide reproductive health care and education to this group of women through basic education and family planning is also being missed.[48]

Lack of Recognition of Prior Victimization

Closely related to these mental health needs is the need to recognize the impact of the physical, sexual, and emotional abuse experienced by women who are in prison. Studies of women in prison establish that many women have been violently victimized both as children and adults. Joycelyn Pollock-Byrne has summarized this research by saying:

> Some researchers suggest female inmates come from families marked
> by alcoholism, drug addiction, mental illness, desertion and child
> abuse. Several studies show that in a sample of incarcerated women, a
> majority had been physically and sexually abused as children, had
> greater difficulties in their interpersonal relationships with family and
> peers than others and had been treated for mental problems.[49]

Studies consistently report a high incidence of physical, sexual, and emotional victimization in the personal histories of women prisoners; 30 to 80 percent of the women in these studies have a background of abuse.[50] In our studies, we found that physical, sexual, and emotional abuse is a defining experience for the majority of women in California prisons. In our sample, which included the category of emotional abuse, 80 percent of the women interviewed reported experiencing some kind of abuse. With the exception of sexual assault, most women indicated that they were harmed by family members and other intimates.[51] Most prisons lack programs to deal with this fundamental problem.[52]

Lack of Substance Abuse Treatment

The vast majority of imprisoned women have a need for substance abuse services. National and statewide surveys consistently demonstrate that women in prison are quite likely to have an extensive history of drug and alcohol use. This research concludes that drug use acts as a multiplier in interaction with criminality.[53] Even in the face of this significant problem, providing prison-based services for women has only recently been considered throughout the nation.[54] A national survey of drug programs for female prisoners found that a relatively small percentage of women prisoners in prisons and jails receive any treatment while incarcerated. In a review of treatment strategies for drug-abusing female offenders, Jean Wellisch and colleagues argue that in-prison treatment must be designed specifically to address the needs of women offenders and that current substance abuse services are not sufficiently tailored to meet the needs of women prisoners. These researchers found that programs were hampered by insufficient individual assessment; limited treatment for pregnant, mentally ill, and violent women prisoners; a lack of appropriate treatment; and insufficient vocational training of program providers.[55] These findings are supported by a recent study released by the National Center on Addiction and Substance Abuse (CASA). CASA found that women substance abusers are more prone to intense emotional distress, psychosomatic symptoms, depression, and low self-esteem than male inmates. The CASA report examines the cost and consequence of the war on drugs and concludes that, nationwide, women substance abusers are not receiving an adequate level of treatment.[56]

Insufficient Mental Health Services

Mental health disorders are equally neglected in U.S. prisons. Although few studies accurately assess the prevalence and incidence of these needs, estimates suggest that 25 percent to over 60 percent of the female prison population requires mental health services.[57] Many inmates are often diagnosed as experiencing both substance abuse and mental health problems.[58] Singer and others report that many incarcerated women have had experience with both the criminal justice system and the mental health system.[59] Teplin, Abraham, and McClelland found that over 60 percent of female jail inmates had symptoms of drug abuse, over 30 percent had signs of alcohol dependence, and one-third had post-traumatic stress disorder.[60] These problems and other problems associated with imprisoned women are best managed outside the punitive environment of U.S. prisons.[61]

Lack of Educational and Vocational Programs

In addition to inadequate substance abuse programs and mental health services, educational and vocational programs are also in short supply. In 1990, Joycelyn Pollock-Byrne found that female prisons offered fewer vocational and educational program opportunities than did prisons for men.[62] The situation today is not much better. Morash, Haarr, and Rucker reviewed prison programs for men and women and found that, in general, women across the country lack programming adequate to their needs.[63] One aspect of this inadequacy is that many vocational programs for female inmates emphasize the traditional roles of women and women's work.[64]

Conclusion

In 1994, Bloom, Chesney-Lind, and Owen offered this explanation for the incredible increases in the female prison population:

> The increasing incarceration rate for women in the State of California, then, is a direct result of short-sighted legislative responses to the problems of drugs and crime—responses shaped by the assumption that the criminals they were sending to prison were brutal males. Instead of a policy of last resort, imprisonment has become the first order response for a wide range of women offenders that have been disproportionately swept up in this trend. This politically motivated legislative response often ignores the fiscal or social costs of imprisonment. Thus, the legislature has missed opportunities to prevent women's crime by cutting vitally needed social service and educational programs to fund ever-increasing correctional budgets.[65]

Today I continue to argue that the problems and issues women who have been sent to prison have experienced—abuse and battering, economic disadvantage, substance abuse, and unsupported parenting responsibilities—are best addressed outside the punitive custodial environment.[66] Under current policy, these complex problems are laid at the feet of the prison by a society unwilling or unable to confront the problems of women on the margin. As a whole, the prison system is designed to deal with the criminality of men and their behavior while incarcerated. The women confined in U.S. prisons are enmeshed in a criminal justice system that is ill-equipped and confused about handling the problems of women—the problems that brought them to prison and the problems they confront during their incarceration. The prison, with its emphasis on security and population management and lack of emphasis on gender-specific treatment and programs, is nevertheless left to deal with the failings of society's institutions. In the United States we expect too much from prisons. Prisons are called upon to deal with deep and complicated problems that society ignores. The number of imprisoned women will continue to rise until the reality of their lives on the streets, and inside the prisons, forces a reexamination of prison policy and its gendered consequences.

NOTES

1. Russ Immarigeon and Meda Chesney-Lind, *Women's Prisons: Overcrowded and Overused* (San Francisco: National Council on Crime and Delinquency, 1992).

2. John Irwin and James Austin, *It's About Time: America's Imprisonment Binge* (Belmont, Calif.: Brooks Cole, 1997).

3. Human Rights Watch, *All Too Familiar: Sexual Abuse of Women in U.S. Prisons* (New York: Human Rights Watch, 1996), 23.

4. Nancy Kurshan, "Women and Imprisonment in the U.S.," in *Cages of Steel*, ed. W. Churchill and J. J. Vander Wall (Washington, D.C.: Maisonneuve Press, 1992), 331–58.

5. Ibid., 331.

6. Barbara Owen, *In the Mix: Struggle and Survival in a Women's Prison* (Albany: State University of New York Press, 1998), 13-14.

7. Mona J. E. Danner, "Three Strikes and It's Women Who Are Out," in *Crime Control and Women,* ed. S. Miller (Thousand Oaks, Calif.: Sage Publications, 1998), 1-11.

8. Ibid., 5.

9. Peter W. Greenwood, C. Peter Rydell, Allan F. Abrahamse, Jonathan P. Caulkins, James Chiesa, Karyn E. Model, and Stephen P. Klein, *Three Strikes and You're Out: Estimated Benefits and Costs of California's New Mandatory Sentencing Laws* (Santa Monica, Calif.: The RAND Corporation, 1994).

10. Danner, "Three Strikes," 8.

11. Darrell Steffensmeir and Emilie Allan, "The Nature of Female Offending: Patterns and Explanations," *in Female Offenders: Critical Perspectives and Interventions,* ed. R. Zupan (Gaithersburg, Md.: Aspen Publishing, 1998), 10.

12. Ibid., 11.

13. Elliot Currie, *Confronting Crime: An American Challenge* (New York: Pantheon, 1985).

14. Ibid., 107-108.

15. Danner, "Three Strikes," 6.

16. Bureau of Justice Statistics, *Women in Prison* (Washington, D.C.: U.S. Department of Justice, 1994).

17. Barbara Owen and Barbara Bloom, *Profiling the Needs of California's Female Prisoners: A Needs Assessment* (Washington, D.C.: National Institute of Corrections, 1995).

18. Ibid., 22.

19. Barbara Bloom, Meda Chesney-Lind, and Barbara Owen, *Women in California Prisons: Hidden Victims of the War on Drugs* (San Francisco: The Center on Juvenile and Criminal Justice, 1994); Human Rights Watch, *All Too Familiar;* Mark Mauer and Tracey Huling, *Young Black Americans and the Criminal Justice System: Five Years Later*

(Washington, D.C.: The Sentencing Project, 1995); Stephanie Bush-Baskette, "The War on Drugs as a War on Black Women," in *Crime Control and Women*, ed. S. Miller (Thousand Oaks, Calif.: Sage Publications, 1998), 113–29.

20. Barbara Owen, *In the Mix*.

21. Bureau of Justice Statistics, *Women in Prison*, 1994; Bureau of Justice Statistics, *Prisoners in 1989* (Washington, D.C.: U.S. Department of Justice, 1990); Bureau of Justice Statistics, *Prisoners in 1990* (Washington, D.C.: U.S. Department of Justice, 1991); Bureau of Justice Statistics, *Special Report: Women in Prison* (Washington, D.C.: U.S. Department of Justice, 1991); Bureau of Justice Statistics, *Women in Jail in 1989* (Washington, D.C.: U.S. Department of Justice, 1992); American Correctional Association (ACA), *The Female Offender: What Does the Future Hold?* (Washington, D.C.: St. Mary's Press, 1990); Sue Klien, "A Profile of Female Offenders in State and Federal Prisons," in *Female Offenders: Meeting the Needs of a Neglected Population*, ed. American Correctional Association (Laurel, Md.: American Correctional Association, 1993), 1–6.

22. Bureau of Justice Statistics, *Women in Prison*, 1994.

23. Klien, "Profile of Female Offenders," 1–6.

24. Barbara Bloom, "Triple Jeopardy: Race, Class, and Gender as Factors in Women's Imprisonment" (Ph.D. diss., University of California-Riverside, 1996).

25. Bush-Baskette, "War on Drugs," 119.

26. Ibid., 113.

27. Cora Mae Mann, "Women of Color in the Criminal Justice System," in *The Criminal Justice System and Women*, ed. B. Price and N. Skoloff (New York: McGraw-Hill, 1995), 118–35.

28. Sharon McQuaide and John Ehrenreich, "Women in Prison: Approaches to Studying the Lives of a Forgotten Population," *Affilia: Journal of Women and Social Work* 13, no. 2 (1998): 233–47.

29. Ibid., 236.

30. Jeffery Reiman, *The Rich Get Richer and the Poor Get Prison* (Needham Heights, Mass.: Allyn and Bacon, 1990).

31. Owen and Bloom, *Profiling Women Prisoners*.

32. The Women's Institute for Leadership Development for Human Rights (WILDHR), *Human Rights for Women in U.S. Custody* (San Francisco, Calif.: WILDHR, n.d.).

33. Joycelyn Pollock, *Counseling Women in Prison* (Thousand Oaks, Calif.: Sage Publications, 1998), 32–33.

34. Dorothy McClelland, "Disparity in the Discipline of Male and Female Inmates in Texas Prisons," *Women and Criminal Justice* 5, no. 2 (1994): 71–97.

35. Pollock, *Counseling Women in Prison*, 35.

36. Human Rights Watch, *All Too Familiar*.

37. Ibid., 1.

38. Barbara Bloom and Meda Chesney-Lind, "Women in Prison: Vengeful Equity," in *It's a Crime: Women and Criminal Justice*, ed. R. Muraskin (forthcoming).

39. Owen, *In the Mix*, 119-20.

40. Bureau of Justice Statistics, *Special Report: Women in Prison*, 1991.

41. Bloom and Chesney-Lind, "Women in Prison."

42. Barbara Bloom and David Steinhart, *Why Punish the Children? A Reappraisal of the Children of Incarcerated Parents* (San Francisco, Calif.: National Council on Crime and Delinquency, 1993).

43. Susan Phillips and Barbara Bloom, "In Whose Best Interest? The Impact of Changing Public Policy on Relatives Caring for Children of Incarcerated Parents," *Child Welfare: Special Issue—Children with Parents in Prison* 77 (1998): 531-41.

44. Leslie Acoca, "Defusing the Time Bomb: Understanding and Meeting the Growing Health Care Needs of Incarcerated Women in America," *Crime and Delinquency* 44, no. 1 (1998): 49-70.

45. Ibid., 51.

46. Bureau of Justice Statistics, *Surveys of Inmates in State Correctional Facilities, 1995.* (Washington, D.C.: U.S. Department of Justice, 1997).

47. Acoca, "Defusing the Time Bomb," 54.

48. Acoca, "Defusing the Time Bomb."

49. Joycelyn Pollock-Byrne, *Women, Prison and Crime,* (Pacific Grove, Calif.: Brooks/Cole, 1990), 70.

50. Bureau of Justice Statistics, *Women in Prison;* Bureau of Justice Statistics, *Special Report: Women in Prison;* American Correctional Association, *The Female Offender;* Klien, "Profile of Female Offenders," 1-6; Owen and Bloom, *Profiling the Needs of California's Female Prisoners;* Pollock-Byrne, *Women, Prison and Crime.*

51. Owen and Bloom, *Profiling the Needs of California's Female Prisoners*, 30-31.

52. Pollock, *Counseling Women in Prison;* Beverley Fletcher, Lynda Dixon Shaver, and Dreama Moon, *Women Prisoners: A Forgotten Population* (Westport, Conn.: Praeger, 1993); Owen and Bloom, *Profiling the Needs of California's Female Prisoners.*

53. Owen, "In the Mix," 44-45; National Center on Addiction and Substance Abuse, *Behind Bars: Substance Abuse and America's Prison Population* (New York: Columbia University, 1998).

54. Jean Wellisch, M. Douglas Anglin, and Michael Prendergast, "Treatment Strategies for Drug-Abusing Women Offenders," in *Drug Treatment and the Criminal Justice System,* ed. J. Inciardi (Thousand Oaks, Calif.: Sage Publications, 1994), 5-25.

55. Ibid., 20-22.

56. National Center on Addiction and Substance Abuse, *Behind Bars.*

57. Acoca, "Defusing the Time Bomb," 54.

58. Acoca, "Defusing the Time Bomb."

59. Mark Singer, Janet Bussey, Li Yu Song, and Lisa Lunghofer, "The Psychosocial Issues of Women Serving Time in Jail," *Social Work* 40, no. 1 (1995): 103–14.

60. Linda Teplin, Karen Abraham and Gary McClelland, "Prevalence of Psychiatric Disorders among Incarcerated Women," *Archives of General Psychiatry* 53 (1996): 505–12.

61. Owen, *In the Mix,* 16–17.

62. Pollock-Byrne, *Women, Prison and Crime.*

63. Merry Morasch, Robin Haarr, and L. Rucker, "A Comparison of Programming for Women and Men in U.S. Prisons in the 1980s," *Crime and Delinquency* 40, no. 2 (1994): 197–221.

64. Pamela Schram, "Stereotypes about Vocational Programming for Female Inmates," *Prison Journal* 78, no. 3 (1998): 244–67.

65. Bloom, Chesney-Lind, and Owen, *Women in California Prisons,* 2.

66. Owen, *In the Mix,* 17.

REFERENCES

Acoca, Leslie. "Defusing the Time Bomb: Understanding and Meeting the Growing Health Care Needs of Incarcerated Women in America." *Crime and Delinquency* 44, no. 1 (1998).

American Correctional Association. *The Female Offender: What Does the Future Hold?* Washington, D.C.: St. Mary's Press, 1990.

Bloom, Barbara. "Triple Jeopardy: Race, Class and Gender as Factors in Women's Imprisonment." Ph.D. diss., University of California-Riverside, 1996.

Bloom, Barbara and Meda Chesney-Lind. "Women in Prison: Vengeful Equity." In *It's a Crime: Women and Criminal Justice,* edited by R. Muraskin. Forthcoming.

Bloom, Barbara, Meda Chesney-Lind, and Barbara Owen. *Women in California Prisons: Hidden Victims of the War on Drugs.* San Francisco: Center on Juvenile and Criminal Justice, 1994.

Bloom, Barbara, and David Steinhart. *Why Punish the Children? A Reappraisal of the Children of Incarcerated Parents.* San Francisco, Calif.: National Council on Crime and Delinquency, 1993.

Bureau of Justice Statistics. *Prisoners in 1989.* Washington, D.C.: U.S. Department of Justice, 1990.

———. *Prisoners in 1990.* Washington, D.C.: U.S. Department of Justice, 1991.

———. *Special Report: Women in Prison.* Washington, D.C.: U.S. Department of Justice, 1991.

———. *Women in Jail in 1989.* Washington, D.C.: U.S. Department of Justice, 1992.

———. *Women in Prison.* Washington, D.C.: U.S. Department of Justice, 1994.

———. *Survey of Inmates in State Correctional Facilities, 1995.* Washington, D.C.: U.S. Department of Justice, 1997.

Bush-Baskette, Stephanie. "The War on Drugs as a War on Black Women." In *Crime Control and Women,* ed. S. Miller. Thousand Oaks, Calif.: Sage Publications, 1998.

Chesney-Lind, Meda. *The Female Offender: Girls, Women and Crime.* Thousand Oaks, Calif.: Sage Publications, 1997.

———. "Patriarchy, Prisons and Jails: A Critical Look at Trends in Women's Incarceration." *The Prison Journal* 71, no. 1 (1991).

Currie, Elliot. *Confronting Crime: An American Challenge.* New York: Pantheon, 1985.

Danner, Mona J. E. "Three Strikes and It's Women Who Are Out." In *Crime Control and Women,* edited by S. Miller. Thousand Oaks, Calif.: Sage Publications, 1998.

Fletcher, Beverly, Lynda Dixon Shaver, and Dreama Moon, eds. *Women Prisoners: A Forgotten Population.* Westport, Conn.: Praeger, 1993.

Greenwood, Peter W., C. Peter Rydell, Allan F. Abrahamse, Jonathan P. Caulkins, James Chiesa, Karyn E. Model, and Stephen P. Klein. *Three Strikes and You're Out: Estimated Benefits and Costs of California's New Mandatory Sentencing Laws.* Santa Monica, Calif.: The RAND Corporation, 1994.

Human Rights Watch. *All Too Familiar: Sexual Abuse of Women in U.S. Prisons.* New York: Human Rights Watch, 1996.

Immarigeon, Russ, and Meda Chesney-Lind. *Women's Prisons: Overcrowded and Overused.* San Francisco: National Council on Crime and Delinquency, 1992.

Irwin, John, and James Austin. *It's About Time: America's Imprisonment Binge.* Belmont, Calif.: Brooks Cole, 1997.

Klien, Sue. "A Profile of Female Offenders in State and Federal Prisons." *In Female Offenders: Meeting the Needs of a Neglected Population,* edited by American Correctional Association. Laurel, Md.: American Correctional Association, 1993.

Kurshan, Nancy. "Women and Imprisonment in the U.S." In *Cages of Steel,* edited by W. Churchill and J. J. Vander Wall. Washington, D.C.: Maisonneuve Press, 1992.

Mann, Cora Mae. "Women of Color in the Criminal Justice System." In *The Criminal Justice System and Women,* edited by B. Price and N. Skoloff. New York: McGraw-Hill, 1995.

Mauer, Mark, and Tracey Huling. *Young Black Americans and the Criminal Justice System: Five Years Later.* Washington, D.C.: The Sentencing Project, 1995.

McClelland, Dorothy. "Disparity in the Discipline of Male and Female Inmates in Texas Prisons." *Women and Criminal Justice* 5, no. 2 (1994).

McQuaide, Sharon, and John Ehrenreich. "Women in Prison: Approaches to Studying the Lives of a Forgotten Population." *Affilia: Journal of Women and Social Work* 13, no. 2 (1998).

Morash, Merry, Robin Haarr, and Lila Rucker. "A Comparison of Programming for Women and Men in U.S. Prisons in the 1980s. *Crime and Delinquency* 40, no. 2 (1994).

National Center on Addiction and Substance Abuse (CASA). *Behind Bars: Substance Abuse and America's Prison Population.* New York: Columbia University, 1998.

Owen, Barbara. *In the Mix: Struggle and Survival in a Women's Prison.* Albany: State University of New York Press, 1998.

Owen, Barbara, and Barbara Bloom. *Profiling the Needs of California's Female Prisoners: A Needs Assessment.* Washington, D.C.: National Institute of Corrections, 1995.

Phillips, Susan, and Barbara Bloom. "In Whose Best Interest? The Impact of Changing Public Policy on Relatives Caring for Children of Incarcerated Parents." *Child Welfare: Special Issue—Children with Parents in Prison* 77 (1998).

Pollock, Joycelyn. *Counseling Women in Prison.* Thousand Oaks, Calif.: Sage Publications, 1998.

Pollock-Byrne, Joycelyn. *Women, Prison and Crime.* Pacific Grove, Calif.: Brooks/Cole, 1990.

Reiman, Jeffery. *The Rich Get Richer and the Poor Get Prison.* Needham Heights, Mass.: Allyn & Bacon, 1990.

Schram, Pamela. "Stereotypes about Vocational Programming for Female Inmates." *Prison Journal* 78, no. 3 (1998).

Singer, Mark, Janet Bussey, Li Yu Song, and Lisa Lunghofer. "The Psychosocial Issues of Women Serving Time in Jail." *Social Work* 40, no. 1 (1995).

Steffensmeir, Darrell, and Emilie Allan. "The Nature of Female Offending: Patterns and Explanations." In *Female Offenders: Critical Perspectives and Interventions,* edited by R. Zupan. Gaithersburg, Md: Aspen Publishing, 1998.

Teplin, Linda, Karen Abraham, and Gary McClelland. "Prevalence of Psychiatric Disorders among Incarcerated Women." *Archives of General Psychiatry* 53 (1996).

Wellisch, Jean, M. Douglas Anglin, and Michael Prendergast. "Treatment Strategies for Drug-Abusing Women Offenders." *In Drug Treatment and the Criminal Justice System,* edited by J. Inciardi. Thousand Oaks, Calif.: Sage Publications, 1994.

Women's Institute for Leadership Development for Human Rights (WILDHR). *Human Rights for Women in U.S. Custody.* San Francisco, Calif.: WILDHR, n.d.

Transformative Justice versus Re-entrenched Correctionalism
The Canadian Experience

Karlene Faith

Introduction

THE PURPOSE OF THIS CHAPTER is to give an overview of women's imprisonment in Canada during the 1990s, an eventful decade for women in prison in this country. Although national officials speak of "restorative justice" and issue declarations about how prisons destroy far more lives than they save, their solutions are to hire more police and prison guards and to build more prisons. The renewed commitment by the state to correctionalism in practice contradicts their rhetoric. The current expansion of correctional practices also defies the vision and solicited recommendations of various consultant groups over the decade.

As of March 1997, 14,448 persons of a total Canadian population of approximately 30 million were serving federal prison sentences. Of this number, 357 (2.5 percent) were women.[1] The first text to be published in Canada on the subject of women in prison was *Too Few to Count: Canadian Women in Conflict with the Law*,[2] a title that well described the Canadian situation until the mid-1990s. As has been true in many countries, because of their small numbers and the inappropriateness of the rigid, militaristic, masculinist, hierarchical model of male prisons, women have been an afterthought in the correctional enterprise.

There are forty-two federal prisons for men in Canada,[3] generally allowing for placement according to security classification and proximity to

family. By contrast, until the mid-1990s, only one prison had been constructed for federally sentenced women who were serving prison terms of
two years to life. Prior to 1934, when the Prison for Women (P4W) in
Kingston, Ontario, was opened, women were confined to small, dark, cold,
bug-ridden attics and cells in men's prisons.[4] The anachronistic P4W, a
large, foreboding, domed, limestone structure surrounded by eighteen-
foot-high stone walls, the interior a dark maze of cells and corridors, offered
little improvement in terms of comfort or civility. Between 1938 and 1978,
eleven of twelve government-appointed investigative bodies agreed that
P4W should be closed and the women dispersed to minimum security
regional facilities in order to be closer to their families.[5]

In 1979, Simon Fraser University sponsored the first Canadian conference on women in prison, organized by Margit Nance, a director of continuing studies, and Curt Griffiths, a professor of criminology. One of the
speakers was the Honorable Jean-Jacques Blais, then the Solicitor General
of Canada; he prematurely announced, to cheers, that P4W would soon
be phased out. Claire Culhane, now a Canadian legend as a researcher-
advocate-activist on behalf of prisoners' rights, was then newly involved in
prison work. She, Lorraine Berzins (a long-time prisoners' rights activist),
Marie-Andrée Bertrand (a Montreal professor whose research produced the
first scholarly Canadian article on gender and crime),[6] and others among us
organized a radical caucus. We lobbied other conference attendees to contribute to a critical analysis of prisons with sensitivity to gender issues. We
didn't use diplomacy in exposing violations of women's rights within the
prison; we spoke forthrightly in the presence of correctional officials. In
1981, spurred by feminist activists, the Canadian Human Rights Commission concurred that the physical structure and custodial practices at P4W
were discriminatory. Correctional Service of Canada (CSC) funded cos-
metic improvements, but nothing changed substantively.

The landmark 1979 conference set in motion a small but growing
national network of activists, former prisoners, advocates, and academics
whose work is meant to serve the interests of women in prison. This work
has had very mixed results, as will be discussed later in this chapter. On the
one hand, it has been a demoralizing era, and the end is not yet in sight.
The government, contrary to the progressive rhetoric of top officials, seems

as committed as ever to confining lawbreakers in destructive environments that exacerbate the problems of crime. On the other hand, more people throughout this vast nation are serving a watchdog function and are determined to turn the penal tide. Throughout Canada, an Australian poster saying "Women Don't Belong in Cages . . . Prisons Are the Real Crime" is displayed illustrating an international coalition of concern for the problems of imprisoned women in our respective countries.

At a strategy meeting in 1997 (referred to as the Gatineau Gathering), former prisoners, lawyers, researchers, and community activists, from different cultures and from all over Canada, met for two days to discuss strategies to address human rights violations in the prisons and to join forces for transformative changes in the justice system. The background for those meetings was a series of 1990s events, some of which aroused the public to a recognition of abuses in women's prisons and others of which raised hopes among human rights activists for more sensible ways of responding to law-breaking.

The Exposé

A videotape of abuses against eight women in segregation cells at P4W, committed in April 1994 by an emergency response team from a neighboring men's prison, was televised in February 1995. The clandestine video obtained by the Canadian Broadcasting Corporation (CBC) was taped according to official policy of the Correctional Service of Canada; restraint incidents that could produce personal injury were recorded for later evidence of unprofessionalism. When CSC learned that a popular news commentary television program, *The Fifth Estate*, was planning to air the tape, they filed an injunction. Months later the courts ruled in favor of public access.

The images televised across the nation included, first, a silent, late-night platoon of six or seven men (the exact number was never reported), wearing identical Darth Vader outfits. They are unidentifiable behind helmets, heavily padded combat suits, masks, shields, and enormous boots. Part of this platoon's function is to intimidate, and they are successful. On orders of the prison warden to conduct emergency strip-searches and cell extractions in the segregation unit, they burst into the cell of a woman who is asleep on her cot. They rouse her by slamming her onto the cement floor, then cut and rip off her night clothing and underwear. They confine her with leg irons and handcuffs. Two or three of the "team" hold her naked body to the cement floor with their padded knees pressed into her back. They stand her against the cement wall, banging their batons right next to her ear. They repeat this procedure from one cell to the next. Some women scream, clearly terrorized. Others, their more experienced friends, call out reassurances, though in desperate voices; they tell the other women that if they just obey they won't be hurt. One woman pleads in vain for her glasses, which are kicked underfoot. After the televised scene, the women were led away, one by one, for "body cavity" searches. Their cells were overturned; their meager belongings were taken away; and the cots, mattresses, and bedding were removed.

Following the strip-searches in the cells and the body cavity searches, "the women were left in shackles and leg irons, wearing paper gowns, on the cement floors of empty cells."[7] Nothing at all was found. None of the eight women had been guilty of holding contraband of any kind. But their punishment continued because they had been judged to be threatening to the guards in the days preceding the assault. As reported later in the official inquiry,[8] one prisoner was accused of throwing urine at a guard, which she said was untrue. Apparently some women were yelling insults from their cells to the guards in response to what they construed as verbal abuse against themselves. Guards claimed they knew of an escape plan, but it was proven to be a false claim. Another guard insisted she had been pricked by an HIV-infected needle, though the accused prisoner said that that definitely did not happen and no evidence was found. Two Native women testified that a guard told them they should go hang themselves, as several of their friends had recently done. The guard vehemently denied having said it. Meanwhile, coinciding with these events inside the prison, the guards' union was demonstrating with pickets outside the prison, expressing serious anger about management decisions and demanding policy changes. As detailed in the Arbour report,[9] tensions and hostilities produced by prison culture itself were pervasive prior to and following the assault on the eight women in segregation in April 1994.

The women in segregation were denied bedding, mattresses, showers, telephone calls, reading or writing material, hot water, radios, adequate feminine hygiene products, legal counsel, and clothing. Some of them were transferred to men's prisons, including men's mental hospital prisons and wards for sex offenders, where they have been ensconced in isolated, grim conditions amid men they fear, and have been subjected to debilitating drug treatments and continual "programming." Some of the assault victims were confined in segregation at P4W for as long as nine months, although expert witnesses who testified at the Arbour Commission Inquiry agreed that anything over a month poses a serious health risk to almost anyone.[10]

John Edwards, the commissioner of corrections, publicly defended the actions of the emergency response team (ERT). It was disclosed that this team included a woman whose uniform made her indistinguishable from the men. She apparently assisted with some of the strip-searches, and observed others. The commissioner thought the team had behaved very professionally, and the prison warden echoed his point of view. Both withheld information and attempted to cover up the details of what had occurred. The warden kept her job for a time, until pressured to leave under charges of giving prison contract jobs to her daughter. The commissioner was pressured to resign in the course of the investigation.

The CSC mission statement includes five core values, none of which was honored in the actions of the ERT. These core values are:

1. We respect the dignity of individuals, the rights of all members of society, and the potential for human growth and development.

2. We recognize that the offender has the potential to live as a law-abiding citizen.

3. We believe that our strength and our major resource in achieving our objectives is our staff and that human relationships are the cornerstone of our endeavour.

4. We believe that the sharing of ideas, knowledge, values and experience, nationally and internationally, is essential to the achievement of our mission.

5. We believe in managing the Service with openness and integrity and we are accountable to the Solicitor General.[11]

The atrocities, the clear helplessness of the women, naked in their vulnerability to armored, faceless men, aroused Canadian public interest in women prisoners in a way that nothing had before. On the video, the frightened women are stripped not only of clothing but also of dignity. They are degraded. In later televised interviews, they are well dressed, poised, some very young, small, feminine, all articulate, not the least bit fearsome. They describe how the assault brought back memories of rape and other painful events in their lives.

Gayle Horii, a former prisoner at P4W who watched the strip-search on television, said "Please understand that the events of April 1994 at P4W were not as shocking to those of us who had already experienced prison, as to those who have not. However, the immediate condemnation by humanist groups across Canada, who easily recognized that women forced into positions of degrading submission is sexual violence, helped to legitimize our feelings."[12]

That prisons often operate outside the law did not come as a revelation. But correctional critics and journalists were nonetheless surprised at the willingness of CSC representatives to tell blatant lies in televised interviews, such as the new warden's insistence that none of the men with the emergency response team had removed women's clothing, and contradicting herself as to whether she'd seen the video at the time of making that statement. As one observer summed up the conclusions of the Arbour report: "Left to itself, the CSC is incorrigible."[13]

The Arbour recommendations included numerous demands that the legal and criminal justice systems increase surveillance of prison wardens and staff just as the staff and the wardens want more eyes on prisoners; everyone under the continuous, multidirectional gaze of the postmodern era.[14] And yet, within several years, prison violence was again inflicted and blamed on women who were incarcerated—in men's prisons in Saskatchewan and Nova Scotia, and in two of the new women's prisons—again bringing in unwarranted "emergency" responses. Old habits die hard (that is, using force to address an "emergency"), and the standard for what constitutes an "emergency" (that is, justifying force) has not risen in the 1990s.

The P4W assault event was a historical milestone in public education in Canada regarding women's prisons and that event is bracketed by other significant events in the 1990s, most of which have promised changes in the way "corrections" are done to women in this country.

Other Significant Events of the 1990s

1. In 1990, a task force appointed by the Solicitor General to evaluate federal corrections for women produced its report, *Creating Choices*. This document represented the work of hundreds of people, primarily women — many feminists; First Nations women; and representatives of many national women's organizations, including the national Elizabeth Fry association, which provides leadership for effective prisoner advocacy work and human rights monitoring. Prisoners were also directly involved in the research. Like the task forces that preceded them, this task force first recommended the closure of the federal Prison for Women (P4W) in Kingston, Ontario, an archaic structure situated thousands of miles from most women's families. To replace it, they recommended regional minimum security facilities that would make room for children and that would draw on noncarceral community resources to assist women in rebuilding their lives.

Five of the "woman-centered" principles by which the task force formulated their recommendations, as discussed by Margaret Shaw,[15] were based on the women's needs for personal empowerment, meaningful choices, respect and dignity, a supportive environment, and shared responsibility. The success of the regional centers would depend on the implementation of those principles.

2. The Solicitor General promised to close P4W by 1994 and to follow the task force recommendation for small, low-custody, regional, cottage-style "homes" for women "in conflict with the law." Local communities submitted proposals for four of the new prisons and the sites were selected: Edmonton, Alberta; Joliette, Quebec; Truro, Nova Scotia; and Kitchener, Ontario. In addition, a Healing Lodge for Aboriginal women was to be constructed outside Maple Creek, Saskatchewan.

3. Meanwhile, in 1993, the Burnaby Correctional Centre for Women opened in British Columbia (capacity of 120), with responsibility for both provincially sentenced women and federally sentenced women from British Columbia and the Yukon and Northwest Territories. In an exchange of services agreement, the federal government helps fund the new prison, which

houses both women prisoners serving up to two years provincial time (including weekends) and federal prisoners serving up to life sentences. The provincial authorities govern the prison according to provincial regulations, which are often more punitive and restrictive than federal regulations, and which deny long-term prisoners their rights under federal law. The concern is that other regional prisons will be similarly abandoned by the federal government to the control of the host province to the detriment of federally sentenced women.

4. By 1995, P4W was still crowded with women but the new prisons were under construction. The rhetoric of the five newly appointed wardens was generally in the direction of community involvement and allocation of attention and resources to the issues women face in and out of prison concerning children; employability; housing and transportation; drug and alcohol dependencies; and unresolved issues such as rape, battering, or childhood sexual abuse. When the evidence of abuse at P4W was televised, CSC rushed completion of the new prisons. It was announced that when the remaining prisoners were transferred, P4W would definitely close.

5. In 1995, spurred by the public outcry over the televised strip-searches, the Solicitor General commissioned an official "Inquiry into Certain Events at the Prison for Women," chaired by an appeals court judge, the Honorable Louise Arbour (who later became the chief justice in the United Nations war tribunal court). As commissioner, Judge Arbour was meticulous in her investigation, seeking perspectives and information from the prisoners, guards, and management on the inside and from researchers, activists, lawyers, and academics on the outside. In documenting the events before, during, and after the assaults, Judge Arbour and her two assistants, Dr. Tammy Landau and Dr. Kelly Hannah-Moffat,[16] presented abundant evidence of law-breaking on the part of the correctional service.[17] The very act of the ERT entering the segregation unit was illegal because with women in bed in their cells, there was no emergency.

Although Judge Arbour's focus was primarily on the particular need of prison authorities to observe and strictly adhere to the law and to function under the direct eye of the judiciary, she also examined evidence of practices that were legal but nevertheless inhumane. For example, she was outraged at the abuses permitted through extended segregation practices and she referred to corrections as a "deplorable defensive culture."[18]

CSC's defiance in responding to so few of the recommendations has been met with scorn. For example, Saskatchewan Member of Parliament Chris Axworthy wrote to the deputy commissioner with two pages of examples of human rights abuses in women's prisons, in particular the transfer of women to men's mental hospital prisons. He concludes, "My astonishment at CSC's disregard for the observations and recommendations of the many task force reports, most notably the Arbour Commission Report and Creating Choices, cannot be overstated."[19] On 1 April 1997, the Elizabeth Fry association issued a public "report card" on the performance of CSC in the year since the Arbour review. The CSC got an F-minus, especially for the racist policy of excluding Native women from the Healing Lodge on the grounds of classification. On 18 April 1997, Ovide Mercredi, the national chief of the Assembly of First Nations (AFN), said that the CSC is "going back a hundred years in its treatment of women prisoners."[20]

The only potentially significant recommendation offered by Judge Arbour that has been implemented to date is the establishment of the position of deputy commissioner in charge of women's prisons. The appointee, Nancy Stableforth, is well qualified but because ninety-five staff are answerable to the commissioner, not to her, there are many questions about how effective she can be. In her first years she has served more as a diplomatic broker of information and a consultant than as a policy maker. She is, nevertheless, frequently approached with recommendations from community groups that urge her to take action on such issues as classification inequities; the need for culturally sensitive programming and job training; and peer-based services to address substance abuse, the effects of physical (including sexual) abuse, self-injury, and problems with parenting.

Although feminists opposed the action, the CSC did heed another recommendation from the Arbour report: They created all-female emergency response teams. This is regressive because it wrongly assumes that women, as men's "equals," have need for these teams. Giving women the entitlement and skills to conduct forced strip-searches of other women is not a step forward for women in either role.

Community coalitions have also pushed for proactive reduction of the numbers of women who are incarcerated. In a discussion paper, the deputy commissioner affirmed her agreement with this principle,[21] making reference to one of the key recommendations of the 1990 *Creating Choices* Task Force, namely "the development of a release strategy which would enhance community resource and support networks for women released from federal custody,"[22] with the valid implication that parole boards may release women earlier if practical resources are awaiting them. With practical support, women are also less likely to violate parole and be returned to prison. Because the government itself is cutting rather than increasing funds for such resources while investing increasing resources in prisons, such pronouncements may be heard as a self-rebuke.

6. In late 1995, the Okimaw Ohci Healing Lodge was opened to thirty First Nations women. The brochure for the opening states: "Healing for Aboriginal women means the opportunity, through Aboriginal teachings, spirituality and culture, to recover from histories of abuse, regain a sense of self-worth, gain skills and rebuild families." Planned and designed by members of various First Nations, the buildings are arranged in the shape of an eagle seen from the sky, situated in a beautiful prairie setting near aspen woods and green hills; they are staffed mostly by Native people who have no history with corrections. The Healing Lodge posed a significant challenge to punishment models, yet CSC gave considerable latitude to the planning committee and did not object to the plans for healing circles; the steady availability of elders for personal counsel; or the absence of locks, fences, and walls.

For two years following its opening, women testified about the nurturing they received at the lodge and the spiritual strengths they gained that have assisted them since their departures. In the past few years, however, more women have been reporting that it has become "more like a prison," more punitive than healing. Rather than CSC letting itself be led by the principles of the Healing Lodge in setting policy for the other women's prisons, as Arbour and many others have advised, "corrections" is imposing its timeworn penal principles onto the Okimaw Ohci "Healing" Lodge. Perhaps this was inevitable given the line of state authority.

7. In 1996, shortly after the opening of the new prison in Edmonton, a

woman was killed. She had been suicidal and had made several failed attempts. This time she persuaded a friend who was also in prison to help her. The friend was convicted of manslaughter; the event was interpreted as an act of institutional violence because the suicide was not a solitary act. There were also half-hearted escape attempts by other women. The immediate conclusion drawn by the CSC, which did not address the reasons why the women were so eager to get away one way or another, was that the prison needed tighter security. The prison was virtually shut down for several months and opportunistically transformed into a maximum security prison. The prison outside Halifax likewise became a maximum security prison after a woman walked away and others were in conflicts with staff and each other. All the other new "minimum security facilities" followed suit, hiring more staff, constructing high, double chain-linked fences topped with coiled razor wire and installing radar detection, cameras, tape recorders, and other security devices.[23] Once on the grounds, having passed through a security check, these prisons appear very attractive until one recognizes the level of technological surveillance or hears cries from segregation units. The voices of women who have been isolated in men's mental illness prison wards can scarcely be heard at all. As Kim Pate said, "We face a situation now where corrections for women is basically back at the turn of the century."[24]

Through the use of euphemisms, CSC has avoided clear communication about the nature of the new prisons; the segregation units, for example, are called the "enhanced" units. Pastel walls and "living units" notwithstanding, the negative consequence of these new prisons has been to illustrate the impossibility of creating a "community" involving freedoms, responsibilities, and choices within a "correctional" penological enterprise. These new prisons serve as both empirical and symbolic evidence that punishment and healing practices are incompatible.[25] Some women do heal in prison, not through institutional regimens but with self-help such as peer counseling or through the Native Sisterhood groups organized by First Nations women in Canadian prisons.

In the new prisons, planned as alternatives to the penitentiary model, guards now unapologetically use pepper spray on women who are disruptive and exercise the control that is fundamental to a total institution. In 1996, a woman in one of the regional prisons became very agitated and cut herself. Jo-Ann Mayhew, a former prisoner, reports that "the staff responded by using pepper spray, placing the woman in shackles and handcuffs, locking her in an isolation unit, stripping her naked, repeated use of pepper spray, then left her in the shackles, handcuffs, naked on a steel frame without a mattress or blanket for several hours."[26] The Board of Investigation concluded that all this punishment, force, and restraint was "not seen as excessive and appears reasonable." They did say that leaving her naked on the cell floor was unjustified.[27]

Who is Affected?

The profile of women in prison in Canada reflects that of women elsewhere in the Western, carceral world. The majority are young, under thirty-five. Political minority groups are overrepresented. In Canada this minority group is First Nations women, who constitute up to 100 percent of women in some provincial and territorial jails. They make up 18.7 percent of the federally imprisoned women's population (the proportion of Black women has increased to 11.5 percent and the proportion of Asian women to 3 percent). Although Natives represent just 4 percent of the total population of Canada, almost 30 percent of federal prisoners overall are Native.[28] Although they commit fewer crimes, Native women are incarcerated in jails and prisons at a higher rate than Native males; generally they are women who have left the reserves, who are disconnected from Native traditions, and who drift into the inner cities without shelter or skills. The majority of women sent to prison (of all ancestries) are single mothers. The majority have histories of illegal drug dependency and childhood sexual abuse.[29] Many suffer from inner pain, often produced by the prison itself; "slashing" (self-injury) is not uncommon.[30]

The crimes of women in Canadian prisons run the gamut. Women commit up to 15 percent of all violent assaults and homicide. They are convicted of 14 percent of cocaine charges and over two-thirds of charges involving pharmaceuticals. They engage in petty theft, chronic larceny (shoplifting), writing bad or fraudulent checks, and welfare fraud. Since the 1980s, increasing numbers of African American and Caribbean women have been incarcerated in Canada for drug trafficking offenses, usually cannabis related. Overall, federal sentences of women average less than six years, but for the less serious crimes they serve longer sentences than do men.[31] The number of federally sentenced women in prison is constantly fluctuating, but is now generally between 300 and 350. From the mid-1970s to the late 1990s, up to half of these women were incarcerated in the Prison for Women. Most others, not always by their choice or to their liking, have been held in provincial jails through exchange of services agreements (ESA). For example, beginning in 1982 women from Quebec—one-fifth of federal prisoners[32]—have been locked in the Maison de Tanguay in order to remain in a French language environment. Now the federally sentenced women are at the new prison in Joliette.

Progressive Rhetoric/Regressive Practices

In 1998, Solicitor General Andy Scott and Commissioner of Corrections Ole Ingstrup spoke in various public venues, to the press, and in Parliament about the futility of prisons as a response to illegal behaviors. Both came into office following the decisions for new prison construction. The Solicitor General acknowledged that prison "can be detrimental or counterproductive" for most people. He stated that offenders "could be more safely and effectively handled through community programs." And he spoke of the "need to develop effective alternatives to incarceration for offenders." Scott argued that public safety, his number one priority, would be better met with community programs that include education and job training and that interpersonal conflicts involving illegal behaviors should be resolved through restorative justice methods.[33]

Ingstrup, in charge of fifty-six prisons and camps, halfway houses, and other aspects of "corrections," is unequivocal: "Prison is a costly and often destructive response to social ills. Harsher penalties do not lead to safer communities. We must deal with the public perception, and fear, that crime is greater than it actually is."[34] Notions of various forms of restorative justice, either innovative or based on traditional aboriginal practices, have officially entered the lexicon of criminal justice agencies.

In his report evaluating the performance of CSC over the previous year, the then Solicitor General Andy Scott concluded decisively,

Keeping offenders in prison for long periods of time is costly. There does not, furthermore, appear to be any clear link between crime in society and levels of incarceration. In addition, community-based interventions appear to equal or outperform institutional measures in the safe reintegration of offenders. There is a growing acceptance of the principle that incarceration should be reserved for higher risk offenders who have committed violent crimes, and that non-violent offenders are best managed through community-based supervision and programs.[35]

Echoing Scott, the National Parole Board states in its manual, "The lowest recidivism rates occur when incarceration is used as a last resort and treatment is offered by programs outside the correctional system."[36] And in a discussion paper the Canadian Criminal Justice Association (CCJA) has this to say:

> We need to recognize that the retributive approach is not the most effective. The fact that Canada is over-reliant on incarceration as a response to crime is well documented. Canada is outranked only by the United States. While the number of adults charged has decreased, the rate of those charged who are being incarcerated has increased.[37]

The report notes that the passage of Bill C-41 in 1996 requires courts to consider "all available alternatives to imprisonment and to use imprisonment only if no other course of action can ensure the protection of society."[38] This significant legislation was perhaps fiscally motivated, but it suggests a political will to move away from a punishment model. Because relatively few women prisoners are a threat to public safety, the increased use of incarceration (for both men and women) suggests that courts are still operating on the basis of "prison as the norm" and community-based alternatives are not yet sufficiently developed to provide the courts with new options. Because of cutbacks in social services state funding for alternative justice services is very limited. Victims' rights groups, via the media, have aggressively persuaded "the public" of a need for more stringent incarceration practices. Law-and-order politicians respond to their constituents by putting pressure on parole boards to withhold releases.[39]

Even as the rhetoric of officials has shifted to a decarceration philosophy, the ratio of guards to prisoners has increased, and women's cell space in Canada has nearly tripled since 1992. In addition to the new prisons in Truro, Edmonton, Kitchener, Joliette, Vancouver, and Maple Creek, women have been incarcerated and drugged in solitary confinement in a variety of men's prisons, a return to the barbarism of the nineteenth century. Having installed maximum security technology in each of the new women's prisons and transferred all but seventeen of the women from P4W to the new facilities, at the first signs of trouble CSC then transferred all the women with maximum security classification to isolated segregation units and psychiatric wards in men's prisons. Over time, women have been sent to the Saskatchewan Penitentiary, the Regional Psychiatric Centre in Saskatchewan, Ste-Anne-des-Plaines in Quebec, and the Springhill Institution in Nova Scotia. At one point, women were incarcerated in eleven different prisons.

Far from the vision of the "Creating Choices" Task Force, and far from the stern judgment of the Honorable Louise Arbour that "corrections" lawlessness had to cease, some of the new women's prisons perpetuated many of the same old abuses: "illegal strip searches, no access to counsel, excessive use of force and segregation, illegal involuntary transfers."[40] The departure of maximum security women prisoners from the new prisons left primarily minimum and medium security women in the chain of new maximum security prisons. Even the Healing Lodge, contrary to its intended mission, and despite the recommendations of the Arbour Commission and initial CSC agreement, was not permitted in the end to accept women with a maximum security classification.

Most remarkably, the archaic Prison for Women is still open. In late 1999, over twenty women are incarcerated there with up to ninety men and women on the staff to guard them day and night. P4W is costing CSC and the taxpayers Can$300,000 per year per woman.[41] Instead of being closed, the P4W now has a growing population, perhaps in part to justify its budget. Many of the determined women who were never transferred out of P4W have served virtual life sentences for incremental or steady failure to adapt to prison. They would act up, get write-ups, and be denied parole. The plan was to send them to the notoriously "masculinist" Kingston Penitentiary across the street, which houses sex offenders. Construction of a segregated women's section in the psychiatric ward was already under way when four of these women developed a court case against CSC. With public support for the women, represented by Elizabeth Fry Societies across Canada,[42] CSC relented, permitting the women to stay at P4W. Now other women are being returned to P4W if they do not adapt to their new prison, and some new prisoners are being sent to P4W direct from sentencing. As cynics predicted after each new delay of the promised closure, P4W has become the CSC dumping ground for women with maximum security classification, almost half of whom are Native women and most of whom do not represent a threat to public safety. In addition to containing unruly women who assert their rights and those of other prisoners, the maximum classification is assigned to women who have not learned how to be compliant prisoners, but who, instead of "fighting the system," retreat into drugs, injure themselves, or attempt suicide.

Although it continues to expound on a decarcerative philosophy to pacify its more liberal critics, in practice CSC traveled full circle in reentrenching correctionalism in the women's system. Despite its purported commitment to the principles of the *Creating Choices* recommendations, despite the findings of a federal commission of inquiry that CSC was breaking the law, despite the men at the top who profess a belief in community-based restorative justice, more women are being locked up—without an increase in their crime rate. Instead of giving women choices for turning their lives around, the punishment industry, which leads to a dead end, is thriving as never before.

The Cruel Farce of Classification

The population mix of high security, low security, long-term, and short-term prisoners has negative effects on virtually every woman in a mixed federal-provincial Canadian prison. Short-termers may be traumatized, but they are just passing through. Long-termers are there to stay; it's their home, their community. Technically, every woman in prison is classified as a minimum, medium, or maximum security risk. The classification is not generally based on the seriousness of the crime or the length of her sentence but rather on the woman's behavior as a prisoner. If she is passive and compliant, she is a good prisoner. Many women entering prison have been oversocialized to be dependent, and have formed self-destructive dependency patterns involving men, social services, and drugs. These women are often highly adaptable to prison, being very obedient. They are credited with "institutional adjustment" or "adaptive behavior." Overdependency, the very problem that led them to prison, is exacerbated by the prison experience.

Officially, classification is constructed from the level of risk represented by each woman: risk that she will attempt to escape and risk that, if she is successful, she will cause harm. But there is no clear way to predict risk.[43] It is the independent, unruly, opinionated women who are more likely to be classified maximum security, along with women who feel defeated. Maximum security women are at higher risk for suicide as a response to the conditions of maximum security confinement, and it is primarily Native women who are dying.[44] Collectively resistant to the White man's prison, Aboriginal women are disproportionately classified as maximum security, at 41 percent,[45] though they represent less than 20 percent of federally sentenced women. Although it observes the "antisocial attitude" among maximum security women, especially toward law enforcement and other criminal justice agencies and institutions,[46] CSC fails to acknowledge the reasons why Native women, in particular, might be alienated from the White man's law and order.

Women classified as maximum security—8.1 percent of the imprisoned women's population[47]—have limited opportunities for prison jobs, study, interaction with others, vocational rehabilitation programs, and self-help groups. Another issue eliciting protest from prisoners and advocates is the reclassification of women with mental health needs to maximum security as a means of justifying more control over them and sending them to men's prisons for "medical" care.[48] In 1996, the CSC identified twenty-six federally sentenced women whom they deemed to be mentally unstable, but a psychiatrist's independent review found that just eight women had need of mental health intervention.[49] Although some women who are classified as maximum security do have assault on their record, or more serious violent offenses, their crimes are highly situational and they are not commonly violent within the prison. Like women classified as medium or minimum security who have also assaulted or killed, most of the maximum security women are not characterized as women at risk of committing violence, either inside or out of prison. It is their classification, rather than anything about themselves, that suggests their "dangerousness."

The Importance of Place

The place of incarceration matters to the woman who is locked up. In the 1980s, Gayle Horii, then a lifer at P4W in Ontario, went on a fast that, when it was clear that her life was at risk, resulted in the authorities meeting her demand that she be transferred to an all-male prison across the country in British Columbia so she could be near her husband, who had serious heart trouble. She later successfully avoided transfer to the new Burnaby women's prison in the same region on the grounds that she could not obtain the higher education at the women's prison that was available to her in the men's prison. She currently has a case pending which, if heard, will call on the Supreme Court of Canada to consider gender equality issues in corrections.

Other women have similarly fought successfully to stay in their home province through exchange of services. In a Saskatchewan case, a federally sentenced Native woman was held by the Court to be in danger if sent to P4W, citing evidence of the ill health, disorder, and fear that pervades that institution. For example, it was noted that between late 1988 and early 1992 seven women at P4W committed suicide, and that six of those were Native women.[50] This woman was kept in her home province for her own safety and protection.

A primary reason for building regional prisons is to give imprisoned women closer proximity to their children and extended family. Although the geographic dispersal of imprisoned women has brought some women closer to their children, many others, including those from the far north who are incarcerated in a southern province, are still thousands of miles from their families. Also, the new facilities have not addressed the parenting issues that cause grief to so many imprisoned women; nor have they facilitated unsupervised time for mothers with their children. In every respect, the state persists in withholding consideration for the ultimate victims of incarceration: the children of prisoners.

Political Signals

One effect of this string of new maximum security women's prisons in Canada is to falsely convey that we now have many more women committing crime and that they are dangerous and need to be kept away from us, under guard and behind bars and fences. A likely effect of all the new beds, from 30 to 80 in each of the five newest prisons and 120 in Burnaby, is that judges will send more women to prison for less serious crimes. This is what has happened in the United States over the past twenty years, where a burgeoning prison industry is justified in part by the war on drugs. Judges routinely pronounce sentences according to options familiar to them. For all the rhetoric about restorative justice, when new prison cells become available, judges fill them. Create more space and the net widens. Previously insignificant petty charges now receive a lock-up punishment.

Prison reform movements are as old as the history of prisons. It is essential that when we learn of a human rights abuse within a prison we seek to end it. But every effort to reform the punitive features of imprisonment results in more bureaucracy, yet more punitive policies, and more societal dependency on the prison system not only to contain the bad guys but to reentrench a punitive, adversarial approach that disproportionately criminalizes low-income and political minority communities.

Reforming specific injustices within prisons is often necessary for the basic human needs of those who are incarcerated. They are paying for their crime with banishment and imprisonment. Inhumane practices beyond confinement are not generally respected by either the prisoner or the law, but prison illegalities are seldom prosecuted. To embark on reforms based on the assumption that prisons themselves can change from houses of punishment to beneficent, nurturing, educational, community environments that promote human growth and solid ethics is to avoid the fundamental contradiction. Healing and punishment methods are antithetical. They cannot be reconciled under the conditions of incarceration.

NOTES

My appreciation to SISter-friends Liz Elliott, Gayle Horii, Kris Lyons, the late Jo-Ann Mayhew, and Kim Pate for their direct or unwitting assistance with this chapter.

1. Correctional Service of Canada, *Basic Facts About Corrections in Canada* (Ottawa: Solicitor General, 1997), 14.

2. Ellen Adelberg and Claudia Currie, eds., *Too Few to Count: Canadian Women in Conflict with the Law* (Vancouver: Press Gang Publishers, 1987).

3. Correctional Service of Canada, *Basic Facts,* 9.

4. See Sheelagh Cooper, "The Evolution of the Federal Women's Prison," in *Conflict with the Law: Women and the Canadian Justice System,* ed. Ellen Adelberg and Claudia Currie (Vancouver: Press Gang Publishers, 1993), 33-49.

5. See Karlene Faith, *Unruly Women: The Politics of Confinement and Resistance* (Vancouver: Press Gang Publishers, 1993), 140.

6. Marie-Andrée Bertrand, "Self-Image and Delinquency: A Contribution to the Study of Female Criminality and Woman's Image," *Acta Criminologica* 2 (1969): 71-44.

7. Allan Manson, "Scrutiny from the Outside: The Arbour Commission, the Prison for Women and the Correctional Service of Canada," *Canadian Criminal Law Review* (1997): 321-37.

8. Louise Arbour, *Commission of Inquiry into Certain Events at the Prison for Women in Kingston* (Ottawa: Solicitor General, 1996).

9. Ibid.

10. Ibid., 185-87.

11. Correctional Service of Canada, *Basic Facts,* 8.

12. Gayle Horii, "Twelve Proposals with Regard to Policy Which May Govern the Future of Incarcerated Women in Canada" (Brief submitted to the Commission of Inquiry into Certain Events at the Prison for Women in Kingston, 31 December 1995), 1.

13. Des Turner, "Letter to the Honourable Herb Gray, then Solicitor General, 6 November 1996," *Accord* (January 1997): 2.

14. Michel Foucault, *Discipline and Punish: The Birth of the Prison* (New York: Vintage Books, 1979).

15. Margaret Shaw, "Is There a Feminist Future for Women's Prisons?" in *Prisons 2000: An International Perspective on the Current State and Future of Imprisonment,* ed. R. Matthews and P. Francis (London and New York: Macmillan Press Ltd., 1996), 183-84.

16. Kelly Hannah-Moffat, "From Christian Maternalism to Risk Technologies: Penal Powers and Women's Knowledges in the Governance of Female Prisons" (Ph.D. diss., Centre of Criminology, University of Toronto, 1997).

17. Arbour, *Commission of Inquiry.*

18. Ibid., 174.

19. Chris Axworthy, Letter to Nancy Stableforth, Deputy Commissioner of Women's Corrections, 18 March 1997 (Copies sent to the National Elizabeth Fry Association).

20. Assembly of First Nations, "National Chief Supports Elizabeth Fry Society Call for Stop in Transfer of Prisoners from P4W," *Bulletin* (18 April 1997): 3.

21. Nancy L. Stableforth, "Community Strategy for Women on Conditional Release: Discussion Paper." (Ottawa: Correctional Service of Canada, February 1998).

22. Task Force on Federally Sentenced Women, *Creating Choices: Report of the Task Force on Federally Sentenced Women* (Ottawa: Correctional Service of Canada, 1990).

23. "Prison Not Prepared for Violent Women," *Globe and Mail* (Toronto), 20 September 1997, A3.

24. Kim Pate, quoted in Marni Norwich, "When Will Prison Reform See the Light of Day?" *Herizons* (Spring 1997): 24-27.

25. See Kathleen Kendall, "Therapy Behind Prison Walls: A Contradiction in Terms?" (paper prepared for Prisons 2000 Conference, University of Leicester, April 1994).

26. Jo-Ann Mayhew, "A Working Paper on the Status of Women Incarcerated at Nova and Springhill Institutions" (Halifax: Nova Scotia Status of Women, April 1997), 3.

27. John Alderson, "Administrative Investigation on Minor Disturbance and Use of Force" (Nova Institution, Ottawa: Correctional Service of Canada, 16 January 1997), 14-15.

28. Correctional Service of Canada, *Basic Facts,* 19.

29. Faith, *Unruly Women;* Karlene Faith, "Aboriginal Women's Healing Lodge: Challenge to Penal Correctionalism?" *Journal of Human Justice* 6, no. 2 (Spring/Autumn 1995): 79-104; Correctional Service of Canada, *Basic Facts,* 17.

30. Canadian Association of Elizabeth Fry Societies, "Regarding the Classification and Carceral Placement of Women Classified as Maximum Security Prisoners" (Position Paper. Ottawa: Canadian Association of Elizabeth Fry Societies, March 1998), 5.

31. Correctional Service of Canada, *Risk and Need Among Federally-Sentenced Female Offenders: A Comparison of Minimum-, Medium-, and Maximum-Security Inmates* (Ottawa: Correctional Service of Canada Research Branch, 1997), 23-24; Faith, *Unruly Women;* Alison Hatch and Karlene Faith, "The Female Offender in Canada: A Statistical Profile," in *Crime in Canadian Society,* ed. R. A. Silverman, J. J. Teevan Jr., and V. F. Sacco (Toronto: Butterworth, 1991), 225-38.

32. Karlene Faith, *Unruly Women,* 140.

33. Solicitor General, "Speaking Notes for the Honourable Andy Scott, Solicitor General of Canada, to the Beyond Prisons International Symposium" (Kingston: Solicitor General, 17 March 1998).

34. "Incarceration Rates Too High, Official Says," *Globe and Mail* (Toronto), 17 March 1998, B1.

35. Solicitor General, *Correctional Service Canada: Performance Report* (Ottawa: Solicitor General, 31 March 1997), 12.

36. National Parole Board, *Risk Assessment Manual* (Ottawa: Solicitor General, 1997), 13.

37. Canadian Criminal Justice Association, "Prison Overcrowding and the Reintegration of Offenders" (Discussion Paper. Ottawa: Canadian Criminal Justice Association, March 1998), 4.

38. Ibid.

39. Ibid., 2.

40. Kim Pate, *Executive Director's Report* (Ottawa: Canadian Association of Elizabeth Fry Societies, 1997), 3.

41. "Prison to Cost $5.1 Million," *Whig-Standard* (Kingston, Ontario), 20 December 1997, A3.

42. Pate, *Executive Director's Report.*

43. Hannah-Moffat, "From Christian Maternalism to Risk Technologies, 197–209.

44. Correctional Service of Canada, *Risk and Need,* 18–19.

45. National Parole Board, *Risk Assessment Manual,* 70.

46. Ibid., 23.

47. Correctional Service of Canada, *Risk and Need,* 21.

48. Canadian Association of Elizabeth Fry Societies, "Regarding the Classification and Carceral Placement."

49. Ibid., 5; National Parole Board, *Risk Assessment Manual,* 14.

50. Pate, *Executive Director's Report.*

REFERENCES

Adelberg, Ellen, and Claudia Currie, eds. *Too Few to Count: Canadian Women in Conflict with the Law.* Vancouver: Press Gang Publishers, 1987.

Alderson, John. "Administrative Investigation on Minor Disturbance and Use of Force." Nova Institution, Ottawa: Correctional Service of Canada, 16 January 1997.

Arbour, Louise. "Commission of Inquiry into Certain Events at the Prison for Women in Kingston." Ottawa: Solicitor General, 1996.

Assembly of First Nations. "National Chief Supports Elizabeth Fry Society Call for Stop in Transfer of Prisoners from P4W." *Bulletin* (18 April 1997): 1.

Axworthy, Chris. Letter to Nancy Stableforth, Deputy Commissioner of Women's Corrections, 18 March 1997. (Copies sent to the National Elizabeth Fry Association.)

Bertrand, Marie-Andrée. "Self-Image and Delinquency: A Contribution to the Study of Female Criminality and Woman's Image." *Acta Criminologica* 2 (1969): 71–144.

Canadian Association of Elizabeth Fry Societies. "Regarding the Classification and Carceral Placement of Women Classified as Maximum Security Prisoners." Position Paper. Ottawa: Canadian Association of Elizabeth Fry Societies, March 1998.

Canadian Criminal Justice Association. "Prison Overcrowding and the Reintegration of

Offenders." Discussion Paper. Ottawa: Canadian Criminal Justice Association, March 1998.

Chapman, Jane. "Violence against Women as a Violation of Human Rights." *Social Justice* 17, no. 2 (1988): 54-65.

Cooper, Sheelagh. "The Evolution of the Federal Women's Prison." In *In Conflict with the Law: Women and the Canadian Justice System,* edited by Ellen Adelberg and Claudia Currie, 33-49. Vancouver: Press Gang Publishers, 1993.

Correctional Service of Canada. *Basic Facts about Corrections in Canada.* Ottawa: Solicitor General, 1997.

Correctional Service of Canada. *Risk and Need among Federally-Sentenced Female Offenders: A Comparison of Minimum-, Medium-, and Maximum-Security Inmates.* Ottawa: Correctional Service of Canada Research Branch, 1997.

Faith, Karlene. *Unruly Women: The Politics of Confinement and Resistance.* Vancouver: Press Gang Publishers, 1993.

Faith, Karlene. "Aboriginal Women's Healing Lodge: Challenge to Penal Correctionalism?" *Journal of Human Justice* 6, no. 2 (Spring/Autumn 1995): 79-104.

Foucault, Michel. *Discipline and Punish: The Birth of the Prison.* New York: Vintage Books, 1979.

Hannah-Moffat, Kelly. "From Christian Maternalism to Risk Technologies: Penal Powers and Women's Knowledges in the Governance of Female Prisons." Ph.D. diss., Centre of Criminology, University of Toronto, 1997.

Hatch, Alison, and Karlene Faith. "The Female Offender in Canada: A Statistical Profile." In *Crime in Canadian Society,* edited by R. A. Silverman, J. J. Teevan Jr., and V. F. Sacco. Toronto: Butterworth, 1991.

Horii, Gayle. "Twelve Proposals with Regard to Policy Which May Govern the Future of Incarcerated Women in Canada." Brief submitted to the Commission of Inquiry into Certain Events at the Prison for Women in Kingston, 31 December 1995.

Kendall, Kathleen. "Therapy behind Prison Walls: A Contradiction in Terms?" Paper prepared for Prisons 2000 Conference, University of Leicester, April 1994.

Manson, Allan. "Scrutiny from the Outside: The Arbour Commission, the Prison for Women and the Correctional Service of Canada." *Canadian Criminal Law Review* (1997): 321-37.

Mayhew, Jo-Ann. "A Working Paper on the Status of Women Incarcerated at Nova and Springhill Institutions." Halifax: Nova Scotia Status of Women, April 1997.

National Parole Board. *Risk Assessment Manual.* Ottawa: Solicitor General, 1997.

Norwich, Marni. "When Will Prison Reform See the Light of Day?" *Herizons* (Spring 1997): 24-27.

Pate, Kim. *Executive Director's Report.* Ottawa: Canadian Association of Elizabeth Fry Societies, 1997.

Shaw, Margaret. "Is There a Feminist Future for Women's Prisons?" In *Prisons 2000: An International Perspective on the Current State and Future of Imprisonment,* edited by R. Matthews and P. Francis, 179-200. London and New York: Macmillan Press Ltd., 1996.

Solicitor General. *Correctional Service Canada: Performance Report.* Ottawa: Solicitor General, 31 March 1997.

Solicitor General. "Speaking Notes for the Honourable Andy Scott, Solicitor General of Canada, to the Beyond Prisons International Symposium." Kingston: Solicitor General, 17 March 1998.

Stableforth, Nancy L. "Community Strategy for Women on Conditional Release: Discussion Paper." Ottawa: Correctional Service of Canada, February 1998.

Task Force on Federally Sentenced Women. *Creating Choices: Report of the Task Force on Federally Sentenced Women.* Ottawa: Correctional Service of Canada, 1990.

Turner, Des. "Letter to the Honourable Herb Gray, then Solicitor General, 6 November 1996." *Accord* (January 1997): 2.

Women's Imprisonment in England
Current Issues

Pat Carlen

Introduction

THE MAJOR CONCERNS about women's imprisonment in England in the late 1990s are those provoked by: the rapid increase in the female prison population and the consequent overcrowding in the women's establishments; the special plight of imprisoned mothers; and the continued failure of the prisons to recognize that the needs of women prisoners are different from those of their male counterparts.

Throughout the 1990s, financial restrictions have resulted in a series of cuts in the operating budgets of all English prisons. At the same time, the continuing steep increases in the female prison population together with the security measures introduced after two major and well-publicized escapes from men's prisons[1] have combined to make women's prisons more oppressive. For, whereas in the early-1980s the discipline of the women's penal institutions centered around a complex of concerns relating to the domesticizing and feminizing of women prisoners,[2] by the mid-1990s the main custodial priorities were the maintenance of tight security and the creation of more punitive prison environments.[3]

In the 1990s changes in the women's prisons have stemmed primarily from the introduction of the opposite sex posting policy in 1988, security measures taken after the escapes from Whitemoor and Parkhurst men's prisons, cuts in amenities as a result of decreases in prison operating budgets, and a determination on the part of government that the public should be convinced that prisons are unpleasant places.

The Female Prison Population

As the twentieth century draws to its close, the numbers of women in penal custody in England and Wales continue to rise. In 1997 the average female population increased by 19 percent from 2,260 in 1996 to 2,680.[4] Forecasts predict that it will rise to 3,500 by 2005.[5] Throughout the period the gaols have contained disproportionate numbers of women from British ethnic minority groups, as well as increasing numbers of foreign nationals convicted of drugs offenses. In June 1995, 24 percent of female prisoners were from ethnic minority groups (as compared with 17 percent of male prisoners) and 16 percent were foreign nationals (as compared with 8 percent of male prisoners).

Furthermore:

> 11 percent of British national female prisoners were black and 1 percent were South Asian compared with 1 percent and 2 percent respectively of British national females aged 15–64 in the general population.[6]

In 1997 sixteen penal establishments in England were holding women prisoners. Yet, at the time of writing (March 1998) the range of amenities for women prisoners is still much narrower than it is for men—with long-term prisoners often spending inordinate amounts of time in one institution, and with regimes being organized so that all inmates are forced to comply with the security or disciplinary requirements thought necessary for the most disturbed or high-risk inmate.

Until the mid-1990s a majority of women in prison in England at any one time had convictions for property crime. However, in the Prison Statistics in England and Wales 1996 it was reported that:

> The main offence groups at mid-1995 were drug offences (30 percent of all offences excluding offences not recorded), theft and fraud (29 percent) and violence against the person (21 percent) . . . the main changes over the last decade have been that the proportion serving sentences for violent and drug offences has increased while the proportion serving sentences for theft and fraud has decreased.[7]

The female prison population at the same date (30 June 1996) was still only 4 percent of the total prison population, and although immediate custodial sentences for violence against the person were as high as 20 percent in the female establishments as compared with 22 percent in the males', the relative totals were 355 sentences for convictions for violence against the person being served in the women's prisons as against 9,230 in the men's.[8]

The women's prison population is very different from the men's and despite the recurrent media claims that women are becoming much more violent, the Penal Affairs Consortium concluded that "most women sentenced to imprisonment are non-violent offenders and many have committed minor offences."[9]

In June 1995 over twice as many women as men were serving sentences for a first offense,[10] though of all women remanded in custody in 1995 only 34 percent subsequently reentered prison as sentenced prisoners, as compared with 47 percent of men.[11] This latter finding provokes speculation as to whether accused women in England are more vulnerable to punitive custodial remands than men.

Mothers in Prison

When women go to prison, a mesh of informal controls that silently coerce and define women outside prison is immediately intertwined with formal penal sanctions.[12] As a result, women usually experience a much heavier penal burden than men. The most obvious effect these informal controls have on women's imprisonment is manifested in the pain that mothers experience as a result of being either pregnant and in prison or of being deprived of their children while serving their sentences.[13]

In 1997 there were four mother and baby units (MBUs) in English prison establishments. Between them they provided sixty-eight places for mothers with babies (up to the age of nine months in the seventeen places at Holloway Prison, and up to eighteen months at the other MBUs). Much of the more recent and detailed investigative work on conditions in mother and baby units has been done by the Howard League.[14] The most worrying of their findings are:

- that in one MBU in September 1995 eleven out of seventeen mothers (i.e., 65 percent) had been imprisoned for nonviolent offenses.[15]

- that one prison stated that the prison budget only allowed babies half the amount allocated for adults. This amounted to 70p per day.[16] (Four years previously, in a very critical Report of a 1990 Inspection of MBUs, a Department of Health Inspection Team had tellingly remarked that they had "understood that both the budget and the variety of meals provided for mothers was less than at the male prisons.")[17]

- since the tightening of security after the Woodcock Report[18] babies have been searched more frequently, the searching involving both rubdown and strip-searches.[19]

Other commentators on babies in prison have drawn attention to the paucity of stimulating materials for children,[20] the difficulties that mothers face in establishing their own routines for babies while they themselves are subject first and foremost to the prison's routines, and also to the traumas of separation when the child is no longer allowed to stay in the prison (either because it has reached the leaving age, or is taken from the mother as a punishment for the mother's transgression of a prison rule).

Prison rules and the thin geographical spread of the women's prisons make it particularly difficult for mothers of older children to maintain good quality contact with children outside. Furthermore, eleven of the problems outlined below are likely to be amplified when the mother is a foreign national.[21]

It is difficult to get accurate information about the number of women prisoners with children under sixteen who were actually living with them at the time of their admission to prison. This is because some mothers fear that, if they admit to having children, both the children and their carers will become recipients of unwelcome attentions by the social services, and that the children may even be taken into state care.

In 1985 the National Association for the Care and Resettlement of Offenders (NACRO) reported that over 1,600 children under the age of sixteen had mothers in prison,[22] and there have been various surveys since, either based on one prison[23] or on a random sample drawn from all the women's prisons.[24] The most up-to-date and comprehensive figures available are to be found in the data provided by the Prison Department for the Chief Inspector's *Thematic Report.* These data were collected from all women in the fifteen prison establishments holding females in October and December 1996 and it was revealed that:

> 55% of all women had at least one child under sixteen years of age
> (83% of those with children). Over a third of the mothers had one
> child or more under 5 years old. 43% had children between 11 and 15
> years and 42% had children 16 years or over. 4% of the women had a
> child of up to 18 months old in the prison with them.[25]

But it is not clear how many of the mothers of children under sixteen had their children living with them immediately prior to their imprisonment. The National Prison Survey 1991,[26] which was based on a random sample of 20 percent of the female prison population (and 10 percent of the male) interviewed in January and February 1991, found that:

> One third of all prisoners had dependent children living with them just
> before they came into prison, with the proportion much higher among
> female prisoners (47%) than among male prisoners (32%).[27]

Some of the most interesting findings of this survey were in relation to the differences between the domestic responsibilities of male and female prisoners both prior to their imprisonment and while they were serving sentence. For instance:

> Male prisoners were more likely than female prisoners to have been liv-
> ing with their parents prior to imprisonment (20 per cent as against 11
> per cent). This was not simply because the male prison population is
> somewhat younger than the female population; in all age groups up to
> the age of thirty male prisoners were more likely than female prisoners
> to have been living with parents. By contrast, female prisoners were
> much more likely than male prisoners to have been living with depen-
> dent children and no other adult (14 per cent against 1 per cent).[28]

Furthermore:

> There were considerable differences between men and women with
> dependent children in the child care arrangements that had been made.
> Male prisoners with dependent children usually said that their spouse
> or partner (64%) was involved. . . . By contrast, of female prisoners
> with dependent children, just 19 per cent said that at least one of their
> children was being looked after by their spouse or partner, and 4 per
> cent by an ex-spouse or ex-partner.[29]

In fact it is a distinct feature of women's imprisonment that many
women in prison are expected, or feel obliged, to try to run their homes
and families while they are inside; by contrast, male prisoners are much
more likely to expect to be shielded from family and domestic burdens
while they are serving their sentences.[30]

> I've had twenty years of males, and in 99 percent of cases, when a man
> comes into prison and he's got a home and family, he comes in with the
> certain knowledge that those kids are being looked after by the wife or
> whatever, and that the DSS is paying the rent. When the females come
> in, it's quite often the case that if they are attached to a male, he is in
> the prison system somewhere anyhow, so, of course, then they're losing
> their houses, and quite often they're losing the children to foster care.[31]

Because they are closer to the children and the home, females lose far
more when they come into prison than male prisoners do. The females
have a closer bond with their children and it affects them far more. When
males come to prison, the wife is at home looking after the children;
whereas, when women come in, quite often the husband's not there or not
capable of looking after a kid. So social services becomes involved, probation becomes involved.

When a woman is in prison, far more pressure is put on her by the
spouse than a female spouse will put on a male prisoner. The greatest
worry with male inmates is, "What's she getting up to while I'm inside?"
whereas women are more concerned about domestic things, the house, the
family, the child's education, "what am I going to do when I get out?" sort
of thing.[32]

When a woman goes to prison she still manages the family. The male partner very often dumps the kids with somebody else, or into care, and goes off with the blonde down the road. Whereas, when a man goes to prison, the female partner looks after the kids, hauls the children all over the country for a visit, and so forth. One of the things which struck me about visits when I came here [women's prison], was the way in which the women would get all dressed up for the partner who was expected, and then he wouldn't come. She would be lucky if she got a phone call to say, "Sorry, love, there was a dart match, or football match," or "I was under the car," whatever, "See you next week." To him it was nothing. To her it was the end of the world.[33]

The problems that women have got inside are far greater than men inside because very often the women are left to cope with extended family responsibilities. I mean, men don't go to prison for a rest, but certainly their families are sort of at a distance and their [the men's] needs are expected to be catered for rather than the other way round. I've found men very selfish in that respect, in the demands they place on their families.[34]

Women are very demanding, and, with the baggage they have, a lot more complex. For instance, they'll say: "I look after my partner's health. If he needs a doctor, I'm the one that rings up the doctor. If he needs a prescription, I'm the one that will go and get it." Women still worry about that when they're in custody. They literally run their homes from within the prison. For example, there was one in May who used to ring home every morning to make sure everyone was up, to make sure the kids were dressed, to make sure they'd had their breakfast and to make sure they'd gone to school.

Men go into custody and it's like them having a rest. They've always got somebody outside. If it's not the female partner or the wife, the mother will be doing it or the sister. Men don't carry that excess baggage along with them.[35]

Despite the foregoing comments from prison personnel suggesting that there is a new understanding of women prisoners' special family-related problems, staff and inmates agreed that it was very difficult to deal effectively with family crises while a woman is in prison. Rather, it was claimed, the additional security measures brought into play in the 1990s made keeping in contact with families much more difficult.

Over the past twenty years I have visited many women's prisons—in the United Kingdom, United States, Canada, Australia and New Zealand—and always the dominant story has centered round the intractability of the prisoners' family problems or desperate social circumstances on the one hand, and, on the other, the inappropriateness of prison as a site for addressing either the prisoners' immediate problems or the bureaucracies outside the prisons within which the problems of the poor are, ironically, as frequently inflated and maintained as ameliorated.[36]

Many of the English prison officers who talked with concern about prisoners also stressed to me that these were "ordinary decent women, bringing up families." Maybe so. Nonetheless, and from a different standpoint, a statistical picture of the women's prison population in England indicates that women prisoners have been disproportionately victims of family violence, sexual abuse, poverty and mental illness; and disproportionately in local authority care. They may indeed be decent mothers, but in many cases their own family histories will not have been happy ones. That being so, it seems to me that, while mothers continue to be locked up for relatively minor offenses, the official concern about families in the women's prisons in England is at best nothing more than an empathic collusion in the still-dominant ideological illusion of "happy familyness." At its worst, it is either sheer muddled-headedness or institutionalized hypocrisy.

The Refusal to Recognize Women's Difference

Despite all the adverse publicity that women's prisons have attracted in recent years, in England there still is no womanwise, principled, coherent and holistic strategy for the management of women's imprisonment.[37] In this final section, therefore, I identify four of the most recent effects of the Prison Department's continuing failure to recognize that biological and gender differences result in women experiencing many aspects of prison life both differently and with greater pain than men.

Mandatory Drug Testing

> Powers to require prisoners to provide a sample for drug testing purposes were introduced as part of the Criminal Justice and Public Order Act in January 1995.[38]

Mandatory Drug Testing (MDT) was introduced in prisons in 1995 for the following five reasons: as part of a monthly 10 percent random drug testing of the population of a prison; on suspicion that a prisoner has illicitly used a controlled drug; as part of a frequent testing ordered at the adjudication of a prisoner found guilty of a drug-related offense; as part of the risk assessment when a prisoner is being granted temporary release or transferred to lower security; and upon first reception, or on transfer and admission to a different prison.[39] According to the Prison Service Security Group:

> The MDT Manual allows women's prisons a high level of discretion to create their own procedures to meet the perceived threat of adulteration in each establishment. As a consequence, sample taking practices do vary between establishments. At Holloway, women are allowed complete privacy in a closed cubicle. Other prisons have adopted a system whereby the cubicle has a stable door arrangement; the bottom half is closed and the top half left open. The woman is asked to place one hand on the door whilst holding the sample cup with the other. In all cases the woman is allowed to wear a gown so that observation of the genitalia whilst urinating is not possible. Male staff are not allowed to collect samples from women.[40]

But the "closed cubicle" system in Holloway was introduced only after both staff and prisoners had objected to a system involving officers watching women while they were urinating. Moreover, although the mode of testing described above may seem unexceptional to many people, the Chief Inspector of Prisons was told that women who had previously been sexually abused did take exception to it:

> Many of the women . . . complained, not of being tested but of having to provide a sample of urine while being observed by a prison officer.

In some cases this was felt to be comparable to and bring back memories of previous sexual assault.[41]

Dedicated Search Teams

Both Woodcock[42] and Learmont[43] recommended that dedicated search teams should be established in prisons and that they should be assisted in their prison searches by dogs trained in the detection of firearms, explosives and drugs. In 1997 the Chief Inspector of Prisons found that in the women's prisons:

> Many managers and staff felt that personal searching was one of the most difficult areas to manage. One specific difficulty was the concealment, particularly of drugs but also other illicit articles, in prisoners' vaginas. Internal searching by prison staff is not permitted even when there is a very strong suspicion that prisoners have concealed contraband internally. Prison staff can require prisoners to bend or squat . . . but none of the staff to whom we spoke considered that this was at all effective with women prisoners.[44]

Nonetheless, as late as 1997 some women prisoners were being made to bend over during strip-searches, and strip-searching, although accepted as an inevitable and justifiable part of prison life by many prisoners, was seen as a violation of personal autonomy and modesty by others, especially those who had never taken drugs, who had suffered sexual abuse, who were from countries where feminine modesty is rigorously enforced, or who already agonized over their body shape. To these latter groups of women strip-searching continues to cause deep distress, and, in some cases, provokes extreme acts of resistance to what is experienced as an assault.

In his *Thematic Report* the Chief Inspector argued that "[T]he reasons justifying the use of dedicated search teams in male establishments apply equally to secure establishments for females."[45] Many informed commentators, including some prison staff, would beg to differ.

One of the greatest causes of resentment in the women's prisons of the late 1990s is that dedicated search teams, like many of the other new and restrictive measures of the 1990s, were set up after serious breaches of security in men's prisons, and that there have never been any comparable threats to security in women's prisons. Thus, the increased emphasis on strip-searching in women's prisons is but another example of the way in which the women's prison system is carelessly treated as being nothing more nor less than a codicil to the men's.

Handcuffing

> Handcuffs [have] a history of use that paid no heed to age or sex. . . . There was, also a special mode of restraint reserved to women called "hobbling," which consisted "in binding the wrists and ankles of a prisoner and then strapping them together behind her back."[46]

The increased security measures which followed upon the escapes from Whitemoor and Parkhurst men's prisons have also resulted in fewer prisoners being allowed to work outside, and, when they are allowed out for hospital, family, and other appointments, handcuffing has become the norm rather than the exception in some establishments. Indeed, stopping the cuffing of women in labor and at other hospital appointments became the *cause célèbre* of anti-prison campaigners in 1996 and 1997, a cause which the Chief Inspector unequivocally backed in his *Thematic Report:*

> Prior to the Woodcock Inquiry women prisoners were handcuffed only in exceptional cases. Since then the increased focus on security and the application of policies arising from incidents at high security prisons for men to all prisoners, including women, has placed unwarranted restrictions on woman under escort. The vast majority of women are not an escape risk, nor do they pose serious danger to the public.
>
> We have heard of women refusing hospital treatment for serious conditions because they did not want to be cuffed in public. For similar reasons women have not attended child custody hearings. In the latter circumstances, they felt, not unreasonably, that appearing in handcuffs might influence decisions about the custody of their children. Regrettably, there is still no clear statement from the Prison Service about the policy of handcuffing women.[47]

The Prison Service has now at least issued instructions that "women admitted to National Health Service hospitals to give birth should not be handcuffed from the time of their arrival until they leave."[48] However, handcuffing for funerals and other major family occasions (together with strip-searching both before and after they leave) still occurs, and, at the time of writing, continues to deter women prisoners from requesting to be allowed out for some very important life events.

Men Working in the Women's Prisons

When I first began to visit the women's prisons in the early 1980s it was a proud boast of the staff that male officers were only exceptionally brought into the living areas of the establishments. If staff shortages meant that men had to be drafted in, their duties were confined to manning the gate. At that time, the arguments against employing men in women's prisons still owed much to Elizabeth Fry's concern for the protection of inmates from sexual exploitation, though modern-day supporters of single sex prisons were also beginning to marshall statistical evidence that one-half to four-fifths of women in prison are likely already to have suffered abuse at the hands of men.[49] Another widely propagated argument against both "mix nicks" (gaols housing male and female prisoners) and prison staff opposite sex postings contended that while they were in prison neither female nor male prisoners would want to cope with members of the opposite sex—in many cases seen as the source of their troubles outside prison. In 1988, however, the coming into force of the Prison Service's Opposite Sex Postings Agreement put an end to mere conjecture and in 1997 I asked thirty-nine female prisoners and thirty-one prison staff about their experiences of male staff working in the women's institutions.

My main conclusion was that the official discovery of gender difference by the Prison Service has focused on issues traditionally associated with maternity, nurturance of the young, and domesticity. Male officers were, as we have already seen, especially loquacious about women prisoners' family responsibilities. By contrast, there was almost a silence on the part of the male staff about issues of gender, penality and the conventional regulation of sexuality. Yet, as some women staff and prisoners talked about male patrols in the women's houses, dormitories, and other living spaces, unease was repeatedly expressed about these symbolic and actual violations of physical privacy which were seen, also, as being sexually threatening.

> You go to bed with no underwear on, and during the night you kick off the covers and a male patrol comes and looks through the hatch — (with the best intentions, to make sure you're OK) — but you're exposed, or could be sitting on the toilet seat. (Female prison officer)

Prisoners were worried by the ambiguity of the cross-gender surveillatory gaze, and resented the consequent edginess they experience when men patrol cell blocks. They were always careful to say that they did not object to men per se working in the prisons. But they did most vocally object to being kept under surveillance by men in the most intimate details of their daily lives, including times when they are naked (when they are washing) or engaged in performing bodily functions which are conventionally required to be completed in private.

> I've no objection to the employment of men in prison. But I do object when two men do the patrols on the houses at night. They either tip the curtain back and shine a torch in, or they actually walk into the room. (Amanda, aged 48)

> In single cells here there's no curtains, nothing to shield the toilet. They can look in and see you straight away. (Liz, aged 19)

> If you've got a single cell and the toilet is there, if they open your door they can see you. I couldn't care less if they saw me with no clothes on, but watching you go to the toilet is a different matter. (Carol, aged 37)

> There's no curtains, not even round the bloody toilet. If you're on the toilet and a man opens the door, it's terrible. (Jill, aged 45)

Women also objected to having to talk to males about matters of female hygiene that they did not talk to anybody about outside prison; and they resented being obliged to name body parts (that they usually only discussed with their doctors) to male gaolers who had no medical qualifications at all.

None of the prisoners reported that male officers were abusing their positions of trust by becoming sexually involved with women, though prison managers readily disclosed that some male officers had been disciplined for unprofessional conduct with inmates. The dominant view of inmates on illicit liaisons between staff and prisoners was that "it takes two to tango."

Women prisoners' primary concern, therefore, was not that male staff might sexually molest them or behave unprofessionally. It was that all prison staff in the normal course of their duties are licensed to gaze on women's bodies and that prisoners have no control whatsoever over the guardianship of what, outside prison, would be considered to be not only their most private parts, but also their most private moments.

Prison personnel recognized women prisoners' fear of the unsolicited, prurient sexual gaze, but discussed it only in terms of officer professionalism, insisting that professional prison officers do not ogle women whom they unwittingly happen upon in a state of undress. So long as only female officers do strip-searching and MDT, and all officers, especially males, knock on the doors of women's cells, then, they claimed, there is no cause for concern. These points, made by staff at all levels, were summed up by a male governor:

> The important point is to get men in who are good role models, because
> a lot of these women have never met a decent man or a man who can
> keep his trousers zipped up. Men—well, all staff—are directed to knock
> before they go into rooms unless there is a security consideration.

Sensitive and relevant as these comments are, they only deal with one aspect of the issue. For while the women themselves expressed no concern that they would be raped by male officers, they were adamantly opposed to the routine violation (by all prison staff) of the social convention that dictates that women should hide their sexual parts from all but their chosen sexual partners or their doctors. Exposure to either of these categories of inspection is usually voluntary. However, when a woman is forced to expose her body to a woman in a strip-search, to engage in supervised (by a woman) urinating (in the MDT test), or to live in constant fear that she will be involuntarily exposed to the surveillance of a prison officer (male or female) who may or may not look upon her with the gaze of a voyeur—but who will cer-

tainly look upon her with a legitimated punitive stare—it is arguable that
she, sensing a perversion of both legitimate punishment and conventional
sexual proprieties, will experience a pervasive and intense humiliation.

> In the mornings, male officers . . . look through and see what you are
> doing. When you are in that situation you know that they've got total
> control. (Karen, aged 21)

That is the nub of the matter—the vulnerability of women prisoners'
naked bodies or exposed sexual parts to the possible lusts, derision or
merely coldly casual inspections of their gaolers—whether those gaolers be
male or female, heterosexual or lesbian.

Prisoners claimed, moreover, that male prison staff were lacking in
even a most basic understanding of female hygiene needs. For instance, I
was in discussion with four long-term prisoners who mentioned that they
could not have as many baths as they needed. The male deputy governor,
who was also present, contradicted them, saying: "That's not true. You can
have as many showers as you like."

In their eagerness to explain, all four prisoners spoke at once: "Yes,
Mr. . . . but showers are not the same. Women sometimes need a bath, not
a shower." Yet, as one discussant remarked later, "the Dep didn't get it, did
he?" And she mimicked his insistence that, "a shower gets you clean, even
though you might prefer a bath." A similar tale was told by a woman
officer at another prison:

> [U]ntil men have the bodily functions of women, they won't under-
> stand it. The main thing the male governors thought of when we said
> we needed baths was that women just wanted to lie in a bath, not that
> they want to give all places to be cleansed a good soaking. They [prison
> management] don't take into account periods and things like that.

> We had an instance when a woman asked a male staff for a sanitary
> towel and he went away and brought a Lillet back, and she said, "I can't
> wear one of them." He said, "Of course you can, it's for the same
> thing." And he didn't know the difference; that some people cannot
> physically wear something without any applicator. It just shows how
> naive some of the men are. (Female prison officer)

Yet, despite all the reservations currently being expressed about mixed prisons, the debate about whether women should be held in wings of men's prisons continues. Like other current issues about women's imprisonment, the continuing debate about "mix nicks" nicely illustrates the complete lack of a coherent holistic policy toward women in penal custody—the Learmont Inquiry Report arguing in 1995 that the women's wings in male prisons should be closed as soon as practical,[50] and since that time two more wings for women being opened within, or adjacent to, male prisons. The usual justification is that these additional wings allow women to be imprisoned nearer to their homes. But in 1997 the rapid growth in the numbers of women being given custodial sentences actually meant that women from Essex could be found down at Eastwood Park near Bristol, women from Hampshire up in the North East, and women from Wales (which has no prison for women) all over the place. Each imprisoned woman, of course, gives the lie to the 1970 Home Office prediction that

> it may well be that as the end of the century draws nearer penological progress will result even in fewer or no women at all being given prison sentences.[51]

NOTES

1. Home Office, *The Escape from Whitemoor Prison on Friday 9th September (The Woodcock Enquiry).* CM 2741 (London: HMSO, 1994); and Home Office, *Review of Prison Security in England and Wales and the Escape from Parkhurst Prison on Tuesday 3rd January (The Learmont Inquiry).* CM 3020 (London: HMSO, 1994).

2. Pat Carlen, *Women's Imprisonment* (London: Routledge & Kegan Paul, 1983).

3. Pat Carlen, *Women's Imprisonment at the Millennium* (London: Macmillan, 1998).

4. Home Office, "The Prison Population in 1997," *Home Office Statistical Bulletin* 5 (1998).

5. Home Office, "Projections of Long-Term Trends in the Prison Population to 2005," *Home Office Statistical Bulletin* 7 (1997).

6. Home Office, *Prison Statistics in England and Wales 1995.* CM 3355 (London: HMSO, 1996), 121.

7. Ibid., 80. These are the latest full statistics available at the time of writing.

8. Home Office, "The Prison Population in 1996," *Home Office Statistical Bulletin* 18 (1997).

9. Penal Affairs Consortium, *The Imprisonment of Women: Some Facts and Figures* (London: Penal Affairs Consortium, 1996), 2 (169 Clapham Rd. London SW9 OPU).

10. Home Office, "The Prison Population in 1995," *Home Office Statistical Bulletin* 14 (1996): 80.

11. Home Office, *Prison Statistics in England and Wales,* 39.

12. Pat Carlen, "Virginia, Criminology, and the Anti-social Control of Women," in *Punishment and Social Control,* ed. Thomas Blomburg and Stanley Cohen (New York: Aldine de Gruyter, 1995) and Carlen, *Women's Imprisonment at the Millennium.*

13. See Carlen, *Women's Imprisonment,* and Roger Shaw, ed., *Prisoners' Children: What Are the Issues?* (London: Routledge, 1992).

14. Howard League, *The Voice of the Child* (London: Howard League, 1993); Howard League, *Families Matter* (London: Howard League, 1994); Howard League, *Prison Mother and Baby Units* (London: Howard League, 1996).

15. Howard League, *Prison Mother and Baby Units,* 7.

16. Ibid., 9.

17. Department of Health, *Inspection of Facilities for Mothers and Babies in Prison* (London: Department of Health, 1992).

18. Home Office, *The Woodcock Enquiry.*

19. Howard League, *Prison Mother and Baby Units,* 10.

20. Lisa Catan, "Infants with Mothers in Prison," in *Prisoners' Children: What Are the Issues?* ed. Roger Shaw (London: Routledge, 1992).

21. Olga Heaven, "Hibiscus: Working with Nigerian Women Prisoners," in *Drug Couriers: A New Perspective,* ed. Penny Green (London: Quartet Books, 1997).

22. National Association for the Care and Resettlement of Offenders, *Mothers and Babies in Prison* (London: NACRO, 1985).

23. See, for example, Prison Reform Trust, *Women in Prison: Recent Trends and Developments* (London: Prison Reform Trust, 1996).

24. Home Office, *The National Prison Survey 1991: Main Findings.* Home Office Research Study 128 (London: HMSO, 1992).

25. HM Chief Inspector of Prisons, *Women in Prison: A Thematic Review* (London: Home Office, 1997), Appendix 3.

26. Home Office, *The National Prison Survey 1991,* 17.

27. Ibid., 17.

28. Ibid., 18.

29. Ibid., 17.

30. See Laura Fishman, *Women at the Wall* (Albany: State University of New York Press, 1990).

31. Male governor of women's prison (Interviewed in 1997).

32. Male prison officer in women's prison (Interviewed in 1997).

33. Male governor of women's prison (Interviewed in 1997).

34. Male governor of women's prison (Interviewed in 1997). See also Fishman, *Women at the Wall.*

35. Female prison officer (Interviewed in 1997).

36. See Carlen, "Virginia, Criminology, and the Anti-social Control of Women."

37. See Pat Carlen, *Alternatives to Women's Imprisonment* (Buckingham: Open University Press, 1990) and *Women's Imprisonment at the Millennium.*

38. Prison Service Security Group, *Mandatory Drug Testing* (London: Home Office, 1996), 2.

39. Ibid.

40. Ibid., 4.

41. HM Chief Inspector of Prisons, *Women in Prison: A Thematic Review.*

42. Home Office, *The Woodcock Enquiry.*

43. Home Office, *The Learmont Inquiry.*

44. HM Chief Inspector of Prisons, *Women in Prison: A Thematic Review,* 46.

45. Ibid., 47.

46. Philip Priestley, *Victorian Prison Lives* (London: Methuen, 1985) quoting from Mrs. F. E. Maybrick, *Mrs. Maybrick's Own Story—My Fifteen Lost Years* (New York and London: Funk and Wagnalls, 1905).

47. HM Chief Inspector of Prisons, *Women in Prison: A Thematic Review,* 45.

48. Ibid.

49. For the most up-to-date estimates, see Allison Morris, Chris Wilkinson, and Andrea Tisi, *Managing the Needs of Female Prisoners* (London: Home Office, 1995) and Home Office, "The Prison Population in 1996."

50. Home Office, *The Learmont Inquiry.*

51. Home Office, *Treatment of Women and Girls in Custody* (London: Prison Department, 1970).

REFERENCES

Carlen, Pat. *Alternatives to Women's Imprisonment.* Buckingham: Open University Press, 1990.

———. "Virginia, Criminology, and the Anti-social Control of Women." In *Punishment and Social Control,* edited by T. Blomburg and S. Cohen. New York: Aldine de Gruyter, 1996.

———. *Women's Imprisonment.* London: Routledge & Kegan Paul, 1983.

———. *Women's Imprisonment at the Millennium.* London: Macmillan, 1998.

Catan, Lisa. "Infants with Mothers in Prison." In *Prisoners' Children: What Are the Issues?* edited by Roger Shaw. London: Routledge, 1992.

Department of Health. *Inspection of Facilities for Mothers and Babies in Prison.* London: Department of Health, 1992.

Fishman, Laura. *Women at the Wall.* Albany: State University of New York Press, 1990.

Heaven, Olga. "Hibiscus: Working with Nigerian Women Prisoners." In *Drug Couriers: A New Perspective,* edited by Penny Green. London: Quartet Books, 1997.

HM Chief Inspector of Prisons. *Women in Prison: A Thematic Review.* London: Home Office, 1997.

Home Office. *The Escape from Whitemoor Prison on Friday 9th September (The Woodcock Enquiry).* CM 2741. London: HMSO, 1994.

———. *The National Prison Survey 1991: Main Findings.* Home Office Research Study 128. London: HMSO, 1992

———. "The Prison Population in 1995." *Home Office Statistical Bulletin* 14 (1996).

———. "The Prison Population in 1996." *Home Office Statistical Bulletin* 18 (1997).

———. "The Prison Population in 1997." *Home Office Statistical Bulletin* 5 (1998).

———. *Prison Statistics in England and Wales 1995.* CM 3355. London: HMSO, 1996.

———. "Projections of Long-Term Trends in the Prison Population to 2005." *Home Office Statistical Bulletin* 7 (1997).

———. *Review of Prison Security in England and Wales and the Escape from Parkhurst Prison on Tuesday 3rd January (The Learmont Inquiry).* CM 3020. London: HMSO, 1994.

———. *Treatment of Women and Girls in Custody.* London: Prison Department, 1970.

Howard League. *Families Matter.* London: Howard League, 1994.

———. *Prison Mother and Baby Units.* London: Howard League, 1996.

———. *The Voice of the Child.* London: Howard League, 1993.

Maybrick, Mrs. F. E. *Mrs. Maybrick's Own Story—My Fifteen Lost Years.* New York and London: Funk and Wagnalls, 1905.

Morris, Allison, Chris Wilkinson, and Andrea Tisi. *Managing the Needs of Female Prisoners.* London: Home Office, 1995.

National Association for the Care and Resettlement of Offenders. *Mothers and Babies in Prison.* London: NACRO, 1985.

Penal Affairs Consortium. *The Imprisonment of Women: Some Facts and Figures.* London: Penal Affairs Consortium, 1996.

Priestley, Philip. *Victorian Prison Lives.* London: Methuen, 1985.

Prison Reform Trust. *Women in Prison: Recent Trends and Developments.* London: Prison Reform Trust, 1996.

Prison Service Security Group. *Mandatory Drug Testing.* London: Home Office, 1996.

Shaw, Roger, ed. *Prisoners' Children: What Are the Issues?* London: Routledge, 1992.

Addressing Women's Needs or Empty Rhetoric?

An Examination of New Zealand's Policy for Women in Prison

Allison Morris and Venezia Kingi

Introduction

NEW ZEALAND CONSISTS of two islands that together make up a country about the size of the United Kingdom. However, it has only three prisons for women. Although these are adequate in size to house New Zealand's women prison population, inevitably women are incarcerated far from their homes, families, and friends.

The three prisons are Mount Eden, which can hold 54 women and is situated in Auckland at the upper end of the North Island; Arohata, which can hold 105 women and is situated in Wellington at the bottom of the North Island; and Christchurch Women's Prison, which can hold 98 women and is situated in Christchurch in the South Island. These prisons provide a total of 247 prison places for women. At the most recent prison census (20 November 1997) there were 207 sentenced women in prison: a mere 4 percent of all sentenced prisoners.[1]

The small size of the women's prison population in New Zealand and the small number of women in individual prisons raises a number of questions about what prison regimes can offer women. Added to this is the fact that most women will serve their sentence far from their homes and families. This chapter profiles the women in these prisons, asks whether or not prison is really the only alternative for them, and questions the adequacy of the prison system's response to the small number of women who make up the women's prison population. Questioning the prison system's response in relation to women's prisons is particularly relevant now as prison regimes become more restrictive in response to the perceived threat posed by the increasing male prison population.

The Number and Profile of Women in New Zealand's Prisons

The women's prison population in New Zealand has not always been so small in comparison to the male prison population. During the latter part of the nineteenth century, women comprised around 20 percent of the New Zealand prison population. These women were primarily sentenced for theft, drunkenness, and prostitution. In more recent years, the female prison population has fluctuated considerably. The average daily population increased gradually from 1985 to 1990, but for the years from 1991 to 1997 the number of women in prison was lower than the 1990 figure. A 20 percent increase, however, occurred between 1996 and 1997. This may mean that New Zealand is starting to reflect the trend in women's imprisonment apparent in other Western jurisdictions. Only time will tell.

There are a number of possible reasons for this recent increase: Women may be committing more serious offenses; women may be experiencing more "equal" sentencing; the "type" of women sentenced to imprisonment may have changed; sentences may have increased; or it may simply be a random fluctuation. The increase is too recent for explanatory data to have been collected, so we do not know which, if any, of these explanations are valid. What we do know from the biennial prison censuses, however, is that the profile of women in prison has changed little over the last ten years. This profile is also significantly different from that of the male prison population.

From the 1997 prison census we know that more than half of women in New Zealand's prisons were there for the first time and that more than one-quarter had no previous convictions at all. Almost two-fifths had two or less previous convictions. For 60 percent of those with previous convictions, the major previous offense was traffic. Two-fifths of the women were in prison for property offenses, about one-third were there for violent offenses, and 14 percent were in prison for drug offenses. Generally the women are serving relatively short prison sentences; more than one-third were serving less than twelve months in 1997. But the proportion serving longer sentences has increased in recent years: 7 percent of women were serving more than five years in 1997 compared with 2 percent in 1989. There has also been a 10 percent increase in the number of women serving sentences of life imprisonment since 1987 (from 7 percent to 17 percent). Most of these women are in prison for killing their partners, their children, or people they believe have harmed their children. Men in New Zealand prisons, generally speaking, have had more prior custodial experience and more previous convictions. A higher proportion of men have been sentenced to imprisonment for violent offenses, and men are serving longer sentences. These differences are reflected in the fact that more than three-quarters of the women in prison in 1997 were classified as minimum security status, compared with 59 percent of male prisoners.

Most of the women in New Zealand's prisons are quite young; in 1997, 15 percent were under twenty years old, more than one-third were under twenty-five, and half were under thirty. Maori—the indigenous population of New Zealand—are overrepresented; more than two-fifths of the women in prison in 1997 identified as Maori, though Maori make up only around 12 percent of the total population of New Zealand. Women in New Zealand prisons, like female prisoners elsewhere, tend to have few educational qualifications, to have been living on low incomes (primarily on state benefits), to have poor or no work records, to have had child care responsibilities (often as single parents), to have histories of drug and alcohol abuse, and to have experienced high levels of victimization. The major difference between female and male prisoners is the proportion of female prisoners who are single parents. In the 1997 census, 76 percent of female prisoners were single parents, compared with 28 percent of male prisoners.

This profile of female prisoners raises the question of whether or not women in prison have special needs that require different policies and practices from those of men in prison. The Ministerial Committee of Inquiry into the Prisons System (referred to as the Roper Committee)[2] rejected in 1989 the claim that women in prison had special needs. It argued that women's needs were only "special" if men's needs were used as the yardstick, and that, historically if not currently, women's supposed special needs had been used against them rather than for them. Instead, the committee recommended "humane containment" that promoted "self-responsibility and self-respect regardless of gender."[3] We agree with this recommendation, but we do not entirely agree with the rejection of women's *additional* special needs, in particular their child care responsibilities. Presumably current prison administrators disagree with the Roper Committee on this too, because there is now in existence in New Zealand a national policy for female prisoners in addition to the various policies that apply to all prisoners. The next section describes this policy and examines the extent to which it has been implemented.

National Policy for Female Prisoners and Related Performance Standards

A national policy and related performance standards, drafted and trialed in New Zealand in 1993, were put in place generally from 1 December 1994, and were to be reviewed by 30 November 1997. The policy still remains in place and is in the current *Policy and Procedures Manual.* The policy states:

> Women inmates are contained in separate secure facilities and are managed in [a] manner which respects women as adults, takes into account their particular needs as women and acknowledges their family/whanau circumstances and personal histories.[4]

Twelve performance standards (included in full in Appendix 1) then follow. These are obviously a useful guide to what is seen as good practice in New Zealand's women's prisons. We have not commented on all of these standards, but some clearly recognize the particular needs of women in prison (for example, performance standard (e) refers to the provision of contraceptive services for women released from prison, including temporary release; performance standard (d) refers to the appointment of nurses with training specific to women's health issues; and performance standards (i) and (j) acknowledge the prevalence of sexual abuse among female prisoners). Performance standard (c) reflects the particular cultural mix of prisoners in New Zealand.

Practice, of course, may deviate from these performance standards. The following sections discuss the extent to which these performance standards seem to be currently met. For this discussion we have grouped together some of the key performance standards under three headings—the separation and management of women's prisons, maintaining family ties, and the provision of employment and vocational training.

Separate Facilities and Management

On a number of occasions the integration of women into men's prisons has been actively promoted in New Zealand (for example, by the Penal Policy Review Committee in 1981 and by the Department of Justice in 1988).[5] However, performance standard (a) states that women should be housed in separate secure facilities and managed independently of male prisoners. As a result of a report commissioned in 1994 by the Department of Justice, explicitly to make cost savings in the prison system,[6] this standard was breached when the management of the women's prison at Christchurch was transferred to Rolleston Prison for men, several miles down the road. However, this situation has since been changed and all the women's prisons are now managed by site managers (all of whom are female)[7] who, like the site managers at most men's prisons, report to a regional manager. Thus the women's prisons are all autonomous units within a regional structure. This does mean, however, that they can become a *regional* resource for male as well as female prisoners, and on a number of occasions in recent years male prisoners have been placed in both Arohata prison and Christchurch Women's Prison to solve overcrowding in men's prisons.

One of the consequences of this for the women in Arohata and Christchurch Women's Prison was that some of them lost their jobs in the laundry to male prisoners. In addition, curtains were placed round the outside of the windows on the *women's* wings of Christchurch Women's Prison recently to prevent the women looking out at the male prisoners, thereby also restricting the women's view of their limited world.

What this seems to indicate is that the needs and interests of female prisoners, and therefore the conditions under which they serve their sentences, have on occasion taken second place to the needs and interests of male prisoners, *even when they are held in separate prisons.* Thus, despite the existence of a national policy for female prisoners, this policy was breached very quickly to deal with the needs of the managers of men's prisons; that is, finding a solution to the overcrowding in men's prisons. This concern that the interests of the majority — male prisoners — would take priority over the interests of female prisoners was the primary reason for the rejection of mixed institutions by the Roper Committee in 1989. Having said this, it is important to acknowledge that practically all of the women in Kingi's sample[8] stated that they would not mind being housed in a "men's" prison, if it meant that they could stay in their home area.

> Who cares, as long as you got to see your kids. . . . If they could put me in a prison closer to my son . . . I wouldn't give two shits (about the men) . . . as long as I was seeing my son. (Woman who did not get visits because of the distance the caregiver lived from the prison)[9]

> I don't think women would have a problem with that if they could be closer to their families . . . and when women have had a terrible deal with men, it's "a man" it's not "men." (Woman who had only one visit from her family due to the distance they had to travel)

Sadly, being housed close to family is the opposite of what happens.

Maintaining Family Ties

When men go to prison, their children tend to be looked after by their current or ex-partner. In contrast, only a few of the children of female prisoners are cared for by their partners. Also, women's children are often separated from one another, especially if the woman is a single parent and is solely responsible for the financial support of those children living with her. As a result, one of the principal worries that women have when they are imprisoned is what is happening to their children.

Some of the women in Kingi's sample said that they had received little or no information about their children, that they were concerned their children were bonding with others rather than with them, and that they were worried about their children's health, safety, or care situations.

> I don't know who's fucken' got them, you know. I don't know. I haven't seen these people — I haven't seen their house. I don't know if they're

black, blue, or purple. (Woman who had voluntarily placed her children in care when she came to prison)

I don't even remember I'm a mother half the time because I don't even hear from him. (Woman whose child was with caregivers in Australia)

[I know] nothing. I have to make the effort to contact them . . . and if my phone card runs out here in the jail I've got no way of contacting them. (Woman whose children had had three changes of caregivers in the space of three months)

I've rung [the social worker], left messages, asked the [New Zealand Children, Young Persons and their Families Service] to include me to meet the new foster-parents of my daughter. Everyone else [in the family] is invited, except for me because I'm in prison. I feel that I haven't got any rights. (Woman with two children in separate long term foster care situations)

These women were also concerned about their older children taking drugs and taking on responsibility for their younger siblings. They felt that they had let their families down because they were not around to offer practical or emotional support.

In addition to the National Policy for Female Prisoners, female prisoners are also covered by prison policies that relate to both male and female prisoners. Two of these have specific relevance for women's relationships with their children and families. First, the national policy on new arrival management states in performance standard (a) that the immediate needs of each inmate should be "identified, recorded and actioned" on entry to prison.[10] This is put into effect by means of an immediate needs checklist that asks prisoners whether or not they need to arrange child care.[11] Second, the national policy on family/whanau relationship maintenance and enhancement states:

As far as is practicable and with consideration to an inmate's security rating, relationships with their family/whanau are maintained and enhanced, in a culturally appropriate manner, to assist their well being and effective reintegration into the community.[12]

The performance standards related to this policy include the provision of culturally appropriate family/whanau visiting areas that reflect the needs of prisoners and their visitors. These include the need for privacy, a play area for child-parent interaction, and a suitable area to feed and change babies and toddlers. In addition, performance standard (b) states that prisoners should be helped to assess their needs in terms of maintaining and enhancing family/whanau relationships and performance standard (d) refers to the encouragement and support of visits by family/whanau.

Sentenced prisoners are entitled to weekly visits (unless they are being punished and are being denied such "privileges") during set visiting hours, usually during the weekend. In special circumstances, and for visitors who have traveled from out of the area, visiting outside of these hours or extended visits may be approved if prior arrangements are made with the prison. Remand prisoners have separate visiting times (usually during weekdays) and are subject to different regulations.

Visits at Arohata and Christchurch Women's Prison take place in the gymnasium where there is minimal, if any, privacy. There is an outside playground at Christchurch Women's Prison—the only women's prison with such a dedicated area. However, women's access to this to play with their children has recently been curtailed in an attempt to stop drugs coming into the prison. At Mount Eden there is a dedicated visiting room that is quite small. There is usually a limited range of toys in all of the visiting areas of the prisons, provided by voluntary groups. Other than these, there are no special facilities for mother and children. As one of the women in Kingi's sample said:

> In the gym it's so impersonal. Like you know, you just have to whisper. And the officers are usually sitting, you know, staring. . . . I don't think it's a relaxing situation at all really, 'cause [the staff are] watching you like hawks you know, to see that you're not smoking or eating.
>
> I don't have enough time to spend with each child and then when the visit's over I haven't even spoken to [my partner], all I've said is "hello" and "goodbye" y'know, I'm hogging the visit with the kids.

According to a Department of Justice submission to the Roper Committee, most of the women in prison come from areas in which there is no prison.[13] Furthermore, only Christchurch Women's Prison takes women convicted of serious offenses in the early parts of their sentence, and Mount Eden can take only women serving relatively short sentences, irrespective of where they lived prior to their sentence. This means that a large proportion of women in prison are far from their families and communities. One-third of the women in Kingi's sample whose children had been living with them at the time they were imprisoned had not had a visit from their children when she interviewed them.

> There are a lot of women in here who haven't had a visit since the day they came in . . . because the people who are looking after their children are their parents and they're old and, you know, they cannot just cope with the drive all the way up here.

Factors contributing to lack of visits included the distance families and carergivers lived from the prison, the time and expense related to visits, financial difficulties when families or caregivers were on benefits or low incomes, and lack of access to private vehicles. The only funding available for the purpose of visiting prisoners is discretionary from agencies such as the Department of Social Welfare or voluntary organizations (such as the Prisoners' Aid and Rehabilitation Society) and so depends on the funding situation of the agency. Applications are assessed on a case-by-case basis. There is no entitlement to funding for visits. Visitors to prisoners are unlikely to be granted funding more than once a year. Consequently, many women in prison in New Zealand experience both geographic and emotional isolation.

Instead of visits, many women have to rely on mail and telephone calls, but these forms of communication are not without their problems—particularly with respect to maintaining contact with young children with limited verbal or reading skills. Phoning their family or children also depends on whether or not they can afford to make the (usually long distance) calls.

> A hell of a lot of us are North Islanders or come from out of town. The people who live in Christchurch and can make local calls can also get visits. So the ones that actually need the phone contact more, have less opportunity to use it. (Woman serving a long term of imprisonment)

Money goes so quickly on the phone cards. I really feel that [the prison system] should do something for people with kids so that they can ring them a couple of times a week. (Woman who had six children and who was serving a long sentence)

In addition, since February 1996 new restrictions have been placed on the number of people prisoners can telephone. A prisoner has to fill out a form on which she nominates a maximum of ten telephone numbers (including her lawyer if she wishes to maintain contact with him or her). Prison staff then check those numbers to ensure that the information provided is accurate (the cost of any overseas calls in this checking process has to be paid for by the prisoner). These approved numbers are the only numbers the prisoner can call and she must pay for all calls. Prisoners used to be able to call collect or make transfer charge calls but this has now been stopped due, in our understanding, to abuses by male prisoners. Calls are limited to fifteen minutes at a time and recipients are advised about who is calling and must agree to receive the call before it is put through. Maintaining contact by writing letters can also be difficult. As one of the women in Kingi's sample said:

I write to my children fortnightly to monthly and I get nothing back, I don't even know if they're getting those letters. (Woman who did not have a good relationship with the caregivers of her children)

Some of the difficulties caused by imprisoning mothers would be eased by the introduction of extended visits for women with dependent children. The Roper Committee in 1989 recommended that children between the ages of two and five years should be allowed to visit their mothers daily on the basis that three visits a week were regarded as the minimum necessary to maintain attachment between a young child and his or her mother. It also recommended all-day visiting on weekends in specially equipped visiting centers. It did not believe that simply putting toys into existing visiting rooms was sufficient.[14] None of these have been implemented, but even if they were, it would be essential to ensure that families had access to adequate funds to take advantage of them.

"Family days" have been introduced at Arohata on an irregular basis so that women can spend time with their families. However, because each wing in the prison has a separate family day and these days are only scheduled to be held every two months, women do not necessarily get to spend quality time with their children every two months. Family days have also been held infrequently at Christchurch Women's Prison. Cost and the distance and the time involved in traveling between the prison and the woman's hometown (or where her children are living) remain issues for women in both of these prisons. There are no facilities to hold family days for women at Mount Eden, but our understanding is that family days have been held for the men there.

Sections 21 and 28 of the Penal Institutions Act 1954 allow women who are likely to give birth while in prison temporary release on parole to church or welfare agencies, and section 91 of the Criminal Justice Act 1985 authorizes the early release of prisoners likely to give birth while in prison. However, not all such women are eligible for release because security considerations are also taken into account. And neither act addresses the issue of women with very young children. According to the 1997 prison census, 15 percent of the women with children had children under one year of age on their entry to prison; a further 41 percent had children between the ages of one and four.

In 1989 the Roper Committee recommended that children up to the age of two should be kept with their mothers in prison in nursery units when the mother was the sole caregiver and wished to continue to care for her child. This has not been implemented. Regulation 55 of the Penal Institutions Regulations 1961 does state that:

> Any female inmate who gives birth to a child, or who on admission has
> a child less than six months old, may keep the child with her until
> proper provision is made for its care.[15]

This does not happen, however, because the Department of Corrections does not see prison as a suitable environment for children. This has resulted in very young children being taken into a women's prison each day to be breast-fed. As one of the women in Kingi's sample commented:

And the little one, well I was breastfeeding her at the time that I came to jail and that just dead stopped, so she lost a lotta weight not taking to the formula straight away. (Woman with four children under five years of age)

In one such case, a young father had left his job, home, and wider family in the North Island to move to Christchurch where he was living in emergency accommodation. His three-year-old daughter was left with the prisoner's sister, who was described as a "young mother already under stress." The father had little money, no transport, and knew no one in the city. He also had no clothing or equipment for the baby. The baby, from the age of five days, was transported with her father each day to the prison.[16] Overall, current practice with respect to women maintaining family ties does not seem to meet the performance standards.

Providing Employment and Vocational Training

Performance standard (h) refers to the provision of employment and vocational training that "reflects the variety of skills which will be of value to [women] upon their return to the community including surviving without paid employment."[17] Again, current practice does not seem to meet this ideal. Partly because of the size of women's prisons, a full range of resources cannot be offered in them, and the nature of the work that is available tends to be rather limited and to focus primarily on servicing the needs of the institution rather than providing the women with skills. For example, the work available for sentenced women in Arohata includes work in the laundry, grounds, kitchen, and garden; and tailoring, sewing, and forestry. In Christchurch Women's Prison, women are employed in the kitchen, garden and grounds, sewing room, laundry room, and as cleaners. For women in Mount Eden Prison, there is little work available other than what can be provided within the women's wing itself. Women may gain useful skills from this type of work and gaining the "habit" of work may be helpful. However, we would suggest that there are more marketable skills that women could gain.

Overall, then, despite the performance standard, the range of work offered in women's prisons does not match that offered in men's prisons. To some extent this has been aggravated by the fact that traditionally work has not been seen as important in women's prisons as it has in men's prisons. As noted earlier, when overcrowding in the men's prison system occurred in New Zealand, men were placed in both Arohata prison and Christchurch Women's Prison and some of the women lost their jobs to the male prisoners. It is also worth noting that, of the women known to be enrolled in programs in 1997, more than one-third were involved in programs involving "leisure/recreational skills" and almost two-thirds were involved in programs involving "personal/social development." Less than one-fifth were involved in vocational training.

Women's Ideas for Improvements in Prisons
and Alternatives to Prisons

The women interviewed by Kingi said that there was a real need for mechanisms by which they could solve urgent problems regarding their families. Staff shortages or absences often meant that by the time they got to see someone the problem had either sorted itself out or had gone away. Nearly all of the women were familiar with the concept of "mother and baby" units in women's prisons and the vast majority were in favor of them.

> If you've just had a baby just before y'come in here . . . that baby sorta doesn't know the mother. . . . [S]ometimes they're breastfeeding y'know. . . . I think there should be a special unit here for especially breastfeeding mothers. (Woman who had six dependent children)

> I wish that they had these sorts of things here so that I didn't have to worry about when I give birth if I'm allowed to go home with my child or not y'know? . . . I want to be with my child. (Woman who was pregnant with her first child)

All of the women were in favor of extended visiting programs that would help them maintain family ties and they suggested that some form of assistance (transport, accommodation, or monetary) should be available to families to make it easier for them to bring children to visit.

> I know it's a lot to ask for. . . . I know we put ourselves in here, but [the criminal justice system is] locking us away from our children. They

should take responsibility for that and pay half [of the fare] so our children can come and visit and set up a facility for them to visit. (Woman who had not seen her son until she had been eligible for home leave — nine months after she had been sentenced)

Houses set up so that like they can come down [and have somewhere to stay] if they're coming from a long way and just to be funded would be nice. . . . [L]ike my Dad he come down and had to sleep in the car because he had nowhere else and he brought all his children. (Young woman who had served numerous terms of imprisonment and whose daughter was in a long-term care situation)

The first priority of the majority of the women was to improve or maintain contact with their families and children.

As we have already noted, only a small number of women are in New Zealand's prisons; many of their offenses are property or drug related and most have had relatively limited prior experience of imprisonment. This raises questions about the continued need for alternatives to imprisoning women (though New Zealand has more community penalties than most jurisdictions). All the women in Kingi's sample were in favor of community sanctions for women who were nonviolent offenders and who had dependent children. This is frequently articulated by penal reformers, too. The Roper Committee, for example, recommended in 1989 the creation of "habilitation centers" in the community.[18] These were intended to be therapeutic centers that would address the treatment of prisoners and their vocational or educational needs. Women would be prime candidates for such centers given the nature of their offenses and their personal circumstances; indeed, the committee recommended that places for women in prison with children up to the age of five years should be included in habilitation centers, thus enabling the women's needs to be met and enabling their children to be engaged in ordinary community activities.

At the time of writing (October 1998), three habilitation centers have been set up for men and one for women, but these are for prisoners on parole rather than alternatives to imprisonment. The women's habilitation center is Aspell House near Wellington, a house that has been in existence in a different guise for a number of years. Its emphasis is on drug/alcohol abuse and it takes female prisoners on parole with drug and alcohol dependence as well as referrals from Community Corrections (women on probation). Between April 1997 and March 1998, only eighteen women had been referred to Aspell House from prison. There are plans to make residence in a habilitation center a sentence in its own right and it will be important to monitor whether women benefit from this or whether, as so often happens, the new sentence becomes just an alternative to other community sanctions.

Conclusion

Despite the critical comments above about aspects of women's imprisonment in New Zealand, it would be wrong not to acknowledge the commitment of many prison staff and the innovations they have introduced. For example, for a number of years now Arohata has had a very active drama and dance group that has put on public performances including material written by the women themselves, and it has also recently introduced a therapeutic unit for drug users who wish to give up drugs. Another innovation is the first "self-care" unit, which was opened in May 1998 in Christchurch Women's Prison. This unit is designed to encourage prisoners at the end of their sentence to take responsibility for their lives in preparation for reentering society.

However, it could be argued that these innovations are simply tinkering around the edges. The number of women in New Zealand's prisons remains relatively small and the "typical" female prisoner has been sentenced for a property or drug offense rather than for violence. Questions can therefore be raised about whether or not they could have been dealt with in a different way. Questions can also be raised about the adequacy of the response of the Department of Corrections to the few women who do have to be imprisoned.

New Zealand does have a national policy and related performance standards specifically for female prisoners—in part, a response to the perceived different needs of female and male prisoners. But it is clear that some of these key performance standards are not being met. At times of overcrowding in men's prisons, men have been placed in women's prisons with the result that some women have lost their jobs and part of their "freedom" within prison. Few women in prison receive training of the kind that might help them get jobs when they leave prison. And because many female prisoners are far from their families and children, maintaining meaningful contact with them — a priority for most women — is simply not feasible. Implementing enhanced visiting programs for children; using modern technology such as videos to enable further contact between women, their families, and their children when visiting is not possible; and dedicated funding to assist family members who wish to visit would all make a difference. But perhaps simply *requiring* the Department of Corrections to meet its stated policy for women in prison would serve well to meet the needs of women in prison as well as the needs of their families and children.

APPENDIX 1: PERFORMANCE STANDARDS

a. Women inmates are housed in separate secure facilities and managed independently of male inmates.

b. The design and furnishing of new women's prisons takes into account the particular needs of women which are identified through consultation with a wide group of people, including women inmates, prison staff and community members.

c. The gender and cultural mix of staff working in women's prisons reflects the need to provide positive role models of both genders for women inmates.

d. Nurses appointed to women's prisons have training specific to women's health issues.

e. Contraceptive services are provided on request from the inmate for temporary releases and/or final release.

f. All women inmates are offered access to, and support in participating in, programmes aimed at reducing or stopping smoking.

g. Programmes offered to women inmates take into account issues impacting on women in New Zealand society which are identified through consultation with women's groups.

h. Employment, industry and vocational training provided to women inmates reflects the variety of skills which will be of value to them upon their return to the community including surviving without paid employment.

i. The prevalence of sexual abuse histories among women inmates is taken into account in both the development of programmes for them and their day to day management.

j. Access for women inmates to information and counselling on abuse related issues is facilitated by prison management.

k. Women inmates have access to the national cervical screening programme.

l. Women inmates over the age of 50 years and/or identified as being at risk have access to a mammography screening programme.[19]

NOTES

1. All figures in this chapter come from the 1997 prison census unless otherwise stated. Barbara Lash, *Census of Prison Inmates, 1997* (Wellington: The Ministry of Justice, 1998).

2. Ministerial Committee of Inquiry into the Prisons System (the Roper Committee), *Prison Review: Te Ara Hou: The New Way* (Wellington: The Crown, 1989).

3. Ibid., 159.

4. Public Prisons Service, *Policy and Procedures Manual* (Wellington: Public Prisons Service, 1998), D.15.

5. Penal Policy Review Committee, *The Report of the Penal Policy Review Committee* (Wellington: Department of Justice, 1981); Department of Justice, *Prisons in Change: The Submission of the Department of Justice to the Ministerial Committee of Inquiry into the Prison System* (Wellington: Department of Justice, 1988).

6. The report was carried out by Peat Marwick, cited in Kathy Dunstall, "Policy and Practice: The Gulf between Intent and Action at the National Women's Prison Christchurch" (paper presented to the Movement for Alternatives to Prisons [MAP] Conference, Auckland, 1994), 9.

7. Almost one-third of the prison officers in women's prisons are male. Performance standard (c) supports the use of male officers to "provide positive role models" for the women.

8. Venezia Kingi, "Mothers in Prison," *Criminology Aotearoa/New Zealand* (newsletter from the Institute of Criminology, Victoria University of Wellington) no. 4 (1995): 7-9.

9. This quote and all other quotes in this chapter from women in prison come from Venezia Kingi's Ph.D. research, unpublished and still in progress.

10. Public Prisons Service, *Policy and Procedures Manual*, A.06.

11. Ibid., A.06.01 F1.

12. Ibid., A.02.

13. Ministerial Committee of Inquiry into the Prisons System (the Roper Committee), *Prison Review*, 160.

14. Ibid., 163-70.

15. Penal Institutions Regulations 1961, Regulation 55.

16. A recent case (cited in Dunstall, "Policy and Practice," 6), signifies an attempt to challenge this policy. In *Singh v. ARCIA,* HC Auckland JP66R95 (13/4/95), the judge allowed an appeal against a five-month prison sentence by a woman with a five-month-old baby she was breast-feeding. The baby was being cared for by the woman's elderly

mother and was being taken to the prison twice a day to be fed. A medical report referred to the effects on the child of separation from its mother and the judge substituted a sentence of 200 hours community service and reparation.

17. Public Prisons Service, *Policy and Procedures Manual,* D.15.

18. Ministerial Committee of Inquiry into the Prisons System (the Roper Committee), *Prison Review,* 32.

19. *Policy and Procedures Manual,* D.15.

REFERENCES

Department of Justice. *Prisons in Change: The Submission of the Department of Justice to the Ministerial Committee of Inquiry into the Prison System.* Wellington: Department of Justice, 1988.

Dunstall, Kathy. "Policy and Practice: The Gulf between Intent and Action at the National Women's Prison Christchurch." Paper presented to the Movement for Alternatives to Prisons (MAP) Conference, Auckland, 1994.

Kingi, Venezia. "Mothers in Prison." *Criminology Aotearoa/New Zealand.* Newsletter of the Institute of Criminology, Victoria University of Wellington, no. 4.

Lash, Barbara. *Census of Prison Inmates, 1997.* Wellington: The Ministry of Justice, 1998.

Ministerial Committee of Inquiry into the Prisons System (the Roper Committee). *Prison Review: Te Ara Hou: The New Way.* Wellington: The Crown, 1989.

Penal Policy Review Committee. *The Report of the Penal Policy Review Committee.* Wellington: Department of Justice, 1981.

Public Prisons Service. *Policy and Procedures Manual.* Wellington: Public Prisons Service, 1998.

On the Margin of Life
Women's Imprisonment in Poland

Monika Platek

A CHILD WAS BORN. A new child was born in prison. In Poland, from the late 1940s until the late 1970s, more than a thousand children were born each year in Grudziadz prison; a cold dark place that had cells with bars in the windows and no running water or sanitation. Over the years, thousands upon thousands of mothers gave birth in Grudziadz. Most were deprived of their children soon after giving birth to them. Others watched their children grow for a year, sometimes two or three years, only to be separated from them once their children were removed to an orphanage. It was not uncommon for a woman who had been born in Grudziaz to return there as a prisoner later in life and, like her mother, to give birth to a new child within those same forbidding walls.

This chapter details several decades of Polish women's experiences behind bars. It contends that their imprisonment reflects the broader stereotyping and vulnerability of women in Poland. As Michel Foucault suggested, prisons provide a sharply detailed picture of the larger social drawing of which they are a part. That is why Foucault became interested in prisons.[1] Although he found criminologists and penologists to be boring and unsophisticated, he turned to exploring the origins of the prison for he believed that this was the place where power structures were most graphically depicted.[2] This is certainly the case in regard to women.

Crime and Imprisonment the Polish Way

In 1981, I was doing research in Fordon, which at that time was the second largest women's prison in Poland (Grudziadz was the largest). My research concerned the failure of conditional release. I had more time than I required, however, and I was therefore able to widen the scope of my research. I was given a little room in the administrative part of the prison, just opposite the women's dormitories. From there I was able to observe the women's lives. Each evening after work there were the same uproars, insults, fights, dances, and caresses. There were usually more than twenty and sometimes more than thirty women in each room, so they had hardly any privacy. There were over six hundred women in Fordon. Most were very young and most were sentenced to be there for a long time.

Most of the women had been imprisoned for petty crimes, the seriousness of which had been exaggerated as a consequence of overblown socialist ideology. Theft in a factory, for example, brought a heavy penalty for it took several years to train such offenders into "socialistic values." The impoverishment of saleswomen, accountants, and housewives, when added to an ideology that placed little value on freedom, resulted in such women being sentenced to many years behind bars.[3] In prison these women worked in the factories producing goods for very little pay. At almost no cost to the government, they were building "their" socialist patrialand (fatherland). There were, however, also other women in the prison.

Over one hundred women were sentenced for murder under Article 148 of the Polish penal code. I was sure that there would be a recognizable pattern; an abused wife with an alcoholic husband who had endured too much and one day had killed him and ended up in Fordon prison. There were such cases, but to my surprise there was no clear pattern as to whom these women had killed. There was a woman with a face like Boticelli's Primavera, who, on the way to visit her lover and in the presence of her elder child, had strangled her younger one. She had not told her lover that she had children, and she was afraid that with two he would not want her. There was another woman who would have been perfect as a Modigliani model. She was so fed up with her mother-in-law that she cut her throat. Not knowing what to do with the body, she put it in bed. She slept in that bed with the body for a week. Was there a pattern? There was a procession of different people killed by these women: lovers, husbands, children, clients, aunts, people they had met by chance who were just unlucky. But characteristically, the sentences meted out to these women were longer than those usually handed down to men who murdered. The judges had not hidden their indignation. Men—yes, that's all right, it happens—but women! For a woman to have done that she must be evil or a pervert and hence deserves a far more severe punishment.

Was there a pattern? Actually there was one. Apart from being sentenced more harshly, hardly any of these women had ever experienced love and respect. Far too many had been bought up in orphanages. Some had been born in prison. Was destiny, a curse, or anathema to blame? No. It was just the negligence of a system that allowed these women to be moved from one institution to the next, depending upon what was deemed necessary. But of course it was they who were blamed for not fitting into the stereotype of the Virgin Saint or honorable mother, and it was they who had to pay. And so they did, until one day . . .

The Voiceless Revolution

For years there were more than 100,000 people in Polish prisons. With an imprisonment rate of over 340 people per 100,000 head of population, Poland had one of the highest imprisonment rates in the world, excluding countries such as the Soviet Union, China, and the United States. From a communist economic point of view, the prison business was part of the state business and the high rate of imprisonment was beneficial to the country. Indeed, prisons were often the only sector to meet their budgetary obligations on time. Women in prison, for example, produced clothing, shoes, food, and other items for general consumption or use. Within the prisons people worked for almost nothing, but a crisis of national proportions was gathering momentum and would soon bring change.

In 1985 the whole ingeniously woven political texture of Poland began to unravel, showing that it was worth little more than scraps of rag. The penal system was the first realm to be touched by economic crisis. Although crucial to the economy, the system was reliant upon state funds and was unable to provide work for all inmates as the number of those imprisoned increased. With the advent of the political crisis, the law came to the rescue of those in power. New crimes were established, heavier punishments were introduced, and speedier trials were ensured. Indeed, all of these practices had begun in preceding years but the new temporary law that came into effect on 1 July 1985 resulted in even more people being deprived of their liberty. The penal system had to organize hundreds of new places to cope with those sentenced under this law. Given increasing imprisonment rates and a social climate that allowed more public discussion of prisons, reform became both possible and unavoidable. A suitable object for reform had to be found and it was women who were chosen.

Women in prison were the first to experience reform, but it was not women or their interests that counted. They were merely used to make other gains, such as the provision of space for more male prisoners. In 1982, for example, partly because of the introduction of martial law and the increase in men's imprisonment that followed, one of the prisons that had traditionally housed women was converted into a men's prison. In 1985 women were once again shifted, only this time they were moved out of the penal system. The minister of justice sent an official letter to prosecutors and judges announcing a new humanitarian policy toward women with respect to the administration of penal law and penitentiary practice. In the new policy women were only to be sentenced to isolation in exceptional cases, and were to be released on license whenever formal prerequisites permitted such release.

Over the previous fifteen years, women had consistently constituted around 5.7 percent of Poland's total prison population. Of the 100,000 Poles in prison at the start of 1985, more than 5,500 were women. This number began to drop suddenly, however, after the practical implementation of the minister's instructions. By the end of 1985 the number of imprisoned women had declined to 5,112. In 1986 the number fell to below 5,000 and the following year it declined further to 4,035. By 30 April 1988 there were 3,301 women in various forms of incarceration. Of this number, 219 were under arrest for misdemeanors, 561 were in detention, and only 2,521 had been sentenced to imprisonment.

How can this dramatic decrease from 5,500 imprisoned women to only 2,500 in just three years be explained? Clearly it was the result of an abrupt reduction in the imposition of long-term sentences of imprisonment, together with more frequent use of conditional release. But rather than focusing on these technicalities, let us try to grasp the reasons for these changes and their merits. Was this new policy toward women really an act of humanitarianism?

One should not fail to recognize those members of the prison service who strive to bring about change. Prison overcrowding, and the inhumane conditions that arise as a consequence of it, are perennial problems confronted by prison administrators. In this part of the world, amnesties have often been declared in order to relieve swelling prison numbers. At times when the penal system has been close to total collapse as a consequence of overcrowding amnesties have been used as a safety valve. The policy of diverting women from prison might be understood as a form of amnesty, but given the increasing numbers of men being sentenced to imprisonment the fundamental problem of overcrowding has persisted, and in some places has become even worse.

From an administrative point of view, beginning the reform process by focusing on a small group of prisoners rather than the system as a whole may have appeared most feasible. Statistics certainly revealed that women were responsible for only one-tenth of total offenses and were therefore less numerous in prisons. Nevertheless, this does not explain adequately why women were chosen as the focus of reform. In Polish stratification data, for example, prisoners are not divided into male and female groups. The rules do not mention sex; rather they specify age, recidivism, mental state, and various other characteristics. If we follow these rules, then at least ten different categories of prisoners, each composed of about 10,000 people, can be distinguished. Women constitute about 10 percent of prisoners within each of these categories. The reason why one of these already defined categories was not selected as the focus of reform remains unclear and suggests that the choice of women warrants further investigation.

Some reasons were given officially for the new policy relating to women. Women, it was stated, should not stay in prison because they constituted a difficult category of prisoner. Prisoners with periods, children, and too many emotions posed a problem for prison managers. Moreover, it was suggested that women were incapable of adapting to prison conditions. Certainly most women do experience problems during imprisonment, but whether this is sufficient to distinguish them as more "difficult" than any other group is highly debatable. Young offenders, for example, have long been regarded as a "difficult" group within Polish prisons. Indeed, they have been specifically referred to in special instructions intended to undermine prison subculture. Significantly, these instructions have failed to recognize the connection between the disruptive prison subculture they seek to weaken and the more general problem of overcrowding. Increases in the number of people held within each cell inevitably generate conflict and aggression among both male and female prisoners. Densely packed prisons are difficult places, and within them every category of prisoner is liable to be "difficult." With this in mind, there seems no real reason why women should have been singled out as the most "difficult" prisoners or as the first focus of reform. If the logic of reform was primarily to remove "difficult" prisoners from the system, then young offenders, both male and female, might just as easily have been nominated.

But there was, of course, another reason given to justify the selection of women. According to official statements humanity required that women be allowed to return home to their families and especially their children. What was blatantly false in this statement was the reference to humanity for the real reason was that economic and other practical benefits would accrue to the state through the return of women prisoners to their homes. Despite the constitutional declaration of equal rights for women and men, women in Poland remain solely responsible for rearing children and taking care of households. Equality of rights, the Polish way—and more broadly, the Eastern European way—means that most women are still required to fulfill their traditional roles as mothers, wives, and housekeepers while also fulfilling new roles as paid workers and family breadwinners.

Given the heavy responsibilities that women are expected to bear, it is hardly surprising that their imprisonment creates problems. When women are imprisoned, men hardly ever take over their responsibilities and duties. These are instead shifted onto the state. It is clearly more convenient for the state to release women prisoners, usually on bail, than it is to provide "care" for these women, their families, and their children. The moment a woman is released from prison these problems cease to exist, at least for state administrators. Women are simply expected to resume their roles and to fulfill their responsibilities and duties. But, at the same time, the difficulties that led them to prison often still exist and have to be confronted once again. These problems frequently include a lack of financial resources, the unavailability of work, an abusive partner, and drug- and alcohol-related difficulties. Although a representative of the state administration is there to shake a woman's hand and to wish her well upon her release, rarely, if ever, is a helping hand offered.

There was also another advantage in releasing or diverting women from prison. Work performed within the prisons was of crucial importance to both the internal economies of the prisons and to the state. In prison, different sorts of work were performed. While men could undertake all the work expected to be performed in the prisons, the same was not true of women. There were some forms of work that women were not able to do. Thus men's labor was more valued than women's, and women as workers were more expendable than their male counterparts.

According to scientific criminological commentary and penal philosophy, imprisonment is meant to deter both offenders and other citizens from engaging in criminal acts. If we follow this reasoning, the sudden reduction in the number of imprisoned women should have sent a message to other women that they were free to do whatever they wanted, even if it was criminal. Under the new policy, the chances of a woman being imprisoned were halved. This reduction should therefore have led to an increase in women's offending, but it didn't. Women continued to commit between 10 and 11 percent of total crimes. There was no marked increase or decrease in their level of offending. Nor was there a change in the types of offenses committed by women. Property crimes, mostly petty ones, continued to predominate, while homicides and aggravated assaults remained relatively few. This lack of change proved that the rate of imprisonment does not necessarily affect the level or type of offending that occurs within a state. It also showed that prisons and crime have very little in common, in the sense that prisons do not prevent crime.

These revelations, however, remained largely unnoticed in Poland. Even when attention was drawn to them they were ignored, especially by policy makers. It was suggested that women, as the objects of reform, were an "incorrect" sample. How could general conclusions be based upon the trends of such an unstable and unknowable group? In the wake of the policy change, the number of women in Polish prisons continued to decline and now stands at approximately 1,500. How, we might ask, have these changes affected women in prison and what does the future hold for them?

Minimum Rules

Until 1956 there was little space in Poland for a human rights discourse concerning prisoners. Inmates were perceived as political enemies, even if their only "crime" had been to steal a bottle of milk or to be consistently late for work. In 1956, however, with the end of the Stalinist period, prison administration was moved from the Ministry of Interior to the Ministry of Justice. An amnesty was declared and many prisoners were released, either as a consequence of court orders or because their cases had been reopened and they had been found not guilty or the charges against them had been dismissed. In that year the number of prisoners in Poland fell to just 35,253—an all-time low. Since that time, increases in the imprisonment rate have occurred regularly, but they have been punctuated by sudden declines. This has happened after each so-called political thaw. It happened after a change in the political leadership in 1970, again in 1980 and 1981 during the Solidarity period, and yet again in 1989 with another change of political regime. In this latter instance, another new amnesty was declared and, as a consequence, the prison population dropped from 100,000 people to only 40,000 in a single year.

Each time the political climate became characterized by "warp, distort, and mistakes," it became fashionable to talk about the resocialization of prisoners. Like the repeated refrain of the same dull song, it was espoused that reformation, or resocialization, would serve to create a new socialist archetype of the good citizen. Preparing to live in an open society while in a closed prison is like trying to learn how to fly in a submarine. Yet this detail did not bother the criminal justice ideologues. Appearance was all that counted. That is why separate prison rules were introduced for women at the end of the 1950s. Introduced also were separate prisons for women and separate classifications that categorized them according to age, criminal career, mental state, and family circumstances.

For years women in prisons had been ignored. From time to time, students who had visited Grudziadz prison—the only one "prepared" for pregnant women—had described the murky conditions inside. The cells were designed for two people but usually held four. They had double bunk beds, no running water, and no sanitation. Pregnant women and those who had just given birth had no choice but to carry heavy buckets filled with either water or excrement to and fro as required. Once a week the women would walk from the buildings that housed them to another where the showers were located. Inadequately clothed for the Polish winter, they often fell ill, but medical attention was scarce and medicine rarely available. The children born in Grudziadz were sometimes taken away soon after birth. Others remained with their mothers for a year or two until they were shifted to an orphanage. Years later some of these children would themselves give birth in prison.[4]

Despite these appalling conditions, it was a long time before any substantial improvements were made inside Poland's women's prisons. In 1966 new prison rules were introduced that did allow some concessions for pregnant women. They were permitted to take longer walks and to rest on a bench during their recreation. They were also given the right to lie down on a bed during the day. In 1974 temporary prison rules that operated for the next fifteen years restricted even these few privileges. Regardless of humanistic slogans, severe discipline has always been dominant in Polish prisons. Wardens were given the right to award special privileges; however, this proved to be more rhetoric than practice. It is enough to mention that it took years for an inmate to earn the privilege to wear personal underwear. Pregnant women were expected to stand in narrow and overcrowded cells that remained devoid of running water or a toilet. Most of these women had been sentenced to many years of imprisonment for petty crimes. Inside, they had no opportunity to maintain adequate contact with the outside world or to prepare for a later life of freedom.

In 1988, instructions were prepared ordering that the women's prisons should be altered to meet minimum rule requirements. Minimum rules are just that; they detail the minimum of what is expected of prisons in terms of the conditions and treatment they afford to inmates. In most cases authorities feel proud when they are satisfied that the reality within prisons meets these minimum rules. Typically, the minimum is treated as both the start and finish of what is required. It is also characteristic for such rules to be called upon when there is a need to meet other goals. The rules serve as an excuse to do what the authorities require in other respects.

The observance of minimum rules in Polish women's prisons commenced in July 1988. A special, more lenient regime was introduced in semi-open labor institutions. Women who for the previous ten years had been locked up twenty-three hours a day were able to enjoy open cells and free movement in the corridors. They were permitted to wear their own clothes, to shower twice rather than once a week, and to use warm water for a wash each day. Unlike other prisoners, women were no longer obliged to come to attention in the presence of a prison guard, and indeed the warden could allow them to stay together in the common room without a guard being present. The women could also watch television for longer periods. They could wear their own clothes when being visited by their children and, unlike other prisoners, they could treat their children to sweets or sandwiches during their visits. There was no limit to the number of letters that women could receive or send. The letters were to remain unbranded by the censor's mark, but in most cases they were censored. If women discovered that their children were in need, they could apply for and, with the warden's approval, gain five days' leave from the prison. Moreover, women were entitled to ten hours' leave from prison twice a month.

The conditions within the women's prisons had improved, but to what extent? The meeting of minimum rules represented another form of experiment and it had obvious benefits for the state. The general atmosphere in the women's prisons had improved and fewer staff were needed. That was important because prison staff were needed elsewhere. Although the women gained greater freedom of movement inside the prisons, they were not provided with opportunities for developing self-respect or skills. There were special rules concerning menstruation, but no special programs to teach women how to get jobs or to manage their relationships with their families, husbands, and children.[5] Although women could also gain greater access to the outside world, no one cared whether or not they had anywhere to go during their periods of leave. The prospects of these women for building better lives for themselves and their children, for finding such necessities as work and accommodation, were not the concern of prison administrators. In fact, they were no administrator's concern.

In Poland Today

The conditions for women in Polish prisons have improved. Grudziadz still serves as a prison for women with newborn children, but it is now renovated and modernized. Women have access to proper medical attention, sanitation is now built into cells, and relations between prisoners and staff hardly ever provoke any complaints. Women can keep their children with them in Grudziadz for up to six months after their birth, and during that time efforts are made to help them develop a meaningful relationship. Efforts are also made to help the women get out of prison if this is possible. It remains the case that most of the women who give birth in prison have other children on the outside as well.

In another prison, Krzywaniec, women can stay with their children for up to three years. Again, the conditions there are relatively good. When you speak to the women there it becomes clear that they want to return to a free life outside with their children. But they also express the fear that they will not be able to provide their children with the necessities they have while in prison. There is clearly something wrong when the conditions women and children experience inside prisons are better than those they can find outside of it. You know when you speak to these women that even though they hope to keep their children, most won't manage to do so. Women's prisons in Poland today may be warm, clean, and almost cozy, but the women inside them have little hope upon release of finding work, a place to stay, and the other necessities required for providing children with adequate care and support.

In Poland's open society women are supposed to manage; they alone are held to blame if they don't. It is rarely acknowledged here that women who are criminals are more often than not also victims.[6] They are simply expected to endure violence, abuse, and poverty in silence. They are expected to listen silently, to serve and, if sent to prison, to be invisible. After all, good women do not commit crimes and good women are not sent to prison. Regardless of whether they have constituted 10 percent of Poland's total prison population, as they did in the 1970s, or just 1.5 percent as they did in 1990, it has remained the case that women's particular needs have never really been acknowledged or addressed. Today there are only 1,343 women in Polish prisons and they are more invisible than ever.

NOTES

1. Michel Foucault, *Discipline and Punish: The Birth of the Prison* (Harmondsworth: Peregrine Books, 1979).

2. Michel Foucault, "Prison Talk," in *Power/Knowledge: Selected Interviews and Other Writings 1972-1977*, ed. Colin Gordon (New York: Pantheon Books, 1980), 37-54.

3. Tadeusz Kolarczyk, Roman Jacek Kubiak, and Piotr Wierzbicki, *Przestepczosc kobeit: Aspekty Kryminologiczne i penitencjarne* (Warszawa: Wydanictwa Prawnicze, 1984).

4. Janina Blachut, *Kobiety recydywistki wswietle badan kyyminologicznych* (Wroclaw: Ossolineum, 1981).

5. Monika Platek, "The Socio-Economic Position of Women in Detention," in *Proceedings of the International Seminar on Women in Detention: Perspectives for Change* (Noordwijk: Dutch Ministry of Justice, 1992), 51-64.

6. Bozena Gronowska and Monika Platek, "On the Victimization of Women in Poland," in *Women: The Past and New Roles* (Warszaw: Centre for Europe, Warsaw University, 1995), 30-41.

REFERENCES

Blachut, Janina. *Kobiety recydywistki wswietle badan kyyminologicznych.* Wroclaw: Ossolineum, 1981.

Foucault, Michel. *Discipline and Punish: The Birth of the Prison.* Harmondsworth: Peregrine Books, 1979.

———. "Prison Talk." In *Power/Knowledge: Selected Interviews and Other Writings 1972-1977*, edited by Colin Gordon. New York: Pantheon Books, 1980.

Gronowska, Bozena, and Monika Platek. "On the Victimization of Women in Poland." In *Women: The Past and New Roles.* Warszaw: Centre for Europe, Warsaw University, 1995.

Kolarczyk, Tadeusz, Roman Jacek Kubiak, and Piotr Wierzbicki. *Przestepczosc kobeit: Aspekty Kryminologiczne i penitencjarne.* Warszawa: Wydanictwa Prawnicze, 1984.

Platek, Monika. "The Socio-Economic Position of Women in Detention." In *Proceedings of the International Seminar on Women in Detention: Perspectives for Change.* Noordwijk: Dutch Ministry of Justice, 1992.

Unheard Voices
Burmese Women in Immigration Detention in Thailand

Carol Ransley

Introduction

If knowledge of female prisoners as a group is thin, knowledge of the strengths and differences of female prisoners of different racial and ethnic backgrounds, the unique needs of particular groups of female offenders, or the interactions between racial and ethnic identity and the prison experience is all but non-existent.[1]

It is useful to place the developments in women's imprisonment and feminist participation in a wider context. One needs to acknowledge the continual tensions between feminist, political, administrative and institutional agendas.[2]

WOMEN'S EXPERIENCES of immigration detention have been largely overlooked by researchers and writers on women's imprisonment. This is particularly disappointing given the growing body of feminist writing and scholarship on women's imprisonment that has developed since the early 1980s.[3] This is also surprising given increasing awareness of the politics of race, ethnicity, and gender in the construction of knowledges about our globalizing world.[4] In short, current writing on women's imprisonment is too narrow in its focus. Even though women who are imprisoned under immigration detention laws are subject to a process similar to criminalization that is no less detrimental to their welfare, the alarming numbers of women in immigration detention continue to be overlooked. Generally immigration detainees are not included in estimates of imprisoned populations throughout the world because breaches of migration laws are usually not understood as being "offenses." This makes it easier to ignore women detainees as an incarcerated population.

In the West we do not see large numbers of undocumented women migrating from newly industrializing countries. We are even less likely to be confronted by the reality of large groups of undocumented women migrants in immigration detention. Inattention to the experiences of women immigration detainees is no doubt partly attributable to the fact that most academic inquiry and activism emanates and is focused upon the West. This chapter argues that consideration of immigration detention should be incorporated into the broader feminist project of naming, understanding, and contextualizing women's imprisonment. It illustrates the necessity of doing this by referring to the complexities and experiences of Burmese women in immigration detention in Thailand. Women immigration detainees are "criminalized" and subjected to penal regimes in ways that are directly related to their gender.

Immigration Detention as Imprisonment

Human Rights Watch draws a distinction between forms of criminal and administrative detention, when, for example, persons kept in immigration detention do not serve a criminal sentence or await trial on criminal charges.[5] Immigration detention is, then, a form of administration detention. Immigration detainees breach regulations governing appropriate administrative procedures for gaining access to a country other than their country of origin and do not commit "crimes." For example, a person entering a country on a false passport, without any kind of passport, or without an appropriate visa is likely to be held in detention. Despite the fact that no crime has been committed by the immigration detainee, more often than not that detainee's experience of incarceration is no different from that of other prison inmates being held on criminal charges.[6] Detention facilities for immigration detainees the world over are not reflective of their "non-accused," "non-criminal" status.[7]

In many circumstances the prison experience is much worse for immigration detainees than for criminal prisoners. For example, Amnesty International found that undocumented migrants from Africa, Asia, and the Middle East who found their way into the United Kingdom were being held in state custody for indefinite periods of time. They claimed that detainees were not adequately informed of the reasons for their detention and were given minimal opportunities, if any, to challenge the legality of their detention. Human Rights Watch has similarly noted that detained asylum seekers who have committed no criminal offense have fewer rights than persons charged with murder, rape, and other serious crimes.[8] According to Amnesty International, it is quite common for inadequately documented migrants or persons seeking asylum to be detained without trial and, in contrast to persons incarcerated for criminal offenses, no provisions are made for granting them bail.[9]

Michael Welch argues that the detention of undocumented migrants is a particular mechanism to control the free movement of peoples and protect First World identity. Questioning of this detention, he states, must be ongoing.[10] Taking such ideas further, Bhabha notes the increasing "criminalization" of undocumented migrants, asylum seekers, and refugees throughout the European Union (EU). She locates immigration detention in the broader political process of defining a new EU, where immigration control is a means of determining who "belongs" — that is, who may lawfully constitute a modern, redefined EU — through a process of inclusion and exclusion.[11] She also explores the implications of this process for women, who are less mobile and less visible as they move beyond borders. Despite the fact that some literature is available on immigration detention as a rising method of social control, very little attention has been given to the problems that face women in immigration detention, or to the development of feminist analyses on the use of immigration detention as a form of social control of women.

While examining the experiences of Burmese women refugees, asylum seekers, and illegal immigrant workers in Thailand, it is important to draw links between aspects of both "women's imprisonment" and "immigration detention" scholarship to identify areas for future scholarship and/or activism. According to Hannah-Moffat,

[f]eminists' failure to challenge the meaning of punishment has amounted to a mere tinkering with a complex institutional network that does not, and cannot, adequately meet women's requirements. Feminists need to devise a concrete understanding of punishment and not simply attempt to compensate existing methods and definitions of punishment, like incarceration, that encompass a number of inherently contradictory goals. Feminism can play a crucial role in the reform process, and we are only beginning to understand the significance, power and authority of this role.[12]

That the specificity of the woman prisoner's experience has been largely invisible to Western governments, legislators, and policy makers has been well documented. An Australian community lawyer and prison activist comments that

[i]n a discussion of prisons, women are usually absent. Women's absence from the study of crime and prisons occurs because of *the narrow view taken of what is crime and what are prisons and, because, as in all other aspects of society, women are marginal and unimportant* [my emphasis].[13]

If more understanding, critical reflection, and debate are to be fostered with regard to women's experiences of immigration detention, it will be necessary to acknowledge how the politics of race, culture, ethnicity, and citizenship can operate to constrain such recognition.

Burmese Women's Migration to Thailand

I have learned that being a woman is very difficult, especially for a Burmese woman.[14]

Widespread state-sanctioned human rights abuses inflicted on both political dissidents and ethnic nationality peoples in Burma have driven at least one million people from their homes in the last fifteen years to neighboring Thailand, Bangladesh, and India.[15] In 1998 the Burmese refugee population in Thailand numbered approximately 110,000; the majority of refugees were women and children. In most cases they were detained in refugee camps still at risk of attack by the Burmese military.[16] A further 500,000 to 1 million unsuitably documented migrants from Burma also fled to Thailand as Burma's economy began exhibiting the more serious effects of a thirty-year-long draconian-style military rule and the use of forced labor and forced relocation by the military became more widespread.[17]

During Thailand's high growth years of the 1980s, its urban-based industries, which included building and construction and sex-related services, attracted rural Thai women, employed in agriculture and the fishing sector, and also to a relatively small number of migrants from Burma, Laos, and Cambodia.[18] As Thai women started to move, refugees and migrant workers from most of Thailand's neighboring countries found that they were able to migrate independently into urban Thailand. Their journeys from their rural villages to the larger Thai industrial zones were facilitated by brokers who increasingly organized "work placements" and took larger and larger commissions for these "placements." Thus, the illegal trafficking process in modern Thailand was born.[19] Although in the past these workers were predominantly male, more recently large numbers of women and children from neighboring countries have traveled and in many cases fled to Thailand as dependent family members. Once there they have engaged in forms of employment less visible than those undertaken by their male relatives.

In recent years, as armed conflict has stepped up along the Thai-Burmese border and as the demand has increased for ever younger women to work in the Thai sex industry, more and more independent young Burmese women have migrated to Thailand. After initially being forced to hide in refugee camps along the Thai-Burmese border, they have been able to migrate deeper into urban Thailand.[20] The Thai government, while fully aware that more and more Burmese women have been migrating to urban areas via a process of trafficking, has consistently failed to acknowledge the "female nature" of the Burmese refugee and migrant populations and to take action to protect this population from exploitation. That there is very little recognition of the sexed nature of Burma-to-Thailand migration has further obscured the ways in which the realities of women's daily experiences can be heard and understood.

Human rights organizations Asia Watch and Images Asia have documented the abuses arising out of the organized process of recruitment, captivity, and slavery of Burmese women migrating or fleeing to Thailand. They have detailed the process of debt bondage and illegal confinement; various forms of sexual and physical abuse; abysmal working conditions that expose women migrants to a significant degree of harm; discriminatory and arbitrary arrests; and violations of due process such as prolonged detention, summary trials, custodial abuse, summary deportation, and forced repatriation to situations of armed conflict.[21] With no country of origin to take responsibility for them, Burmese women have little or no power with which to bargain, to make requests for assistance, or to extricate themselves from situations that they did not anticipate or want.[22] Illegal Burmese women migrants in Thailand have little opportunity to change their situation or to voice opposition to their detention. For everyone except the women, it is convenient that they remain an invisible but nonetheless crucial source of labor for Thailand.[23]

In much of the literature on the population movement of Burmese people in Thailand, two broad conceptual categories are used. Women and children living in refugee camps along the Thai-Burmese border are generally regarded as "refugees" who have been caught in the line of fire between the Burmese military and the insurgent armies along the border.[24] Women and children able to flee further into Thailand are generally understood to be "migrant workers" or "economic migrants" because they are not generally thought of as being "caught in the crossfire." Because of the logistical problems associated with physically migrating deeper into Thailand, most of the latter category of women and children arrived via a trafficking process — a highly organized process of moving larger and larger numbers of men and women into Thailand to fill an increasing need for cheaper unskilled labor.[25] It is the latter group, the migrant worker women and children, who face the most threat from immigration detention.

There are, however, many similarities between Burmese women's experiences as immigration detainees and their experiences as refugees living in camps along the Thai-Burmese border. In the first place, it is frequently the Burmese military's practice of forced labor and forced relocation that drives women from the country. The distinctions, therefore, that are drawn between "migrant workers" and "refugee" women are arbitrary. They do not take into account the similarities of these women's experiences, in particular, the common reasons that so often underlie their flight into Thailand. Their common experiences as women are fundamental; however, it is often difficult to articulate how these experiences relate specifically to gender. As Elizabeth Ferris explains:

> Sometimes women are singled out for persecution, simply because they are women. Women may be captured or tortured as a way of punishing male relatives. Or women may be harassed or abused because of their failure to follow traditional norms for women's behavior in a given society. During flight, refugee women face particular problems of rape and abuse, from those from whom they are fleeing, but also sometimes from those from whom they seek protection. At borders they are more vulnerable to sexual abuse and intimidation. Once they arrive in camps, they face the possibility of violence from camp officials, from other refugees, and from their own families. Women living as urban refugees, particularly when they are undocumented, are often subjected to sexual abuse.[26]

It is not just women's voices that are lost within the theorizing about who is a refugee or migrant worker. The leaders of Burma's ethnic nationality peoples and various Burmese women's organizations have consistently stated that it is impossible to make the simple distinction so often made between Burmese refugees, migrant workers, and trafficked persons. Each of these groups has experienced economic abuses such as being forced into labor and having unfair taxes imposed upon them and each has suffered human rights violations, including the abuse of political and civil rights.[27]

Leading human rights organizations have supported the "Burmese position" by claiming that the distinction made by the international community and Thai officials between migrants and refugees is arbitrary. Human Rights Watch notes that the occurrences of arrest, detention, and deportation of unsuitably documented Burmese persons, some of whom would have a clear claim to refugee status under the UN's Convention on the Status of Refugees (1951) if they were permitted to make such a claim, are increasing steadily.[28] It accuses the Thai government of repeatedly violating international laws that protect a refugee's right to seek asylum with respect to both Burmese refugees and migrant workers and voices concerns that continuing economic and political pressures in both Burma and Thailand will result in further abuses. Meanwhile Thailand continues to step up its border controls and community-based enforcement and surveillance and to impose harsher and harsher fines and sanctions for Burmese people forced to breach immigration laws. The refugee experience that "belongs" to Burmese women falls abruptly through the conceptual abyss created between the two categories of "refugee" and "migrant worker."

Burmese Women's Experiences of Detention

Little has been written about women immigration detainees by Western writers, and what has been written focuses on demographic statistics rather than women's experiences. In Thailand, for example, more has been written, but this is of an anecdotal nature, not the critical analyses required to include these women's experiences in the body of writing about women's imprisonment.[29] Burmese women face a complex range of abuses because they are vulnerable to abuse on many fronts: as women generally; as female refugees; and as migrant workers. Their experiences as women leave them extremely vulnerable to various forms of sexual violence and severe curtailment of their freedom of movement.[30] A Burmese woman interviewed in Samut Sakhorn Province in Thailand stated that

> [t]he police come regularly to raid us and to take us to jail but we try to stay quiet and hide in our dormitory. There are some special places for us to go. We must stay very quiet and not make a noise otherwise the police will come and then we will have to stay in jail.

All roads lead to jail, or the immigration detention centers (IDCs), as they are commonly known. Such detainees are not given an opportunity to challenge the legality of their confinement under local or international laws, let alone tell of the kinds of abuses they are surviving along the way.[31]

For women being detained under immigration laws in newly industrializing countries such as Thailand, the situation is significantly more urgent than in the West—conditions are deplorable. Women are often kept in holding cells that are sometimes so overcrowded that it is not possible to sleep lying down. Women are not provided with opportunities to wash and dress in privacy and are quite regularly detained in cells alongside men. Women are sexually abused and exploited. Without adequate government policies and procedures, resources to implement what policies *do* exist, or adherence to basic and minimum standards for imprisonment of detainees that are embodied in international law,[32] and amid a culture of official corruption, the detention of undocumented migrants from Burma receives little if any attention that goes beyond tokenism. Furthermore, the myriad of sexual abuses inflicted upon Burmese women in immigration detention in Thailand are rarely acknowledged, if ever addressed. The following eyewitness account of the abuses being perpetrated by Thai officials against Burmese women detainees is, unfortunately, a typical account:

[O]n July 21, 1993 between three and four hundred detainees in the IDC were transferred to the Kanchanaburi immigration jail. There were about 50 women and fourteen children in the group. When they first arrived at the jail, they were divided by sex and put into small rooms downstairs. The women were asked to pay 100 Baht for the transportation costs to the border and 100 Baht each for the cell upstairs. Ten women, including two girls aged fifteen, could not pay. One policeman and one male warden called them out and ordered them to take off all their clothes in front of all the other detainees. When several of the women were too slow, the two men pulled off their clothes. The policeman touched the women all over and even checked their vaginas. The police took everything they found on the women: watches, gold and money. Two officers played with the younger girls and after the search sent everyone back to the cell except one girl, about 20 years old. . . . At 7 pm that night all the inmates upstairs could hear the police demanding that the girl left behind sleep with them. She refused and they listened to at least an hour of screaming and beating. Afterwards, the same two officers brought her upstairs to the cell, slapping and hitting her in front of the others. During the following eight days while this group was kept at the Kanchanaburi jail, the policemen came each night to the cell to call a woman or girl down to wash the dishes. Those who refused to go down would be threatened and hit. Eventually all had to go. One evening, he heard the policeman tell the woman downstairs that if she agreed to sleep with him, she could return to Bangkok for free, without having to pay 3,000 Baht fee to return to the capital.[33]

"Aye Aye," a Burmese woman interviewed in Bangkok during 1998, speaks of the central problem and ever present source of tension faced by women detainees in immigration detention: having so few ways to voice the terrible problems they experience.

> The Thais find us and want to punish us for coming here. We have done nothing wrong. We cannot stay in Thailand, but we cannot go home—the Burmese military are everywhere, they make our lives very difficult. If we can't go home, where should we go? We are stuck between two countries with nowhere to go. As women, because we are so afraid of what might happen to us, we can't even talk about these things that are happening to us—who will listen?[34]

Conclusion

The many conceptual and practical difficulties posed by Burmese women facing periods of immigration detention raises two important questions. How do we understand the problems of women's diverse experiences of incarceration? And, how do we go about addressing these issues in practical terms? Indeed, the practice of immigration detention itself is too often overlooked and underreported. Attempts need to be made to identify women's diverse experiences of all forms of incarceration to bridge the many conceptual gaps and to remedy the many wrongs.

For Burmese women who have survived to recount their migration experiences, it is difficult to draw a clear distinction between what "belongs" to their refugee experiences and what "belongs" to their experiences as a "migrant" or a "Burmese woman." The answers to our conceptual difficulties can only be found in the testimony, experience, and understandings of women from Burma. Sharon McQuaide and John Ehrenreich ask:

> [W]hat are the central research questions about women inmates, and what are the appropriate methods to be used in answering these

questions? . . . To understand these women and to design interventions to serve them, a more *experience-near* approach, which takes into account how a particular woman experiences her own unique life as well as how her shared experiences of gender, race and ethnicity, and imprisonment affect her, is necessary. . . . It is necessary to search for and to recognise the different voices with which a woman speaks, to identify the triggers for the various voices, and to perceive and comprehend her inconsistencies. Perhaps most important, the prison voices of the inmate do not necessarily exhaust her repertoire. To see her only as the prison creates her is to falsify her and to reduce her to her current social status.[35]

There is a great deal of scope for further research on women's immigration detention throughout the world, and for feminists and prison activists to "take on board" the problem of women's immigration detention, if we are bold enough to reconceptualize the meanings of the prison experience. In the case of women from Burma who remain at risk of detention in Thailand, there is much scope to advocate for the use of noncustodial alternatives to detention.

NOTES

Thank you to Toe Zaw Latt for his ability to see beyond the complex of problems presented in this paper and for his encouragement and support of my work in Thailand. Additional thanks to John Cox, Lia Kent, Sue Davies, and Sandy Cook for their helpful comments and advice on various drafts.

1. Sharon McQuaide and John H. Ehrenreich, "Women in Prison: Approaches to Understanding the Lives of a Forgotten Population," *Affilia: Journal of Women and Social Work* 13, no. 2 (1998): 236–37.

2. Kelly Hannah-Moffat, "Unintended Consequences of Feminism and Prison Reform," *Forum* 6, no. 1 (1994): 9.

3. See Pat Carlen's exploration of the meanings of women's imprisonment in Scotland and the invisible nature of the social control of women in Pat Carlen, *Women's Imprisonment: A Study in Social Control* (London: Routledge & Kegan Paul, 1983).

4. I do not have time to fully explore the implications made by feminist critiques of globalization and international relations, particularly as it affects immigration detention. Please refer to Jan Jindy Pettman, *Worlding Women: A Feminist International Politics* (Sydney: Allen & Unwin, 1996) for the most comprehensive exploration of a feminist international politics.

5. Human Rights Watch, "Locked Away: Immigration Detainees in Jails in the United States," *Human Rights Watch Report,* vol. 10, no. 1(G) (New York: Human Rights Watch, 1998).

6. Amnesty International claims that in the United Kingdom the number of immigration detainees being held alongside convicted criminal inmates has increased three-fold since 1993, and that increasingly detention centers are being run by private security organizations that run these centers along similar lines to prisons. See Amnesty International U.K., *Cell Culture: Asylum Seekers in the UK* (London: Amnesty International, 1998). Human Rights Watch has noted a similar trend in the United States, where the U.S. Immigration and Naturalization Service (INS) houses more than 60 percent of its 15,000 detainees in local jails inappropriate to their noncriminal status. See also Human Rights Watch, "Locked Away: Immigration Detainees in Jails in the United States."

7. Amnesty International U.K., *Cell Culture.*

8. Human Rights Watch, "Locked Away: Immigration Detainees in Jails in the United States."

9. Amnesty International U.K., *Cell Culture.*

10. Michael Welch, "The Immigration Crisis: Detention as an Emerging Mechanism of Social Control," *Social Justice* 23, no. 3 (Fall 1996): 169-85.

11. Jacqueline Bhabha, "'Get Back to Where You Once Belonged': Identity, Citizenship, and Exclusion in Europe," *Human Rights Quarterly* 20 (1998): 592-627.

12. Hannah-Moffat, "Unintended Consequences," 9.

13. Amanda George, "The Big Prison," in *Women and the Law,* ed. Patricia Easteal and Sandra McKillop (Canberra: Australian Institute of Criminology, 1991), 241.

14. "Moo," a Burmese laborer working in Ranong Province, Thailand as quoted in Images Asia, *Migrating with Hope: Burmese Women Working in the Sex Industry (Thailand)* (Chiangmai: Images Asia, 1997), 21.

15. Human Rights Documentation Unit, *Burma: Human Rights Yearbook 1997-98* (Bangkok: National Coalition Government of the Union of Burma, 1998).

16. Human Rights Watch, "Burma/Thailand: Unwanted and Unprotected: Burmese Refugees in Thailand," *Human Rights Watch Report,* vol. 10, no. 6 (C) (New York: Human Rights Watch, October 1998).

17. Human Rights Documentation Unit, *Burma: Human Rights Yearbook 1997-98.*

18. Aaron Stern, *Thailand's Migration Situation and Its Relations with APEC Members and Other Countries in Southeast Asia* (Bangkok: Asian Research Centre for Migration, Chulalongkorn University, 1998); Kritaya Archavanitkul et al., in *Complexities and Confusion of the Transnational Peoples in Thailand,* ed. Kritaya Archavanitkul, Jarusoomboon Wanna, and Warangrat Unchalee (Thailand: Institute for Population and Social Research, Mahidol University, 1997).

19. Siriporn Skrobanek, Nattaya Boonpakdi, and Chutima Janthakero, *The Traffic in Women: Human Realities of the International Sex Trade* (London: Zed Books, 1997).

20. Images Asia, *Migrating with Hope.*

21. Images Asia, *Migrating with Hope;* Asia Watch and the Women's Rights Project, *A Modern Form of Slavery: The Trafficking of Burmese Women and Girls into Thai Brothels* (New York: Human Rights Watch, 1995).

22. Images Asia, *Migrating with Hope.*

23. Ibid.

24. The United Nations High Commissioner for Refugees in Thailand does not actually refer to these Burmese as refugees, but as persons of concern to their office. The 1951 refugee convention does not apply to their circumstances. They are, at best, regarded as temporarily displaced persons who will be repatriated back to Burma at the earliest opportunity.

25. See Siriporn Skrobanek, et al., *The Traffic in Women.*

26. Elizabeth G. Ferris, *Beyond Borders: Refugees, Migrants and Human Rights in the Post-Cold War Era* (Geneva: WCC Publications, 1993), 111–12.

27. Human Rights Documentation Unit, *Burma: Human Rights Yearbook 1997-98.*

28. Human Rights Watch, "Burma/Thailand: Unwanted and Unprotected: Burmese Refugees in Thailand."

29. Images Asia, *Migrating with Hope;* Asia Watch and the Women's Rights Project, *A Modern Form of Slavery;* All Burma Students Democratic Front, *Burma and the Role of Women* (Bangkok: Research and Documentation Unit, All Burma Students Democratic Front, 1995); Burmese Women's Union, "The Plight of Burmese Women" (paper prepared for and distributed at the Fourth UN Conference on Women, Beijing, September 1995).

30. All Burma Students Democratic Front, *Burma and the Role of Women;* Betsy Apple, *School for Rape: The Burmese Military and Sexual Violence* (Thailand: Earthrights International, 1998); Asia Watch and the Women's Rights Project, *A Modern Form of Slavery.*

31. Human Rights Documentation Unit, *Burma: Human Rights Yearbook 1997-98.*

32. See United Nations Standard Minimum Rules for the Treatment of Prisoners, adopted August 30, 1955, UN Doc. A/CONF/611, annex I, ESC res. 663C, 24 UN ESCOR Supp. (No. 1) at 11; UN Doc. E.3048 (1957), amended ESC res 2076, 62 UN ESCOR Supp. (No. 1) at 35; UN Doc. E/5988 (1977); and the Body of Principles for the Protection of All Persons under any Form of Detention or Imprisonment, adopted by General Assembly, Resolution 43/173 of 9 December 1988.

33. Burmese Women's Union, *The Plight of Burmese Women.*

34. McQuaide and Ehrenreich, "Women in Prison," 243.

35. "Aye Aye," interview by author, Bangkok, 1998.

REFERENCES

All Burma Students Democratic Front. *Burma and the Role of Women.* Bangkok: Research and Documentation Unit, All Burma Students Democratic Front, 1995.

Amnesty International U.K. *Cell Culture: Asylum Seekers in the UK.* London, Amnesty International, 1998.

Apple, Betsy. *School for Rape: The Burmese Military and Sexual Violence.* Thailand: Earthrights International, 1998.

Archavanitkul, Kritaya, Jarusoomboon Wanna, and Warangrat Unchalee. *Complexities and Confusion of the Transnational Peoples in Thailand.* Institute for Population and Social Research, Mahidol University, 1997.

Asia Watch and the Women's Rights Project. *A Modern Form of Slavery: The Trafficking of Burmese Women and Girls into Thai Brothels.* New York: Human Rights Watch, 1995.

Bhabha, Jacqueline. "'Get Back to Where You Once Belonged': Identity, Citizenship and Exclusion in Europe." *Human Rights Quarterly* 20 (1998).

Burmese Women's Union. "The Plight of Burmese Women." Paper prepared for and distributed at the Fourth UN Conference on Women, Bejing, September 1995.

Carlen, Pat. *Women's Imprisonment: A Study in Social Control.* London: Routledge & Kegan Paul, 1983.

Ferris, Elizabeth G. *Beyond Borders: Refugees, Migrants and Human Rights in the Post-Cold War Era.* Geneva: WCC Publications, 1993.

George, Amanda. "The Big Prison." In *Women and the Law,* edited by Patricia Easteal and Sandra McKillop. Canberra: Australian Institute of Criminology, 1991.

Hannah-Moffat, Kelly. "Unintended Consequences of Feminism and Prison Reform." *Forum* 6, no. 1 (1994).

Human Rights Documentation Unit. *Burma: Human Rights Yearbook 1997-98.* Bangkok: National Coalition Government of the Union of Burma, 1998.

Human Rights Watch. "Burma/Thailand: Unwanted and Unprotected: Burmese Refugees in Thailand." *Human Rights Watch Report* vol. 10, no. 6 (C). New York: Human Rights Watch, 1998.

———. "Locked Away: Immigration Detainees in Jails in the United States." *Human Rights Watch Report* vol. 10, no. 1 (G). New York: Human Rights Watch, 1998.

Images Asia. *Migrating with Hope: Burmese Women Working in the Sex Industry (Thailand).* Chiangmai: Images Asia, 1997.

McQuaide, Sharon, and John H. Ehrenreich. "Women in Prison: Approaches to Understanding the Lives of a Forgotten Population." *Affilia: Journal of Women and Social Work* 13, no. 2 (1998).

Pettman, Jan Jindy. *Worlding Women: A Feminist International Politics.* Sydney: Allen & Unwin, 1996.

Skrobanek, Siriporn, Nattaya Boonpakdi, and Chutima Janthakero. *The Traffic in Women: Human Realities of the International Sex Trade.* London: Zed Books, 1997.

Stern, Aaron. *Thailand's Migration Situation and Its Relations with APEC Members and Other Countries in Southeast Asia.* Bangkok: Asian Research Centre for Migration, Chulalongkorn University, 1998.

Welch, Michael. "The Immigration Crisis: Detention as an Emerging Mechanism of Social Control." *Social Justice* 23, no. 3 (1996).

Current Issues in Women's Imprisonment

The New Prison Culture
Making Millions from Misery

Amanda George

Introduction

We'll hopefully make a buck out of it. I'm not going to kid you and say we are in this for humanitarian reasons.

— Australian prison contractor[1]

THE FIRST PRIVATE PRISON for women outside the United States opened in Melbourne, Australia, in 1996. Melbourne is a city of 3 million people; 200 women are incarcerated there. Prison privatization was forced through by a newly elected conservative Victorian state government. In addition to the privatization of prisons, it implemented a massive sell-off of publicly owned utilities—water, electricity, gas, and transport; it contracted out welfare services, health, and housing; and it closed 350 schools and scores of hospitals. The sell-off of prisons was part of an ideological commitment to characterizing government as a business and our community as an economy rather than a society. The prison sell-off went hand in hand with a law-and-order climate of mandatory and longer sentences that handed private prison contractors a guarantee of rising prison numbers (and profits). The decimation of services in the community that support people at risk of incarceration sealed the deal.

The prison experiment that the state of Victoria embarked upon, the largest handover in the world, by which 80 percent of women and 40 percent of men who are incarcerated now receive their punishment at the hands of profit makers, has turned into a disaster. Not only did government hand over management of prisons, it adopted the U.S. model of privatization in which financing, design, construction, and ownership of the prison are awarded to one contractor and the government pays them back for construction over twenty years. This means that it is virtually impossible to remove the contractor because that contractor owns the prison.[2]

The cozy arrangements between government and the corporations over contracts, standards, and accountability have huge implications for outside input into prison policy. Although we—the public—are central to the arrangement because we pay for it, in policy terms we have been squeezed out. The transparency of government activity that is required in a democracy has been sidestepped. Information is no longer public because it has been characterized as commercial. The government has reduced the ability of the public and Parliament to scrutinize the Aust$80 million a year it hands to the corporations at a time when accountability ought to have been strengthened.

There is a new culture in prison policy now and prisoners don't feature in it—neither does the public, unless they are shareholders. Corrections Corporation of America (CCA), the largest private prison company in the world and the parent company of Corrections Corporation Australia (CCAust), which runs the Metropolitan Women's Correctional Centre, the private women's prison in Melbourne, put it nicely in its 1997 Annual Report letter to shareholders:

> [D]uring 1997 CCA expanded its operating territory and profitability, successfully navigated the political landscape, weathered the storm of media scrutiny and forged new rules for our industry's development. . . . [N]et income grew 75% to $54 million, our revenue grew 58% to $452 million. . . . [W]e opened almost 15,000 beds. . . . [O]ur market capitalization is $3.5 billion.[3]

Prisoners themselves didn't rate a mention.

Not Forgetting: The Life Handed Over for Profit to Control

Being inside gives you an unerasable sense of alienation from mainstream society. The sense that what you know is worlds apart from what most people know never leaves you. Your eyes have been opened and you can never forget what you have seen.[4]

Prison is an institution of punishment. It is a frightening place to be. Abuses in prison can take forever to be exposed. All outside communication is monitored. If you want to complain or have a voice, you know that the people you complain about have the lawful power to further punish you: to lock you in isolation for twenty-three hours or for months, put you in canvas, cut you off from the outside, and arbitrarily apply rules. This can destroy your sense of reality. You are never safe. You know that anything can happen to you in your cell and that no one who can do anything about it will know. And would anyone believe you? To be a prisoner is to experience total powerlessness.

Added to this potent mix is the recent decision that 96 percent of Australian prisoners do not have enforceable human rights.[5] Introducing profit into the equation only makes the stakes higher, the reasons to cover up greater, and the resources with which to do this enormous.

This chapter looks at how profits have affected prison issues. The first section, "Women in Prisons: 1956-1996," discusses women's prisons in Victoria during the forty-year period prior to the prison sell-off. It reveals the part that activism by women prisoners and groups on the outside has played in influencing the environment of public discussion of prison policy. The second section, "Secure in Luxury," looks at Australia's first private women's prison, and the final section, "Opening Windows for Profit—Closing Doors on Information," discusses how the profit culture was facilitated by government, and the effect this has had on prison policy and management.

Women in Prisons: 1956–1996

Australia's first purpose-built prison for women, Fairlea Women's Prison, was opened in 1956. Fifty women were sent there. When it closed in 1996 to make way for the private prison, it held 110 women. During its lifetime, 18,000 women went through it and seven women died inside.[6]

Prior to Fairlea's opening, women had been held in men's prisons. The impetus for a stand-alone women's prison resulted from pressure by reformers inside and outside prison.[7] For the next forty years, unpaid "outsiders"—

reformers, charitable matrons, Christians, and volunteer teachers—provided a number of services to women inside. Their work didn't challenge or threaten the prison system and in many ways allowed the injustices of prison to be ameliorated somewhat and hidden. However, to individual women inside they were often extremely important, particularly volunteer teachers and those who assisted with support on leaving prison.

Numbers of women incarcerated hovered between forty and fifty in the 1950s and 1960s.[8] These numbers were somewhat lower than earlier in the century, perhaps due to the restrictive gender and social prescriptions in the postwar period that kept women under surveillance and under control in nuclear families. By the mid-1970s there were only twenty-four women incarcerated at Fairlea, a figure directly related to the prevailing economic conditions of high employment and the introduction of social security payments for women with children outside the nuclear family. At this time there was some discussion of there being no need for a women's prison. It was thought that perhaps alternatives and support on the outside could replace the institutional prison. Women prisoners constituted a group the public knew little about.[9] Their only source of information was from a popular local TV drama called "Prisoner" that was sold worldwide and portrayed women in a stereotypical manner.[10]

In the early 1980s an increase in the number of people prosecuted for drug-related offenses and the adoption of extremely long sentences for these offenses meant that more women went to prison, for years rather than months. This increase did not signal a rise in women's criminality. Rather it reflected the law's continuing focus on poverty, order, and street offenses. The only difference was that drug addiction and prohibition served to provide a new justification for criminalization.

The 1980s was a decade of increasing activism by women prisoners and emerging outside groups. In the early part of the decade, women in prison, who were supported by one of the "reformers" from the outside,[11] were able to get the rule changed that forced women prisoners to relinquish their babies at twelve months old. Fairlea was the first prison in modern Australia to permit children to stay until school age.

The early 1980s also saw the start of a theater group of women prisoners that evolved into Somebody's Daughter Theatre. The group was facilitated by outside drama students. From their first performance, *Bad Women,* they began raising questions about the purpose and justice of punishment and prisons as well as telling women's stories. They had performances every couple of years in the prison that people from the outside could attend. In addition, many publications came out of the education center at Fairlea. In these magazines and books the women talked about their lives before jail; expressed their anger, humor, and loves; and their despair at separation from children, friends, and families and at what was happening inside prison.

In the early 1980s there was much unrest at Fairlea. Women held strikes over wages for sewing, work in the kitchen and prison grounds, and housework. There was a series of fires and staff warned the government that the place was a firetrap. Finally in 1982, a fire that was deliberately lit killed three women in a remand dormitory. Other women in cells watched helplessly.

The extensive damage was seen to make Fairlea "insecure" and most women were moved into two divisions at H. M. Pentridge Prison, a classic bluestone fortress men's prison.[12] Six "high security" women were sent to Jika Jika and the rest to B Annexe. Jika Jika was a high security, electronic, sensory deprivation prison that was opened in 1980. The exercise areas were cages; nearly all interaction with prisoners was via intercom and camera. Even the government called it an "electronic zoo." This prison was so brutal that in five years it was closed, after five men protesting the inhumanity of the prison died in a fire there. B Annexe was a bluestone division that hadn't been used for many years. It was small and damp, with tiered cells and tiny windows, had virtually no exercise area, hadn't been maintained for years, and had an atmosphere that was violent and oppressive. In the five years during which an average of thirty-five women were housed there five women hanged themselves. This was devastating, as these were the first Victorian women to suicide in prison. It was clear that the regime and conditions were the cause.

The practice of putting "difficult women" in men's prisons continued for some years despite the fact that, or perhaps because, the conditions were more brutal. In 1989, a protest by women prisoners at Fairlea about the treatment of a suicidal Aboriginal woman prisoner led to twelve women being sent to G Division, a male psychiatric unit in Pentridge. Men were emptied out of the cells the morning the women were sent over. The women were given men's underclothing to wear and slept on mattresses with masturbation holes and feces on them. The levels of slashing, taunting by officers, and violence in this prison were notorious.[13]

Fairlea was reopened in 1986 after Aust$3.7 million was spent completely remodeling it. Government described it as "the most modern female prison in Australia."[14] There was some amnesia about this later, when the next government said it was "antiquated and overcrowded" and needed replacing with a private prison.[15]

Activism on the Outside: The 1980s and 1990s

In 1982 the Fairlea Research Group, a group of women on the outside, lodged a complaint with the Equal Opportunity Board documenting the discriminatory treatment of women prisoners.[16] Questions were constantly asked in Parliament. This interest preceded a decade of media interest, research, policy changes, and some progress in women's conditions. Nevertheless, despite this attention from the outside, inside Fairlea there were regimes in operation that were fanatically militaristic; one governor donned white gloves for wiping inspections of the insides of ovens.[17]

In the mid 1980s, Women Against Prison was formed. It was made up of women who worked in drug and alcohol services, housing, and community legal centers and women who had been in prison. They wrote letters, leaflets, and newsletters; made public comment; had community radio shows; and organized demonstrations outside Pentridge, when women were held there. They also established Flat Out, a housing support service for women leaving prison and their children.

In 1988 Wring Out Fairlea, the first large-scale action, was held outside Fairlea prison by the Women's Coalition Against Imprisonment.[18] The prison was completely encircled by one thousand people linking hands. We wanted to create an event that brought people to the prison wall, literally and via media, and to use this focus to educate the community about the issues inside and outside prison that needed addressing. We had bands and speakers on the oval outside Fairlea that the women inside could hear, stalls, food, and children's activities. We had negotiated with the prison governor about what we were doing to ensure that the women were not locked down that day and to ensure that visits from friends and family would not be stopped. Community radio covered the day and broadcast prerecorded phone interviews with women inside.

The Wring Out was the culmination of a six-week campaign that brought together many organizations, most of which had previously had little to do with women in prison. It involved community legal centers, refuges, domestic violence networks, centers against sexual assault, poverty action groups, young women's organizations, Aboriginal groups, drug agencies, the prostitutes collective, neighborhood houses, and student groups. We sought to create an awareness for them of the links between the issues they worked on and women's imprisonment.

The media campaign started with the launch of the report *Women and Imprisonment*.[19] The report contained an analysis of the offenses that were landing women in prison and a number of demands aimed at getting policy change within the prison and outside. It showed the relationship between poverty and crime, that many women in prison were victims of sexual and violent crimes, that homelessness is a major factor in crime, and that continuing the criminalization of drunkenness was landing many Aboriginal women in jail. It highlighted the injustice of jailing women for social security fraud committed out of need and demanded that prostitution be decriminalized, that needle exchanges should be in prisons, that women prisoners should have access to a woman doctor, and that visits from children should be a right, not a privilege.

Soon after this campaign, government announced it was setting up its first policy committee to look specifically at the needs of women in prison, and a woman doctor was appointed to the prison.

The Mood Changes: Privatization Announced

The Wring Out Fairlea campaign and circling of the prison continued until 1993, when it was announced that Fairlea would be the first prison to be closed in its privatization sweep. There was already a high level of community interest and information about women prisoners, and in the frenzy of privatization of health, welfare, transport, and utilities people were curious and skeptical about what privatization of prisons would mean. There was a general gut feeling that making a profit from prison was somehow wrong and that abuses were certain to occur. Australia's history as a prison colony to which both government and private contractors shipped convicts is well known. Convicts on the private fleets suffered massive loss of life.[20]

In some ways, though, the privatization battle was diverted when the government decided it wanted to close Fairlea early and tip women and children into the cages and tunnels of Jika Jika inside Pentridge. For many months the government denied officially that it was doing this.

So started the Save Fairlea and Stop the Move to Jika campaigns. These campaigns represented a massive broadening of people working on prisons issues. For eight months, in the midst of a Melbourne winter, a 24-hour camping vigil was held outside Fairlea. People donated food and tents, unions donated a caravan, and churches donated money. People came out of the woodwork, including prison workers who would have no truck with us in the past; 17,000 people signed a petition against the move. The commitment of people was relentless. Not a week went by when there wasn't some media coverage.

We were conscious of the contradiction that many of us who were abolitionists were campaigning to keep a prison open. However, our campaign to save the prison never minimized the problems of Fairlea or the futility of incarceration. We spoke of bashings by former governors and officers, psychological games that were de rigueur, women who were left to rot in observation cells, women who were suicidal being taunted by officers,[21] 13,000 strip-searches of Fairlea's 100 or so women prisoners in the two years before its closure.[22] We leaked a pharmaceutical report indicating the level of chemical control of women — 141 administrations of psychiatric drugs a day for eighty-seven women prisoners.[23]

Central to the legitimacy of the campaigns was that members of Somebody's Daughter Theatre spoke out in the media for the first time as former prisoners, using their names. Some of them had been in Jika Jika when it was a punishment unit, others had been in men's prisons and knew that moving women there would be a disaster. Having the voices of women who had been in prison speaking openly and persuasively gave our concerns life and credibility.

After months of official denials a government document was finally leaked to the media that showed detailed plans to move women and children to Jika Jika. The existence of this document allowed women prisoners to lodge an Equal Opportunity complaint about the move to a men's prison and the Equal Opportunity Commissioner unsuccessfully sought an injunction to stop it. The government then sacked the Equal Opportunity Commissioner and soon after that emasculated the Equal Opportunity Act to effectively stop prisoners from being able to take such action again.

Then, five days before Christmas 1993, with no public announcement and no media release, we learned that the government had backed down about the Jika Jika move. Victory! The timing and failure to make a public announcement, when so much of the campaign had been fought in the media, indicated the government's desire to minimize our victory.

The level of prison activism that preceded private prisons is something that both governments and private corporations choose to ignore. Private prison contractors have cried loud and hard that media and activists target them because they are profiteers. None of us who are prison activists in Victoria are apologists for state-run prisons. We were active and critical of them before private prisons appeared. Prison is a brutal response to social problems. It scapegoats and marginalizes specific groups of people and creates the illusion of safety for people not in prison, while in actual fact it perpetuates violence and compounds alienation.

"Secure in Luxury"[24]

The private Metropolitan Women's Correctional Centre (MWCC) is built on a former rocket fuel testing and explosives site on the edge of the urban sprawl, twenty-six kilometers from the center of Melbourne. There is no public transport to the prison. The area is barren, rocky, and has winds of up to 130 kilometers an hour.[25] The government bought the 217 hectares for Aust$1 million from the defense department. It says the site is not contaminated by chemicals. If this is so, it is curious that such a mammoth site on sale so cheaply was not snapped up by the housing developers across the road.

A number of us toured the MWCC before it opened. We looked at the glossy brochures about the prison that made it seem very attractive. We read that cells have "ensuite facilities" (a toilet and shower next to the bed).[26] The first cell we walked into had a dead bird in it. This was to prove prophetic. In the two years since MWCC opened, two women have died there: One death of "natural causes" is still the subject of a coronial inquiry; the other death was a hanging suicide. At the official opening of the prison we stood outside it, outnumbered by police, to hand out literature to the official guests and shower them with fake bloodstained "hell money." We wore gags with dollar signs on them to symbolize the silencing enforced by legislation that protects commercial confidentiality and that is reinforced by corporate defamation threats.

Private prisons claim that they are cheaper and more innovative because they are not as accountable to public opinion as governments are and they can challenge the old prison culture by employing staff who are "uncontaminated" by the old system.

On the costs issue, no figures whatsoever have been released by government. We do know that government has subsidized the corporation each year.[27] The "innovations" emerged early. The prison centerpiece is a clock so prisoners can watch time pass and a fluttering corporate flag; fifty-five cameras keep an eye on the 160 women and their surrounds. Another innovation involved animals. The first general manager wanted a water buffalo. Head office disapproved. They thought of having an emu farm, but were worried the emus would hurt themselves on the razor wire. They brought in donkeys, but they bucked and kicked their way through the prison and had to be put in their own prison. The geese that were brought in bit, so they were taken to their own prison. A peacock was removed because some women had plucked its feathers. Two small kangaroos were also purchased. One escaped and was run over and killed outside the prison, and no one knows the other one's fate. Now the only animals are domesticated feral cats.

One officer seemed to believe that the women were animals. In an incident with a woman prisoner he asked another officer to take off her belt so he could hog-tie the prisoner. He tied her legs together with a belt, handcuffed her hands behind her back, and then attached the belt to the handcuffs. Hog-tying is illegal in Australia and officers' belts are not "authorized instruments of restraint." The woman prisoner was charged with offenses in an outside court case arising from the incident, yet the officer, who a magistrate said used "an inexcusable amount of force unnecessarily,"[28] was not charged at all.

The company was also "innovative" in its management style, requesting that the helmeted and shield-wielding state emergency management unit[29] attend a relatively minor incident. This resulted in women prisoners being tear-gassed for the first time in Victoria's history.[30] The gassing was authorized by the government. The reason? Three women in a prison van were being taken to a management unit and did not want to get out. They were handcuffed, had stepped through each others' handcuffs so they could not be separated, were unarmed, and were making no threats. The women were gassed in the enclosed van because they wouldn't get out of it, and "the noise and commotion involved (in physical removal) would have a very negative effect on other prisoners."[31]

One of CCAust's other innovations was to cut back the time and the quality of visits women prisoners can have with their children, despite a specific promise made to women by CCAust when women were at Fairlea. Initially women had all-day visits with their children in their units. They could cook with them, sit in their bedrooms, kiss and cuddle in privacy, and just "hang out" together. Now women must have their five-hour visits in a camera-monitored visit center, with straight-back chairs, a video machine, and a vending machine.

The prison said that they stopped the unit visits because the women were using children to bring in drugs. Rather than observing natural justice and punishing the individual offender, they decided on the collective punishment of all women and children. To see how many drug-filled nappies were coming into the prison, we did a freedom of information request of the contraband found on visitors for the time of the ban and the months before it.[32] No contraband was found! No drug-filled nappies!

A coronial inquest in July 1998 into the death of the first woman who died at the prison disclosed for the first time in an open court significant problems at the prison—problems they had been able to hide behind "commercial confidentiality." Cheryl Black, a forty-three-year-old intellectually disabled epileptic asthmatic woman, allegedly died of natural causes. At the inquest it was revealed that the private investigation the prison had into the death was so flawed that the government conducted its own investigation. The MWCC also presented incomplete computer records of the prison's electronics system to the coroner. Also revealed in evidence was that, in a prison of 130 women, a nurse attended one overdose a day.[33] At Fairlea there were perhaps ten attendances on overdoses by medical staff a year.[34]

In September 1998, Paula Richardson hanged herself at the prison while in a management unit. The significance of this was that prior to this event the only hanging at Fairlea in forty years had been in 1991. The other five women who had hanged themselves had been held in appalling conditions inside men's prisons. It seems clear that the more oppressive the environment, the more likely it is that women will kill themselves. The MWCC has had many women cut down from attempted suicides prior to the one that eventually resulted in death—one woman was cut down the day Paula died. Six months earlier, the government had pumped Aust$75,000 into the prison to train officers in suicide prevention. The prison locked women up one afternoon each week while the officers were trained. The first suicide prevention training manual used at the prison was actually written for officers working with male prisoners.[35]

The level of violence at the prison surpasses any level of violence at Fairlea, and even more disturbing is that there are now rapes happening at the prison. At Fairlea there were some incidents where women had their vaginas forcibly entered in the search for drugs, but no assaults happened there that resembled those now happening at the MWCC. One woman was sexually assaulted with fruit and vegetables and forced to eat them. Not only is this development devastating for the victims involved, it is deeply disturbing for other women in the prison to be around these assaults and to wonder if they are at risk. If the prison can not protect its inmates from this type of assault, women can have no confidence in their own security. On a broader level, when news of these sexual assaults hits the media it confirms a misconception that many people have of women prisoners—that they are a bunch of violent dangerous individuals—when, in fact, most are there for nonviolent offenses.

Why is this level of violence happening now? These women are essentially the same women who were in Fairlea prison, so why are they behaving differently now? The problems of violence and sexual assault are occurring because it is a prison reliant on cameras rather than staff, it has ongoing staff turnover from the top to the bottom, and it has chronic understaffing.

Opening Windows for Profit—Closing Doors on Information

One of the major selling points of private prisons to the community was that there would be scrutiny of prison "performance," something that had previously not occurred.[36] Yet in its desire to close off information and ensure that problems not be revealed, the government erected legislative barriers to the flow of information about prison contracts, performance standards, policy, practices, and statistics by claiming that the lives of prisoners are now "commercial secrets." Information that was previously available under Freedom of Information legislation is not available now. Just to make sure groups do not legally challenge claims of the "commercial confidentiality" of information, the government has this year introduced costs into the legislation. This is contrary to the spirit and intention of Freedom of Information laws (created to ensure open, accountable government). So if you lose at court because the commercial interest of the information is seen to override public interest, you can be ordered to pay the legal costs of both the government and the corporation.

In a genuflection to principles of accountability, the government set up a "contract monitor" who is supposed to report on whether the prisons are performing according to the contract. There is no information available on how the monitor assesses the prisons. It seems that they largely look at self-reported data that the prisons file. A monitor's report (released during a court case) that covered the period of the hog-tying and a "riot" at the MWCC did not mention those incidents. In the two years of the contracts, there has not been a skerrick of reporting to Parliament by the monitor. Despite the government's promise that a monitor would be required to report to Parliament, this has not eventuated.[37]

The only official information available has come as a result of coronial inquires, Freedom of Information appeals, and parliamentary committees. From the latter we have discovered that the women's prison had Aust$100,000 of contract money withheld because of inadequate training of staff, illicit drugs levels, and the high number of self-injuries. The desperate desire of the government and companies to keep information out of the public eye creates a deep suspicion and lack of confidence among the public about the integrity of government and the character of the corporations.

Commercial Secrets

"Commercial confidentiality" is a device whereby only parties to a contract can know its terms. Commercial confidentiality supposedly stops the release of financial information that may benefit competitors in a market in which contracts are tendered. Therefore the number of suicides a prison can have before the deaths trigger penalties in the contract is a commercial secret.[38] Presumably, if a contract permits two deaths, then a competitor can bid for just one death — profit at any cost, even life.[39]

Yet the mantra of commercial confidentiality to keep information out of the public arena does not stand up to the slightest analysis. A proper understanding of commercial confidentiality in relation to prisons would surely require that information be released to the public. This is because the community has both a financial interest in the prisons, in that we pay the companies the full amount to run the prisons, and a public interest in what goes on in them, because prisoners are punished by the companies pursuant to laws that are enacted on our behalf. Many years ago individual citizens gave up their personal "right" to punish wrongdoers and handed this function over to the state. The state on our behalf, and only because we gave them authority, now makes the laws, prosecutes offenders, and administers punishment. So how can information about prisons be called a "commercial secret" when the community is pivotal to the legal authority of the private prison and the totality of its financial payments? We are part of the contractual arrangement and therefore must be entitled to know its terms.

In the context of prisons then, the law actually privileges the commercial interests of the corporations over both the human rights of prisoners and the public's interest in knowing what happens to the people we pay the corporations to punish.

Contractual Flexibility

The government maintained that the prison contracts would ensure levels of performance and standards in prisons not seen before. Yet what has become apparent is that there is a contractual scheme that allows the prisons to do just as they please within extremely wide parameters. The government indicated it did not want overly prescriptive contracts, but that the companies would face financial penalties if they didn't achieve certain standards. But the current standards and penalties are a commercial secret. The consequences of this "do as you please" approach did not take long to emerge.

On the day after the women's prison opened, women prisoners had a sit-in on the oval over children's visits. The prison had reneged on all-day children's visits and said it would take a while for them to happen. Following the women's action the visits were brought on sooner than had been indicated. Children's visits were again the cause of a strike and sit-in eighteen months later, when all visits were reduced.

It was then revealed that even though women had had all-day visits with their children in prison in their units for over a decade at Fairlea, a policy that was the most progressive access policy for women in a maximum security prison in the Western world, the government had not required in the contract that the new prison provide for such visits; it was left up to the prison. For the 75 percent of women in prison who have children, this intentional omission was abominable.

Another consequence of this nonprescriptive contract arrangement was a record number of suicide hangings at the private men's prison. The government, in its free market "let them do what they want" mode, had approved the design and construction of cells with obvious hanging points—vertical bars inside cell windows and exposed shower rails. Before the prison opened, these hanging points were the subject of complaint by various community organizations, prison activist groups, the Parole Board, and the Human Rights Commissioner. The government minister responsible called us "bleeding hearts."[40] Four hangings later, after wrangling between the company and the prison over who would pay for cell redesign, the government agreed to pay an undisclosed amount as part of the costs.

The priority of creating profits for shareholders over and above putting resources into prisoners has been financially supported by government through subsidies to the prisons. In addition to paying for the redesign of cells in the men's prison, the government has paid for suicide prevention training of officers and drug treatment programs in the women's prison, a prison run by the world's most profitable prison corporation.

The Commercial Reputation Stranglehold

> Am I now to understand that the transfer of management of
> prisons to private corporations should shield the companies
> from the same essential scrutiny which has hitherto applied to
> state run institutions? — Dr Eileen Baldry's response to defama-
> tion threat[41]

Now that prisons are a business, they have a commercial reputation and profits to protect. Like any autocratic institution, the companies respond to criticism by trying to stifle it with defamation threats.[42]

The power of defamation threats in the prison dialogue is derived from the secretive nature of prisons. What goes on in prison is hidden behind walls. Prisoners are in a vulnerable position if they want to speak out against those who are paid to punish them and, anyway, prisoners are prohibited from talking to the media.

The debate on prisons has always been loud and vigorous in Australia. Our history in being established as one big prison colony influences the way we see ourselves, the distrust we have of authority and institutions purporting to have authority. Many prison inquiries and royal commissions have come about through pressure from interest groups raising their concerns publicly, often for years. These concerns have included deaths, corruption, Ku Klux Klan operations, drug, bashings, and early release schemes. To create an environment of fear on the outside about discussing these matters is extremely dangerous.

The use of defamation law by corporations to protect their "commercial reputation" makes discussion of the lives of the prisoners we pay them to incarcerate much harder. Information sources are being strangled despite company slogans such as "our aim is not to stifle expression, but to encourage it."[43]

Public Interest, Prison Policy? Not Your Business

The quote below comes from an informal chat between the general manager (GM) of MWCC and the author (A) in October 1998:

A: What is happening with the children's visits?

GM: Why are you so interested?

This attitude that "it is none of our business" is what we now face as we endeavor to engage, as we always have, in the prison debate. Prisoners are now "their business." Private corporations have appropriated for themselves prison policy as well as the prisoners. So where does privatization leave prison policy?

It is difficult to know now where to direct our questions and complaints about prison policy. Attempts to question government about the policy implications of private prison practices is met with blanket statements like "the day to day running of the prison is their business."

CCAust, which imprisons 80 percent of women prisoners, has no policy workers and no policy development structures. CCAust's definition of policy is a "[g]eneral plan and or statement of 'what' shall be done, conditions that shall exist and/or requirements that shall be met." "Policy" decisions are made by the prison managers.[44] What they call "policy" I would call rules. Policy, as I understand it, is not a two-line statement of rules. It is clear that private prisons operate in a policy vacuum, although I am sure resources are spent on business expansion policies and strategies.

If MWCC was interested in being truly innovative, as is claimed, it could produce brave programs to deal with the major problem in women's lives, before, during, and after prison—drugs. Prison activists and health researchers have advocated the need for needle exchange programs in prison, as there are on the outside. The illegality of the substance being put into the syringe has not prevented the proliferation of needle exchange programs outside prison—and the public health benefits have been enormous.

Most women prisoners have a history of IV drug use. Prisons are recognized as significant sites of hepatitis C and HIV transmission. It is estimated that 40 percent of prisoners have hepatitis C.[45] Needle exchanges have been safely and successfully trialed in women's prisons overseas.[46]

If the corporations believe that we have no "legitimate" interest in how they run the show, to what extent does the government recognize the value of community input? In the past, community legal centers and other interest groups have made freedom of information requests to assist us in research, policy discussion, and debate. These requests allow us to analyze what is going on and give us information not necessarily published by governments in their publications. But information is power and the government and companies want it all for themselves. We now must go to court to show that public interest overrides commercial confidentiality, and in attempting to do so we have met the full force of the resources available to the government and the multinationals involved.[47]

The Global Punishment Industry

The conflict between the profit motives of the company and the social objectives of government are virtually impossible to reconcile in a contract.[48]

In the past, prison activists have had to engage with both the government and the community to bring about changes in public mindsets about prison and social policies. We have had to challenge the "prison swimming pool photos" that tabloid media invariably run.[49] Now added to the milieu is the global multibillion-dollar "corrections industrial complex." This exponentially expanding conglomerate of private corporations designs prisons, prison fittings, weaponry, tools of punishment, lethal injection chambers, ducted tear gas systems, masks to stop prisoners' spitting, smart cards, and prison management systems. They rely on technology to run prisons. When they do employ humans they pay their prison officers poorly and their executives handsomely.

These companies have none of the broad social objectives that prison policy is part of. It runs counter to corporate interests for government to pursue social policies that deal with crime other than by imprisonment. The only policy of private prison corporations is to make profits and expand. They depend on crime and perpetuate the cycle that reproduces it.

It is increasingly obvious that poverty, unemployment, violence, alienation, homelessness, diminishing public education and health funding, and inappropriate drug laws need to be addressed to reduce "crime." Society can afford to pay for real crime prevention, but prioritizing prison spending leaves less money available for productive crime prevention work. In Australia, the gap between the rich and poor is increasing, more people are being sent to prison, and more people are dying there. Punishing poverty doesn't take it away. Prison gives people a roof for a time but it compounds their homelessness. Prison doesn't stop violence or alienation, it breeds it. Prison doesn't stop drug use, it creates reasons to continue.

We hope that the prisons for profit pustulence[50] is only brief and that instead of following the path of the United States, the most prison-hungry nation in the world, where retribution rules and profit is god, that Australia comes to its senses, even if it is only to realize that it is bad economics to favor policies of punishment over social justice and cohesion.

NOTES

1. Cited in Paul Moyle, *Private Prisons and Police: Recent Australian Trends,* 9th ed. (Sydney, New South Wales: Pluto Press, 1994), 51.

2. Richard Harding, "Private Prisons in Australia: The Second Phase," *Trends and Issues* no. 84 (April 1998).

3. Corrections Corporation of America, 1997 *Annual Report* (Nashville, Tenn.: Corrections Corporation of America, 1998), 3-5.

4. Blanche Hampton, *Prisons and Women* (Sydney: University of New South Wales Press, 1993), 147.

5. *Minogue v. Human Rights and Equal Opportunity Commission and Others,* 1283 Federal Court Australia (12 October 1998). The decision was based on the interpretation of the Australian Constitution that only federal offenders who comprise 4 percent of the prison population are covered by international convention.

6. Emma Russell, *Fairlea: The History of a Women's Prison in Australia 1956-96* (Melbourne: The Public Correctional Enterprise, 1998), 46.

7. Ibid., 4.

8. Statistics from Satyanshu K. Mukherjee et al., *Source Book of Australian Criminal and Social Statistics 1804-1988* (Canberra: Australian Institute of Criminology, 1989).

9. Fairlea was briefly the focus of media attention in 1971 because of protests outside the prison when five women were sent there as part of the Save Our Sons anticonscription campaign. This was at the height of Australia's pandering to the United States by our involvement in the Vietnam War.

10. Called *Prisoner: Cell Block H* outside Australia. It began in 1979 and remains one of the highest-selling overseas TV dramas from Australia, even though it ended production in 1986. It is still rerun in Australia and overseas.

11. Dame Phyllis Frost was one of the outside reformers involved in the establishment of Fairlea. She has been chairman of the Victorian Women's Prison Council for forty years. When privatization was announced, Dame Phyllis's endorsement was essential to the government's claim that privatizing a women's prison was a good idea.

CCAust started its overtures early as well, flying her to Queensland to inspect one of its prisons.

12. Pentridge occupies a piece of real estate worth Aust$100 million in Melbourne—the closing of Pentridge was central to the government's moneymaking privatization plan.

13. Somebody's Daughter Theatre, *Call My Name* (Script and Program) (Melbourne: Somebody's Daughter Theatre, 1993).

14. Attorney-General (Victoria), *"Fairlea Prison Redevelopment,"* 4 July 1986, 2. News Release issued by Jim Kennan, Victorian Attorney-General.

15. Office of the Minister for Corrections (Victoria), *"New Women's Prison Designed on a Village Concept,"* 15 August 1996, 1. News Release issued by Minister Bill McGrath for the opening of the private women's prison. At the time of closing, Fairlea was below its authorized capacity.

16. Fairlea Research Group, *Female and Prisoner: The Double Negative* (Melbourne: Victorian Council of Social Services, 1982).

17. Helen Barnacle, *Don't Let Her See Me Crying* (forthcoming).

18. Wring Out was used to symbolize a woman's hand action in "putting the squeeze on" the Office of Corrections.

19. Amanda George and Jude McCulloch, *Women and Imprisonment: A Report* (Melbourne: Fitzroy Legal Service, 1988).

20. Michael Flynn, *The Second Fleet: Britain's Crime Convict Armada of 1790* (Sydney, New South Wales: Library of Australian History, 1993).

21. Barnacle, *Don't Let Her See Me Crying;* Letters of Rikki Dewans (dec) to the author, from Fairlea Prison; "Governor Rumor Led to Fairlea Escape," *Herald Sun,* 19 June 1986; "Fairlea Governor Had Blackmail File, Court Told," *Herald Sun,* 20 June 1986.

22. Freedom of Information Request by Essendon Community Legal Centre, April 1995.

23. Internal nursing time assessment, Fairlea, 1993.

24. Jim Tennison, "Secure in Luxury—First Look Inside New Women's Prison," *Herald Sun,* 26 July 1996.

25. Chris Evans, "Prison Staff Locked in Jail," *The Mail,* 30 October 1996.

26. Corrections Corporation of Australia, *"Metropolitan Women's Correctional Centre,"* brochure of the Corrections Corporation of Australia released in July 1997, 1.

27. The government paid for women's drug treatment and officers' suicide prevention training. Figures have not been released but are estimated at Aust$150,000.

28. Victoria Button, "Rebuke for Deer Park Warders," *Age,* 4 December 1997, 6.

29. The Emergency Management Unit is the state's paramilitary prison riot squad, which the companies can ask to come into the prison.

30. "Tear Gassing of Women Prisoners," *The Republican,* 10 May 1997. The only other gassing of women prisoners was in Sydney at Mullawa Prison in 1980.

31. Victorian Ombudsman, *Twenty-fourth Report of the Ombudsman (Victoria),* (Melbourne: Victorian Government Publishing Service, June 1997), 57.

32. Freedom of Information Request, Essendon Community Legal Centre, August 1998.

33. Inquest into the death of Cheryl Black, 16 June 1998, Melbourne Coroners Court, transcript page 119.

34. Personal communication with author from staff at Fairlea Medical Centre.

35. Metropolitan Women's Correctional Centre Staff Training, *Suicide Prevention.* Released under FOI to Coburg Brunswick Community Legal Centre, October 1998.

36. In the past there was no "assessment" of how state-run prisons performed. The development of contractual standards created benchmarks of prison performance for the first time, which will now apply to the private and public sector prisons.

37. The Office of the Deputy Premier and Minister for Corrections (Victoria), *"Security to be Upgraded with Three New Prisons,"* 16 December 1993, 6. Press Release of the Office of the Deputy Premier and Minister for Corrections. This press release promised appointment of a contract monitor under Section 9D of the Corrections Act 1986 (Victoria) as amended, but the appointment was not made under this section.

38. Freedom of Information Appeal, *Coburg Brunswick Community and Financial Counselling Legal Service v. State Government of Victoria, Corrections Corporation of America, Group Four, Australasian Correctional,* Victorian Civil and Administrative Appeals Tribunal, November 1998.

39. The two private men's prisons have inside vertical bars in cells, which required extensive cell refitting after a spate of suicides. At the Victorian Civil and Administrative Appeals Tribunal hearing, evidence was given on the level of deaths in contracts (27 October 1998); See also *Jarvis v. Australasian Correctional Management* (ACM), District Court of Queensland, 5 July 1996, where a prison officer was awarded damages because of inadequate training and the ACM's treatment of him as a worker who was called to many suicides in that prison.

40. "Jail Critics Derided as Bleeding Hearts," *Australian,* 10 March 1998, 2.

41. Dr. Eileen Baldry's letter of reply to Australasian Correctional Management's solicitor's letter asserting Dr. Baldry made defamatory statements, 26 July 1994.

42. Corrections Corporation of Australia has been involved in three such incidents, two against the author.

43. Corrections Corporation of Australia, "Excellence in Corrections & Project Management" (brochure. Queensland: Corrections Corporation of Australia, circa. 1990), 2.

44. Metropolitan Women's Correctional Centre, *Policy and Procedures Manual* (Corrections Corporation of Australia, n.d.), 1-101.3.

45. Dr. Nick Crofts, McFarlane Burnett Research Centre, *The Breakfast Show,* Radio National, 23 November 1998.

46. "Heroin Prescription and Needle Exchange in Prison," *The Health Report,* Radio National, 10 August 1998.

47. See note 39 for details of such court action.

48. Harry S. Havens, "Private Sector Ownership and Operation of Prisons: An Overview," (paper presented at a meeting of the Organisation for Economic Cooperation and Development [OECD], Paris, 1994), 8.

49. Newspaper stories on prisons are invariably accompanied by a photo of the prison's swimming pool to show what a pleasant and well-appointed environment prisoners live in.

50. Pustulence is the seepage of a weeping sore.

REFERENCES

Barnacle, Helen. *Don't Let Her See Me Crying.* Forthcoming.

Corrections Corporation of America. *1997 Annual Report.* Nashville, Tenn.: Corrections Corporation of America.

Fairlea Research Group. *Female and Prisoner: The Double Negative.* Melbourne: Victorian Council of Social Services, 1982.

Flynn, Michael. *The Second Fleet: Britain's Crime Convict Armada of 1790.* Sydney, New South Wales: Library of Australian History, 1993.

George, Amanda, and Jude McCulloch. *Women and Imprisonment: A Report.* Melbourne: Fitzroy Legal Service, 1988.

Hampton, Blanche. *Prisons and Women.* Sydney: University of New South Wales Press, 1993.

Harding, Richard. "Private Prisons in Australia: The Second Phase." *Trends and Issues* no. 84 (April 1998).

Havens, Harry S. "Private Sector Ownership and Operation of Prisons: An Overview." Paper presented at a meeting of the Organisation for Economic Cooperation and Development (OECD), Paris, 1994.

Metropolitan Women's Correctional Centre. *Policy and Procedures Manual.* Corrections Corporation of Australia, n.d.

Moyle, Paul. *Private Prisons and Police: Recent Australian Trends.* 9th ed. Sydney, New South Wales: Pluto Press, 1994.

Mukherjee, Satyanshu K., Anita Scandia, Dianne Dagger, and Wendy Matthews. *Source Book of Australian Criminal and Social Statistics 1804-1988.* Canberra: Australian Institute of Criminology, 1989.

Russell, Emma. *Fairlea: The History of a Women's Prison in Australia 1956-96.* Melbourne: The Public Correctional Enterprise, 1998.

Somebody's Daughter Theatre. *Call My Name* (Script and Program). Melbourne: Somebody's Daughter Theatre, 1993.

Victorian Ombudsman. *Twenty-fourth Report of the Ombudsman (Victoria).* Melbourne: Victorian Government Publishing Service, June 1997.

The "War on Drugs"
A War Against Women?

Stephanie R. Bush-Baskette

Introduction

DURING THE 1970S AND 1980S, state and federal legislators initiated stricter enforcement, increased penalties, and mandatory sentencing laws for the violation of drug laws. This "war on drugs," as it was labeled, emphasized arrests of low-level drug dealers and persons engaged in street-level drug offenses such as possession and trafficking.[1] During this time the rate of incarceration for females began to increase at an exorbitant rate. In 1970 the rate of incarceration for women in state and federal prisons was five per 100,000. By 1995 the rate had increased to forty-eight per 100,000. The number of incarcerated females in state and federal prisons increased from 5,635 in 1970 to 63,900 in 1995.[2] Between 1985 and 1995 there was an increase of 200 percent in the number of females incarcerated in state and federal institutions, as compared to an increase of 122 percent for males.[3] Between 1990 and 1997 the average annual rate of growth (8.8 percent) for numbers of females incarcerated in federal or state facilities exceeded that of men (6.9 percent). In 1997 alone, the number of females in state or federal prison increased by 6.2 percent (74,970 to 79,624).[4] Most of the increase in the rate of female incarceration was for nonviolent property crime and drug offenses.[5] Facts such as these have led some feminist criminologists to posit that this war on drugs has actually been a war on women.[6]

This chapter explores the impact of the war on drugs on the imprisonment of women in the United States. It begins by reviewing the origin of and defining the current war on drugs in the United States. The relationship between women and drug use is discussed. The chapter concludes with an analysis of the relationship between the imprisonment of women and the war on drugs. I posit that women were the easy targets of the war on drugs for two reasons: first, because of the history of drug use by women in the general population and the high prevalence of drug abuse among the incarcerated female population; and second, because of a combination of the media's depiction of a crack epidemic and the alleged culprits, the resulting public fear and concern, and political necessity.

The War on Drugs

The United States has a history of enacting antidrug laws at both the local (city and state) and national (federal) levels of government. The first such law was passed as an ordinance in 1875 by the city of San Francisco. This local legislation outlawed the smoking of opium in opium dens. The federal government began to control the use of cocaine in the early 1900s and the use of marijuana in 1937. The Harrison Act of 1914 was the primary legislative vehicle implemented by the federal government to regulate narcotics in the United States.[7]

The "war on drugs" is a popular term that, although frequently used, is seldom defined. Rasmussen and Benson suggest that there are at least two methods by which to determine when a war on drugs begins. The first identifies key legislation or presidential announcements. The second directly measures changes in the allocation of criminal justice resources to the enforcement of drug laws.[8]

If one uses presidential announcements or legislative initiatives as indices for the beginning of the war on drugs, there are four benchmark periods: 1972, 1982, 1986, and 1988. Former President Richard Nixon declared the initial "war on drugs" in 1972.[9] In February 1982, former President Ronald Reagan also declared a "war on drugs." The goals of these wars were to reduce drug use by individuals; to stop the flow of drugs into the country; and to reduce drug-related crimes.[10] The declarations were ignored until 1985.[11] In 1986 and 1988 the Anti–Drug Abuse Acts were enacted into law at the federal level. These acts changed the focus away from the major drug dealers and treatment toward the users and street-level dealers, particularly those using and dealing in crack cocaine. What transpired between the declaration of 1982 and the legislative initiatives of 1986 provides an explanation about why only certain kinds of drugs and drug users were targeted.

The development of the current federal drug policies contained within the acts of 1986 and 1988 resulted from intense media attention that preceded and coincided with national elections. Beginning in 1984 and continuing into 1985, the media began reporting about "rock" cocaine in Los Angeles. In 1985 there was a newspaper account of cocaine abuse in New York. In late 1985 the presence and use of crack cocaine was noted in New York. These reports were rather obscure and the public was not overly concerned. However, in 1986 Len Bias and Don Rogers, two well-known athletes, died, allegedly from their use of cocaine. At that point the media focused its attention on crack as "the issue of the year." All forms of media —newspapers, magazines, and television—began to cover crack cocaine with unprecedented allocations of time.[12] This media attention coincided with an election year. By the November 1986 elections, at least 1,000 newspaper stories had appeared in the national print media alone.[13] The major television networks aired documentary-style programs that defined crack cocaine as a national epidemic.[14] Cocaine and crack cocaine became ideal campaign issues for politicians.

On 27 October 1986, just days before the national elections, the Anti-Drug Abuse Act (ADA) of 1986 was enacted by Congress. This legislation delineated the parameters of the current war on drugs. The ADA of 1986 included mandatory minimum penalties for drug trafficking based on the amount of drugs involved.[15] The legislation also mandated disparate treatments for mere possession of cocaine and possession of crack cocaine. Specifically, a mandatory minimum of five years (up to twenty years) was established for persons convicted of possession of five or more grams of crack cocaine and of twenty years for any offender who was found to be part of a "continuing drug enterprise."[16] In contrast, an offender found guilty of possessing powder cocaine would only be subjected to a five-year mandatory minimum if the amount equaled or exceeded 500 grams.[17]

The emphasis of the ADA of 1986 was on punishment and social control and it incorporated such penalties as increased prison sentences for the sale and possession of drugs, elimination of probation or parole for certain drug offenders, increased fines, and the provision for the forfeiture of assets. Most of the funds made available by the act were directed toward law enforcement, expanded prison facilities, interdiction, and efforts to reduce the supply of drugs. Drug abuse was defined as a national security problem. The war was contrived as being necessary for the survival of the United States.[18]

In 1987, after the national elections and passage of the Anti–Drug Abuse Act of 1986, the media focused its sights on issues other than crack and drug abuse. The public's attention and concern with drugs also declined. The *New York Times*/CBS polls in 1987 found that only 3 to 5 percent of the public opined that drugs were the most pressing social problem.[19] However, in 1988 there was a presidential election and drugs, particularly crack, were again the target of politicians. A subsequent Anti–Drug Abuse Act was passed by Congress on 22 October 1988—approximately one and one-half weeks before the election. As compared with the 1986 act, the 1988 act did include more funding for treatment and prevention and also established the Office of Substance Abuse Prevention as a cabinet-level post. However, most of the funding continued to be directed toward law enforcement and punishment, and enhanced penalties for certain crack cocaine offenses were developed. A first-time offender convicted of possession of five grams of a "substance containing cocaine base" could receive five to twenty years in prison. Second-time offenders could receive five to twenty years for possessing three grams of the substance, and third-time offenders could receive the same amount of time for the possession of one gram. The act also provided for civil penalties for the possession and use of crack.[20]

By 1990 the media's representation of crack had stabilized. Most news accounts focused on the health effects of and treatment possibilities for crack.[21] Consequently, the National Drug Control Strategy of 1991 did not focus on crack and cocaine as vigorously as did the act of 1988. However, the initiatives of the two prior acts were not significantly modified.

The Anti–Drug Abuse Acts of 1986 and 1988 continue to dictate the fate of drug offenders. The acts were developed as political responses to heightened public concern about cocaine and crack that resulted from representations by the mass media. Although the attention has been somewhat diverted from crack, cocaine, and drug abuse in general, these policies continue in full force.

Federal statistics provide substantiation of the federal government's increased and harsher response to drug offenders between 1982 and 1991. In 1982, 81.3 percent of the people who were charged with a drug offense in the federal system were prosecuted. In 1988, the percentage had decreased to 76.5 percent.[22] However, there was a 52.17 percent increase in the number of persons convicted for drug offenses for those two years (6,979 in 1982, as compared with 13,376 in 1988).[23] Furthermore, in 1982, 5,138 of those convicted of drug offenses were sentenced to prison. In 1988 the number rose to 10,599, a 48.48 percent increase.[24] In other words, although there was a decline in the number of people who were charged with drug offenses in the federal system, there was a significant increase in the number of those people who were both prosecuted and sentenced to prisons. Furthermore, the federal drug offenders with minor or no past criminal records received much longer sentences than similarly situated offenders received prior to the Anti-Drug Abuse Act of 1986.[25]

If one uses the allocation of resources as an indicator of the onset of the post-World War II drug wars, it is apparent that 1986 marked a beginning. In 1986, expenditures from federal, state, and local entities for the war on drugs totaled $5 billion.[26] In 1991 the national drug policy initiatives cost more than $10 billion a year. Prior to resigning as the head of the federal government's war on drugs, William Bennett recommended that the budget for the initiatives be doubled in the 1990–1991 fiscal year. He further urged the states to increase their funding for the drug initiatives by $10 billion dollars and to increase the number of prison cells intended to confine drug offenders by 85 percent.[27]

In 1995 the federal government spent $13.2 billion on the drug war. Two-thirds of this money was used for law enforcement. This figure does not include the cost of incarcerating convicted drug offenders. If all the money spent for the direct costs of the war on drugs is accounted for, the total expenditure is approximately $100 billion annually.[28]

Women and Drugs

At the time of the passage of the Harrison Act in 1914, approximately one million of the ten million people then living in the United States were addicted to drugs. Most of these addicts were housewives who were addicted to opiates that they could legally purchase in medicinal remedies over the counter for any number of ailments.[29] Unfortunately, research that focused on the use of drugs focused on males. Some researchers considered that drug abuse was a male problem because they believed that sociocultural factors caused some men to abuse narcotics and at the same time protected females from such activity. During the 1970s, the women's movement and the "American drug crisis" of the 1960s caused attention finally to be paid to drug use by females.

Historically, women have been prescribed drugs such as sedatives and tranquilizers at a much greater rate than their male counterparts. More middle-class women than men are treated in emergency rooms for overdoses of prescription drugs. This has also become a problem for women of lower economic status who are on Medicaid. Initial studies indicated that although females used illegal drugs at a much lower rate than males, the use of drugs by females was much higher than had been assumed previously. During 1967–1972, studies revealed that the rate of increase in the use of drugs by females was much greater than that of males, including during the heroin epidemic of the 1960s.[30]

Researchers have discovered that suburban, middle-class women with drinking problems and their inner-city counterparts who use heroin or crack are both likely to undergo the same process at the onset of drug use. Both groups of women have similar motives for taking drugs and share many of the same experiences that take them from experimentation to addiction. Depression often precedes the use of drugs by women, and drugs of any type may be used to deal with the depression. Some women use drugs as a means of self-medication to cope with the devaluation of women in general and the resultant low self-esteem. Traumas of a personal nature such as rape, incest, and other sexual abuse, as well as economic pressure, may also lead to drug abuse in women. The combination of being devalued because she is a woman, a racial or ethnic minority, and poor has also been posited as the underlying cause for drug abuse by some women. Drug use by any woman, whether she lives in suburban or urban areas, brings with it the psychological, social, and cultural experience of stigmatization that can cause the continued problem of drug use and perpetuate the problematic behavior. This usage and its inherent problems violate the gender expectations established for women by this society. Women have been found to be more likely than men to continue their use of drugs after initial experimentation as a way to cope with situational factors, life events, or general psychological distress.[31]

Poor women who use street-level drugs experience additional stigmatization. They do not have the protective societal buffer enjoyed by women who are insulated by their families, friends, and economic status. Women who use street-level drugs tend to suffer a greater degree of criticism, denigration, and loss of relationships.[32] Those who use street-level drugs on the streets are also less protected from becoming prisoners of the "war on drugs" because of their high visibility.[33] Because the tactics of the drug initiatives' focus on street drugs such as cocaine, crack, and heroin and on street-level offenses such as possession and trafficking, this group of women predictably constitutes a major portion of the incarcerated population who have been sentenced for committing a drug offense.

Drug use forecasting consists of voluntary tests in which the urine samples of arrestees are analyzed on an anonymous basis. These tests are conducted at the time of arrest, which may be a significant period of time after the commission of the alleged offense. During 1994, screening for the use of drugs was performed on a total of 7,839 adult females who were booked at twenty-one sites. As compared to test results in previous years, the data indicated that adult female arrestees had a slight increase in the use of cocaine and relatively unchanged rates for the use of marijuana and opiates. Cocaine proved to be the drug of preference among the adult female arrestees. At all but one site, the percentage of female arrestees testing positive for cocaine exceeded the percentage testing positive for marijuana. In a number of cases the cocaine rate was at least double the rate of marijuana use. This was also found in the data from 1993. The rate of increase in the use of cocaine was also generally higher than that of the adult male arrestees.[34]

The drug use forecasting data also indicated that among younger adult female arrestees aged 15 to 20 years, marijuana was the drug of choice, while cocaine and other drugs were less prevalent. Furthermore, the percentages of these younger adult females testing positive for at least one drug ranged from 23 to 68 percent as compared to 33 to 91 percent of the older adult female arrestees. The range of cocaine use by younger females was 0 to 53 percent, while the range for the older adult females was 19 to 82 percent. The test results for the use of marijuana ranged from 16 to 45 percent for the younger set and 6 to 25 percent for the older group of females. The use of opiates was even less common than cocaine or marijuana for the younger group, for whom the range was 0 to 29 percent. Based on these surveys, the use of cocaine appears to be more prevalent among older female arrestees and the use of marijuana seems to be more prevalent among their younger counterparts.

Because of the prevalence of drug use by women in the general population and the prevalence and frequency of drug abuse by female arrestees, one can expect that there is a high prevalence of drug use/abuse by female prisoners prior to their incarceration. This expectation is supported by research that shows that the use of drugs by women prior to their imprisonment is more prevalent than it is for males who are incarcerated.

Figures show that this use of drugs by women increased after the war on drugs in 1986. In 1986, 50 percent of the women reported using drugs the month before the offense for which they were being incarcerated. By 1991 this had increased to 54 percent. Among those women, the use of cocaine or crack increased from 23 percent in 1986 to 36 percent in 1991. The use of marijuana decreased (30 percent in 1986 to 20 percent in 1991). Female drug users who were serving time, regardless of the amount of drug use, were less likely than nonusers to be serving a sentence for a violent offense.[35] Of the female inmates who reported that they had committed their current offense to obtain money for drugs, only 17 percent were serving time for a violent crime compared to 43 percent for a property crime. Of all the women who had sought to obtain money for drugs, 54 percent were incarcerated for robbery, burglary, larceny, or fraud. Only 22 percent of the women who indicated that they had committed their crimes for reasons other than to obtain money for drugs were sentenced for economic crimes (robbery, burglary, or fraud). Half of the women in state prisons in 1991 reported having never participated in a drug treatment or drug education program.[36]

Although drug abuse may have been prevalent among incarcerated women prior to the war on drugs, women were not incarcerated for their drug abuse or drug offenses at the rate and in the numbers they are today.

The war on drugs was the impetus for the shift in policy that greatly contributed to the increase in the imprisonment of women in the United States. The drug policies contained in the acts of 1986 and 1988 snared more women into the criminal justice system. These policies also subjected more women to greater probability of imprisonment and longer periods of incarceration for low-level drug offenses.

Women, Imprisonment, and the War on Drugs

Nationally, the number of adults who were held in state or federal prisons or local jails skyrocketed between 1985 and 1995. In 1985 the total number of adult inmates in the United States totaled 742,579. Of this number, 21,400 were White females and 19,100 were Black females. By 1995, the total number of inmates in U.S. prisons had risen to 1,577,845. Of this population, 57,800 were White women and 55,300 were Black women. The rate of adult prisoners per 100,000 adult residents throughout the United States increased during this ten-year period from 27 to 68 for White females and 183 to 456 for Black females.[37]

A review of the data of persons who were incarcerated in the federal system in 1985 and 1995 indicated substantial growth in the number of inmates who were incarcerated for drugs. In 1985 there were 27,623 sentenced inmates in the federal prisons; 34 percent of these inmates (9,491) were serving time for drug offenses. Ten years later, the total number of sentenced federal prisoners had almost tripled (79,347) and more than half (48,118) had been sentenced for drug offenses. These statistics indicate that the number of federal prisoners sentenced for drug offenses increased more than fivefold in a ten-year period. In 1985 drug offenders constituted a minority of the federal prison population (34.3 percent); by 1995 a majority of the federal prisoners (60.8 percent) were drug offenders. These statistics are derived from data collected prior to the Anti–Drug Abuse Acts of 1986 and 1988, and during the implementation of these acts.[38] They reveal the exorbitant increase in both the number and percentage of drug offenders in the federally incarcerated population that occurred during the war on drugs.

There was even greater change in the offenses for which females were sent to federal institutions. In 1986, 7.1 percent of the federally incarcerated female population were incarcerated for violent offenses, 28.2 percent for property offenses, and 26.1 percent for drug offenses. By 1991, the percentages had shifted to 2 percent for violent offenses, 6.3 percent for property offenses, and 63.9 percent for drug offenses.[39] Thus, although there were decreases for property offenses and violent offenses, the percentage of women who were incarcerated in the federal system for drug offenses more than doubled during this segment of the war on drugs. Between 1990 and 1996 the number of women who were prisoners sentenced under federal jurisdiction increased by 2,057; 84 percent of the increase was drug related. The corresponding percentage for men was 71 percent.[40]

The ratio of sentenced prisoners to types of offenses also changed significantly between 1985 and 1995. In 1985, 35.1 percent of new commitments to the state system were convicted of violent offenses, 42.4 percent were convicted of property offenses, and 13.2 percent were convicted of drug offenses. By 1995, the percentages had decreased to 29.5 percent for violent offenses and 28.9 percent for property offenses and had increased to 30.9 percent for drug offenses.[41] The increase in commitments for drug offenses, therefore, more than doubled in the state system during this ten-year period.

Not only did the percentage of federal prisoners who were incarcerated for drug offenses increase over the years, but there was also an increase in the length of their sentences. In 1982, the mean sentence length for drug offenders was 54.6 months; for violent offenders it was 133.3 months. By 1991, the mean sentence length for drug offenders had increased to 85.7 months; for violent offenders it had declined to 90.7 months. Therefore, the mean length of sentences for drug offenders increased by 31.1 months; for violent offenses the mean sentence length decreased by 42.6 months.[42]

The federal government has not been alone in the attack on drug offenders. Most states have enacted legislation that either mirrors or is similar to the federal laws. One of the states to enact stringent antidrug laws was New York. New York began its initiatives against drugs with the enactment of the "Rockefeller Drug Laws" in 1973. These laws required severe mandatory sentences of imprisonment for drug offenses and limited plea bargaining. Major components of the Rockefeller Laws were repealed in mid-1976 after they were found to have minimal, if any, effect on drug use or crime in New York.[43] The Rockefeller Laws still require that a person convicted of possessing four ounces of cocaine or heroin or attempting to sell two ounces of cocaine or heroin spend a mandatory fifteen years to life in prison.[44] These laws appear to have had an impact on the increase in the prison population in New York. In 1981, 10 percent of the prison population were nonviolent drug offenders and 60 percent were violent offenders. In 1994, violent offenders constituted only 33 percent of New York's incarcerated population and nonviolent drug offenders constituted 45 percent.[45]

The war on drugs has had a major effect on the composition of the imprisoned female population. Furthermore, the drug policies have increased the incarceration of women at a rate that far surpasses that of men. During the 1980s the number of arrests of women for drug violations increased at approximately twice the rate of arrests of men for drug violations. The number of women arrested for drug-related offenses (for example, possession, manufacturing, or sale) increased by 307 percent between 1980 and 1989. The increase in the number of men arrested for these drug crimes during this ten-year period was 147 percent.[46] The number of women incarcerated in state prisons for drug offenses increased 433 percent between 1986 and 1991 compared with an increase of 283 percent for men.[47] One of every three women in U.S. prisons in 1991 was incarcerated for a drug offense, compared with 1979 when only one in ten women was incarcerated for drug offenses. Drug offenses represented 55 percent of the national increase in women prisoners from 1986 to 1991.[48] Note that although there was an increase of 275 percent in the incarceration of females in federal and state prisons between 1980 and 1992, the arrests of females for violent offenses such as murder, aggravated assault, and robbery only increased by 1.3 percent (from 10 to 11.3 percent). In 1991, 64 percent of the female inmates in federal prisons were incarcerated for a drug-related offense, compared with 26.1 percent in 1986.[49] By the end of 1991 the number of women who were incarcerated in state prisons had increased by 75 percent from 1986. Women serving time for a drug offense accounted for more than half the total growth in the incarcerated female population.[50] In New York between 1980 and 1986, 23.3 percent of the incarcerated females were imprisoned for drug offenses; by 1991 this percentage had increased to 6 percent.[51]

The percentage of females who are incarcerated at the state level for violent offenses has also decreased since the beginning of the current war on drugs. Almost half of the women incarcerated in state prisons in 1991 were convicted for nonviolent offenses. Although they had a prior record of convictions, these too were for nonviolent offenses. Approximately two-thirds of all women incarcerated in state prisons in 1991 had no more than two prior convictions.[52] The proportion of women incarcerated for violent crimes as compared with nonviolent crimes decreased between 1986 and 1991. In 1986, three in ten women incarcerated in the state prisons were there for violent offenses. In 1991, this proportion was four in ten.[53]

Although the war on drugs has significantly affected the imprisonment of women in general, Black women have suffered from the greatest increase in the percentage of inmates incarcerated for drug offenses. At the state level there was an 828 percent increase in the number of Black women who were incarcerated for drug offenses between 1986 and 1991. For Black men the change was 429 percent, for White women it was 241 percent, and for Hispanic women it was 328 percent.[54] Both their race and their gender exacerbate their plight. The war on drugs, with its focus on street-level drug offenses, possession, and crack cocaine, brings Black women into the prison system as ruthlessly as it does their male counterparts. Sentencing guidelines that disallow the use of drug addiction and family responsibilities as mitigating circumstances subject Black females to prison and long sentences under criminal justice supervision, as they do White females. In the 1980s the media focused on Black women as well as Black men as the culprits of the so-called crack epidemic. As such, they were portrayed as "others"—inner-city dwellers who were addicted to crack, were sexually promiscuous, and were giving birth to crack babies. Black women were the perfect targets for the politically derived drug policies contained within the Anti–Drug Abuse Acts of 1986 and 1988.[55]

In summary, the current war on drugs in the United States can be documented as having begun with the Anti–Drug Abuse Act of 1986. These policies were continued with the enactment of the Anti–Drug Abuse Act of 1988 and the National Drug Strategy of 1991, which are currently still in effect. The major focus of the war has been to target low-level street users of drugs, particularly users of cocaine, and specifically users of crack cocaine. The primary weapons that have been used are mandatory minimum sentences and the reduction of judicial discretion in sentencing, sentence enhancement for repeat offenders, and punishment instead of treatment for offenders who are addicted to drugs.

Feinman appropriately summarized the increase of the incarcerated female population as follows:

> The increase from 1983 to 1991 can be attributed to the "war on drugs," mandatory sentencing for drug offenses, mandatory sentencing for second felony convictions, and more women getting involved in both the use/possession and the sale of drugs, especially the cheap, easy-to-produce "crack."[56]

Summary

The war on drugs targeted women intentionally. The increase in the imprisonment of women was a direct result of the drug policies that constituted the war on drugs. The sentencing guidelines, mandatory nature of the imprisonment laws, focus on first-time offenders, criminalization of certain abusers, and mandatory minimums for persons with prior felony convictions brought more women into the criminal justice system and caused a tremendous increase in the number of incarcerated women in the United States. When one considers that women have historically been major consumers and abusers of drugs, whether they be illegal drugs or legal drugs, one can easily understand how policies that include the imprisonment of drug abusers would cause more women to become part of the system. Surveys of prison populations over the years have consistently indicated that most imprisoned women have committed the offenses for which they were incarcerated either in order to obtain drugs or to secure money to buy drugs. These studies have also substantiated the prevalence of the use of hard drugs on an ongoing basis by female arrestees and inmates. However, most of these women did not commit violent offenses. Furthermore, Black women have suffered greatly from these drug policies. The ADAs of 1986 and 1988 were developed during a time of intense media focus on the use of crack and cocaine when there was little or no research on the effects of crack and when policies with popular appeal were being sought by politicians seeking reelection.

Judge Gladys Kessler of the National Association of Women Judges testified before the Senate Judiciary Committee that the majority of women who are imprisoned are there from the "lowest, most easily arrested rung of the drug crime business." Kessler further stated that these women offenders are "ideal candidates for community placement."[57] Unfortunately, current drug policies do not allow for such placements.

Two questions need to be answered:

1. Are the current drug policies meeting their goals of reducing the presence of drugs and drug use?

2. Are the effects of the policies worth the results?

Although mandatory minimum sentencing has been the mainstay of the drug laws for the federal and state governments, many practitioners and researchers agree that behaviors constituting drug law violations are uniquely resistant to the deterrent effects of sanctions.

> The proliferation of mandatory penalties for drug crimes in the 1980s did not demonstrably reduce drug trafficking. . . . There is little basis for believing that mandatory penalties have any significant effects on rates of serious crime. The list of problems with any mandatory penalties, however, only begins with their crime-prevention ineffectiveness. They do great harm to the integrity of case processing and sentencing and often result in the imposition of manifestly unjust punishments.[58]

This position is difficult to refute, particularly when one considers the increasing number of people who continue to be incarcerated for drug offenses and the cost of the construction of prisons to house them. If the policies are effective the number of drug offenders should decline. Instead, the only major impact of the policies has been on the growth of the prison population.

The adverse effects of these drug policies on families and communities are also undeniable. Most incarcerated women are mothers of at least one child.[59] When a mother is incarcerated the effects on her child are similar to the grief and loss experienced when a parent dies.[60]

A complex range of issues and effects must be considered when people, particularly women, are incarcerated because of policies that were developed purely for political gain in an atmosphere of hysteria that was created by the media. Subsequent research indicates that much of the hype that was promulgated by the media has not been substantiated: Crack addiction is not increasing and people addicted to crack are not more violent than other drug abusers.[61] What is true is that the war on drugs in the United States continues to swell the prisons with women who have been convicted of possession and trafficking—low-level drug offenses. What is also true is that most of them have drug problems and have never had treatment. It would be more cost effective, both in monetary and social currency, if the addicted women were treated outside of costly prison walls—walls that separate mothers from children, women from productive futures, and taxpayers from other services.

NOTES

1. Michael Tonry, *Malign Neglect* (New York: Oxford University Press, 1995).

2. Kathleen Maguire and Ann L. Pastore, eds., *Sourcebook of Criminal Justice Statistics*, 490. Available online at: http://www.albany.edu/sourcebook/1998.

3. *Ibid*, 510.

4. Bureau of Justice Statistics, *Correctional Populations in the United States, 1995* (Washington, D.C.: U.S. Department of Justice, 1997), 5.

5. Meda Chesney-Lind, "Rethinking Women's Imprisonment: A Critical Examination of Trends in Female Incarceration," in *The Criminal Justice System and Women*, ed. Barbara Raffel Price and Natalie Skoloff (New York: McGraw-Hill, 1995).

6. Clarice Feinman, *Women in the Ciminal Justice System* (Westport, Conn.: Praeger, 1994); Chesney-Lind, "Rethinking Women's Imprisonment."

7. Eric L. Jensen and Jurg Gerber, "The Social Construction of Drug Problems: An Historical Overview," in *The New War on Drugs: Symbolic Politics and Criminal Justice Policy*, ed. Eric L. Jensen and Jurg Gerber (Cincinnati, Ohio: Academy of Criminal Justice Science/Anderson, 1998), 1–23.

8. David W. Rasmussen and Bruce L. Benson, *The Economic Anatomy of a Drug War* (Lanham, Md.: Rowman and Littlefield Publishers Inc., 1994), 6.

9. Craig Horowitz, "The No-Win War," *New York Magazine,* 5 February 1996, 22–33.

10. Ibid.

11. Steven R. Belenko, *Crack and the Evolution of Anti-drug Policy* (Westport, Conn.: Greenwood Press, 1993), 23.

12. Belenko, *Crack and the Evolution of Anti-drug Policy.*

13. Craig Reinarman and Henry Levine, "Crack in Context: Politics and Media in the Making of a Drug Scare," *Contemporary Drug Problems* 16, no. 4 (1989): 535–77.

14. Belenko, *Crack and the Evolution of Anti-drug Policy.*

15. Katherine Beckett and Theodore Sasson, "The Media and the Construction of the Drug Crisis in America," in *The New War on Drugs: Symbolic Politics and Criminal Justice Policy,* ed. Eric L. Jensen and Jurg Gerber (Cincinnati, Ohio: Academy of Criminal Justice Science/Anderson, 1998), 38.

16. U.S. Sentencing Commission, *Mandatory Minimum Penalties in the Federal Justice System: Special Report to Congress* (Washington, D.C.: GPO, 1991), 16.

17. In 1995 the United States Sentencing Commission recommended to Congress and President Bill Clinton that the disparate treatment between crack and powder cocaine be abolished because there was no valid reason for the difference in penalty and it was having a negative impact on African Americans. Neither Congress nor President Clinton supported the recommendation. See U.S. Sentencing Commission, *Special Report to Congress: Cocaine and Federal Sentencing Policy* (Washington, D.C.: GPO, 1995) and U.S. Sentencing Commission, *Special Report to Congress: Cocaine and Federal Sentencing Policy* (Washington, D.C.: GPO, 1997).

18. Belenko, *Crack and the Evolution of Anti-drug Policy,* 15.

19. Reinarman and Levine, "Crack in Context."

20. Belenko, *Crack and the Evolution of Anti-drug Policy.*

21. Ibid.

22. U.S. Department of Justice, *Federal Criminal Case Processing, 1982–93* (Washington, D.C.: GPO, 1996), 3.

23. Ibid., 9.

24. Bureau of Justice Statistics, *Correctional Populations in the United States, 1993* (Washington, D.C.: U.S. Department of Justice, 1995), 15.

25. Tracey Huling, "Prisoners of War: Woman Drug Couriers in the United States," in *Drug Couriers: A New Perspective,* ed. Martin D. Schwartz and Dragan Milovanovic (London: Quartet Books Unlimited, 1996), 58.

26. Horowitz, "The No-Win War," 27.

27. National Council on Crime and Delinquency, *Drug Policy Statement* (Hackensack, N.J.: National Council on Crime and Delinquency, 1991), 3.

28. Horowitz, "The No-Win War," 26–27.

29. Ibid.

30. James A. Inciardi, Dorothy Lockwood, and Anne E. Pottieger, *Women and Crack Cocaine* (New York: Macmillan, 1993).

31. Ibid.

32. Ibid.

33. Horowitz, "The No-Win War."

34. U. S. Department of Justice, *Drug Use Forecasting: 1994 Annual Report on Adult and Juvenile Arrestees* (Washington, D.C.: GPO, 1995).

35. Bureau of Justice Statistics, *Women in Prison* (Washington, D.C.: GPO, 1994), 8.

36. Ibid., 9.

37. Bureau of Justice Statistics, *Correctional Populations in the United States, 1995,* 13-14.

38. Maguire and Pastore, *Sourcebook of Criminal Justice Statistics,* 506.

39. Stephanie R. Bush-Baskette, "The War on Drugs as a War against Black Women," in *Crime Control and Women,* ed. Susan L. Miller (Thousand Oaks, Calif.: Sage, 1998), 117.

40. Bureau of Justice Statistics, *Correctional Populations in the United States, 1995,* 13.

41. Ibid, 24.

42. U.S. Department of Justice, *Federal Criminal Case Processing, 1982-1993* (Washington, D.C.: GPO, 1996), 22.

43. Michael Tonry, *Sentencing Matters* (New York: Oxford University Press, 1996).

44. Horowitz, "The No-Win War," 26.

45. Ibid.

46. Bureau of Justice Statistics, *Women in Prison* (Washington, D.C.: U.S. Department of Justice, 1991), 5.

47. Barbara Bloom, Cheoleon Lee, and Barbara Owen, "Offense Patterns among Women Prisoners: A Preliminary Analysis" (paper presented at the American Society of Criminology Annual Meeting, Boston, Mass., November 1995).

48. Bureau of Justice Statistics, *Women in Prison,* 1994, 3.

49. American Correctional Association, *The Female Offender: What Does the Future Hold?* (Washington, D.C.: St. Mary's Press, 1993).

50. Bureau of Justice Statistics, *Women in Prison,* 1994, 2.

51. Chesney-Lind, "Rethinking Women's Imprisonment," 111.

52. Bureau of Justice Statistics, *Women in Prison,* 1994, 4.

53. Ibid., 3.

54. Mark Mauer and Tracey Huling, *Young Black Americans and the Criminal Justice System: Five Years Later* (Washington, D.C.: The Sentencing Project, 1995).

55. For a full discussion regarding the war on the drugs and its impact on Black women, see Bush-Baskette, "The War on Drugs," 113–29.

56. Feinman, *Women in the Criminal Justice System,* 47.

57. Laura Flanders, "Locked-Up Woman Locked Out of Coverage," *Extra!* (May/June, 1994).

58. Tonry, *Sentencing Matters,* 141–42.

59. Ruth Glick and Virginia Neto, *National Study of Women's Correctional Programs* (Washington, D.C.: National Institute of Law Enforcement and Criminal Justice, 1977); Bureau of Justice Statistics, *Women in Prison,* 1994.

60. Barbara Bloom and Dorothy Steinhart, *Why Punish the Children? A Reappraisal of the Children of Incarcerated Mothers in America* (San Francisco, Calif.: National Council on Crime and Delinquency, 1993).

61. Gary L. Webb and Michel P. Brown, "United States Drug Laws and Institutionalized Discrimination," in *The New War on Drugs: Symbolic Politics and Criminal Justice Policy,* ed. Eric L. Jensen and Jurg Gerber (Cincinnati, Ohio: Academy of Criminal Justice Science/Anderson, 1998) 45–57.

REFERENCES

American Correctional Association. *The Female Offender: What Does the Future Hold?* Washington, D.C.: St. Mary's Press, 1993.

Beckett, Katherine, and Theodore Sasson. "The Media and the Construction of the Drug Crisis in America." In *The New War on Drugs: Symbolic Politics and Criminal Justice Policy,* edited by Eric L. Jensen and Jurg Gerber. Cincinnati, Ohio: Academy of Criminal Justice Sciences/Anderson, 1998.

Belenko, Steven R. *Crack and the Evolution of Anti-drug Policy.* Westport, Conn.: Greenwood Press, 1993.

Bloom, Barbara, Cheoleon Lee, and Barbara Owen. "Offense Patterns among Women Prisoners: A Preliminary Analysis." Paper presented at the American Society of Criminology Annual Meeting, Boston, Mass., November, 1995.

Bloom, Barbara, and Dorothy Steinhart. *Why Punish the Children? A Reappraisal of the Children of Incarcerated Mothers in America.* San Francisco: National Council on Crime and Delinquency, 1993.

Bureau of Justice Statistics. *Correctional Populations in the United States, 1993.* Washington, D.C. : U.S. Department of Justice, 1995.

———. *Correctional Populations in the United States, 1995.* Washington, D.C.: U.S. Department of Justice, 1997.

———. *Women in Prison.* Washington, D.C.: U.S. Department of Justice, 1991.

———. *Women in Prison.* Washington, D.C.: U.S. Department of Justice, 1994.

Bush-Baskette, Stephanie R. "The War on Drugs as a War against Black Women." In *Crime Control and Women,* edited by Susan L. Miller. Thousand Oaks, Calif.: Sage, 1998.

Chesney-Lind, Meda. "Rethinking Women's Imprisonment: A Critical Examination of Trends in Female Incarceration." In *The Criminal Justice System and Women*, edited by Barbara Raffel Price and Natalie J. Skoloff. New York: McGraw-Hill, 1995.

Feinman, Clarice. *Women in the Criminal Justice System*. Westport, Conn.: Praeger, 1994.

Flanders, Laura. "Locked-Up Woman Locked Out of Coverage." *Extra!* (May/June 1994).

Glick, Ruth, and Virginia Neto. *National Study of Women's Correctional Programs*. Washington, D.C.: National Institute of Law Enforcement and Criminal Justice, 1977.

Horowitz, Craig. "The No-Win War." *New York Magazine*, 5 February 1996.

Huling, Tracy. "Prisoners of War: Woman Drug Couriers in the United States." In *Drug Couriers: A New Perspective*, edited by Martin D. Schwartz and Dragan Milovanovic. London: Quartet Books Unlimited, 1996.

Inciardi, James A., Dorothy Lockwood, and Anne E. Pottieger. *Women and Crack Cocaine*. New York: Macmillan, 1993.

Jensen, Eric L., and Jurg Gerber. "The Social Construction of Drug Problems: An Historical Overview." In *The New War on Drugs: Symbolic Politics and Criminal Justice Policy*, edited by Eric L. Jensen and Jurg Gerber. Cincinnati, Ohio: Academy of Criminal Justice Sciences/Anderson, 1998.

Maguire, Kathleen, and Ann L. Pastore, eds. *Sourcebook of Criminal Justice Statistics*. Available online at: http://www.albany.edu/sourcebook/1998.

Mauer, Marc, and Tracy Huling. *Young Black Americans and the Criminal Justice System: Five Years Later*. Washington, D.C.: The Sentencing Project, 1995.

National Council on Crime and Delinquency. *Drug Policy Statement*. Hackensack, N.J.: National Council on Crime and Delinquency, 1991.

Rasmussen, David W., and Bruce L. Benson. *The Economic Anatomy of a Drug War*. Lanham, Md.: Rowman and Littlefield Publishers, Inc., 1994.

Reinarman, Craig, and Henry Levine. "Crack in Context: Politics and Media in the Making of a Drug Scare." *Contemporary Drug Problems* 16, no. 4 (1989).

Tonry, Michael. *Malign Neglect*. New York: Oxford University Press, 1995.

———. *Sentencing Matters*. New York: Oxford University Press, 1996.

U.S. Department of Justice. *Drug Use Forecasting: 1994 Annual Report on Adult and Juvenile Arrestees*. Washington, D.C.: GPO, 1995.

———. *Federal Criminal Case Processing, 1982-1993*. Washington, D.C.: GPO, 1996.

U.S. Sentencing Commission. *Mandatory Minimum Penalties in the Federal Justice System: Special Report to Congress*. Washington, D.C.: GPO, 1991.

———. *Special Report to Congress: Cocaine and Federal Sentencing Policy*. Washington, D.C.: GPO, 1995.

———. *Special Report to Congress: Cocaine and Federal Sentencing Policy*. Washington, D.C.: GPO, 1997.

Webb, Gary L., and Michel P. Brown, "United States Drug Laws and Institutionalized Discrimination." In *The New War on Drugs: Symbolic Politics and Criminal Justice Policy*, edited by Eric L. Jensen and Jurg Gerber. Cincinnati, Ohio: Academy of Criminal Justice Sciences/Anderson, 1998.

Crime, Sex, and Justice
African American Women in U.S. Prisons

Evelyn Gilbert

Introduction

> *Black women serve as contemporary prophets, calling other
> women forth so that they can break away from the oppressive
> ideologies and belief systems that presume to define their reality.*[1]

THE CRIMINAL JUSTICE SYSTEM in the United States processes more male than
female offenders; however, the rate at which women are incarcerated has
exceeded that of men for almost two decades. Between 1980 and 1993 the
number of women in prison increased by 313 percent, while the comparable increase for men was 182 percent.[2] Women represent the fastest-grow-
ing group in prison, growing twice as fast as the male prison population.
Women were 4 percent of the state prison population in 1986, 5 percent in
1991, 6 percent in 1995, and 7 percent in 1997. Among women who were
federal prisoners in 1997, Whites numbered 3,665 and African Americans
numbered 2,466; however, the rate of incarceration is higher for African
Americans. Similarly, the number of African American women incarcerated
in state prisons has grown faster than the number of White women.

The dragnet cast by current sentencing policies and practices are
bringing into U.S. prisons nonviolent, first-time, and petty criminals who
are disproportionately African American. The increase is attributable to
drug law violations and a willingness by the criminal justice system to adju-

dicate and incarcerate women. Aggressive law enforcement, the "War on Drugs," and mandatory sentences portend a greater emphasis on incarcerating persons on the periphery of the drug market. In the United States, unfortunately, these persons are people of color. For example, 1.1 million persons were in state and federal correctional facilities in 1995. Of this number, Whites, African Americans, and Hispanics comprised 36 percent, 48 percent, and 14 percent respectively of the prison population.[3] Five years earlier in 1990, of the 715,649 persons in prison 38 percent were White, 46 percent were African American, and 13 percent were Hispanic. However, in 1985, of the 480,568 people in prison, 51 percent were White and 44 percent were African American.[4] The rising percentage of African Americans in prison is due, in part, to the imprisonment of Black women. However, the pattern of incarceration over the past fifteen years suggests continued increases in the imprisonment of African American men and women.

Trends in Imprisonment

In 1997 women comprised 10 percent of all jail inmates, an increase of 3 percent since 1983. Women are more likely than men to be in jail for drug, fraud, and theft offenses. However, African American women are more likely than White women to be in jail for drug offenses. Although arrest patterns indicate equal involvement of Black and White women with drugs, African American women are more likely to be jailed than White women. The drug law policy of the United States has subjected property offenders to the punitive response normally reserved for violent offenders. African American women are more likely than White women to be property offenders.

During the five-year period from 1990 to 1995, the prison population increased substantially, escalating by 42 percent for men and 56 percent for women.[5] Rising arrests of women confirm a pattern of increased incarceration of women generally and of women of color specifically. Although women represented only 16 percent of all arrests in 1977, that number increased to 19 percent in 1991 and 21 percent in 1996. The arrests led to convictions of women for property (41 percent) and violent (41 percent) crimes in 1986; violent (32 percent) and drug (33 percent) crimes in 1991; and property (41 percent) and drug (20 percent) crimes in 1995.

Drug use among the women who are arrested appears to be more common than not; cocaine use is more widespread than either marijuana or opiate use. Interestingly, White women were more likely to test positive for drug use. The type of drug use among White and African American women shows variation. Although use of opiates is more characteristic of White women, African Americans are more likely to test positive for marijuana. Both groups of women are equally likely to test positive for cocaine use. The women who are eventually imprisoned, however, are characteristically involved with cocaine. What is quite clear from the current sentencing climate is that diverse lifestyles and experiences play a crucial role in the increasingly high crime figures for African American women. Another explanation suggests that racial bias and discrimination are the factors contributing to the disproportionate involvement of racial/ethnic minorities in the criminal justice system. Both of these explanations, however, are relevant to understanding why more and more members of racial and ethnic minorities are being channeled into the criminal justice system.

For African Americans, the "get-tough-on-crime" laws have not discriminated between men and women. Although African Americans are less likely than Whites to become federal prisoners (39 percent versus 58 percent), over 70 percent of Black federal prisoners (68 percent for Whites) were committed for drug offenses in 1997. The incarceration of women for drug-related crimes is best demonstrated by the practices in federal jurisdictions. In 1997, 71 percent of women committed to federal prisons were there for drug offenses. Although the largest group of women in federal prison is comprised of Whites (58 percent versus 39 percent of African Americans), African American women compose the largest group of women in federal prisons for drug offenses.

The higher representation of African Americans among federal drug offenders should not be interpreted to mean that they have a greater involvement in the drug business or that they are more drug dependent. The sheer range of punishable offenses subsumed under drug laws makes it possible to incarcerate individuals who have no knowledge of drug-related activities. Their proximity to persons involved in the drug business, implication by informants, and snitch naming are enough, under current prosecution practices, to impose a prison sentence. The outcomes of police saturation-surveillance of minority neighborhoods, criminal profiling, and cultural stereotyping ensures a constant supply of prosecutable offenders. Minority population removal, however, is not concluded with the institutionalization of Black males. Recent trends in incarceration tell us that the next casualties are African American women and children.

Conviction offenses for women demonstrate a policy of decarceration for index crimes and a punitive response of institutionalization for drug-related crimes.[6] In the ten-year period ending in 1996, felony convictions for violent crimes were 75 percent less than in 1986. During the same time period, property convictions decreased overall by 3 percent, while drug offense convictions increased by 4 percent. Specifically, in 1994, women comprised 15 percent of felony offenders convicted in state courts;[7] most convictions were for property offenses, followed by drug offenses. The increased processing of drug offenses during the last ten years is no doubt due to the implementation of mandatory minimum sentences and sentencing guidelines. Although women remain primarily property offenders, they are becoming identified as drug offenders and so are imprisoned.

Although these numbers do not necessarily reflect a change in the criminality of women, the racial composition of imprisoned women may reflect disparate stereotypes of women held by prosecutors and members of the judiciary. The traditional stereotypes[8] of women often resulted in a reluctance to exact the full weight of the law upon them.[9] Historically, however, African American women have not benefited from these stereotypes.[10] The United States has maintained a different stereotype for American women, one based on a history of enslavement. Slavery offered no protection to Black women because they were property—not women—whose value was based entirely on their fecundity. The prevailing female stereotype represents a distinctly Eurocentric view of the possible gender roles of White women. The Eurocentric view of Black women is embodied in either the "mammy" or the "matriarch" role. In other words, the Black woman is seen as docile and motherly or aggressive and nonfeminine.[11]

The slavery tradition of the United States withheld the feminine gender role from African American women and endowed them, in perpetuity, with a sex role. The Eurocentric view has never bestowed a gender-role expectation on African American women. Instead, a Black woman role was sown and cultivated. This role emanates from the sexploitation of slave women in the United States and relegates African American women to "object" status—not personhood. It appears that African American women have arrived in prison because of their racial status, sex role, and life circumstances rather than their law violations.

Criminalization of African American Women

The United States has historically had a disproportionate number of African Americans in its prisons.[12] The racial stratification inherent in the American criminal justice system means that African American women have experienced the greatest increase in criminal justice involvement of all demographic groups, particularly when they are convicted of an offense that is drug related.[13] In the federal system, drug law violators serve average sentences of three to five years. The sentencing guidelines and mandatory minimum sentences that took effect in the mid-1980s and 1990s prescribe long prison terms. The gender benefit of the doubt in sentencing is not apparent given the number of women sentenced for drug-related crimes. Perhaps there is a gender benefit, but it is for Whites only. Temin believes judges reserve harsh sentences for women who commit masculine-type offenses, crimes that are serious and depart greatly from traditional female gender-role expectations.[14] Because more African American women in prison have drug-related convictions, it may be argued that judges' sentences are punitive and not paternalistic, as they are in the case of White women.[15]

The disparity between the incarceration of African American and White women has been attributed to African American women committing crimes that are more similar to those of men than to those of women.[16] A closer examination of women's offenses tells us that the crimes committed by African American women are very much like crimes committed by White women.[17] In the past, a female stereotype that permitted the characterization of women as less dangerous or as undeserving of an offending status, justified practices of fewer arrests and incarceration.[18] The crimes for which women are convicted today sustain the historical characterizations and practices when the offender is not African American. The female stereotype reserved for African American women is one that supports a punitive response (imprisonment) to women brought into the criminal justice system. Fishman provides a succinct description of the female stereotype of African American offenders.

> The legacy of slavery also provided images of black women with some gender-specific criminal traits. They were frequently described as wanton, hot-blooded, highly sexed, and erotic, as well as very fertile. Because black women had been forced to do the same hard labor as black men, they also were perceived as possessing an excess of such masculine characteristics as toughness and aggressiveness. They were thought to be assaultive, murderous, uncompassionate, physically strong, and capable of physical abuse. This sexual objectification and defeminization of black women persists today.[19]

Such selective imaging ignores the different life chances of African American women. Poverty, abuse, and limited economic opportunities shape the lives of most female offenders, making them marginal in society. However, African American women also suffer intraracial gender oppression and class oppression. These additional burdens confirm their marginality as objects in society[20] but mask their marginality as females among women offenders. Belknap succinctly describes the impact of multiple marginalities: "As a rule, women of color, poor women, and younger women are afforded less leniency than other females."[21] In fact, the media and its representation of African Americans perpetuate the criminal justice system's punitive response to African American women generally.[22] Fishman describes the representation of Black men as "bogeyman" and suggests that "black women have been similarly demonized."[23]

Arrest and Charging

Excessive police surveillance in African American neighborhoods leads to increased police-citizen contacts that lead to arrest. Aggressive patrol practices coupled with department policies that emphasize proactive policing and law enforcement strategies that prohibit drugs result in large numbers of arrests for crimes feared most by the public. Drug-related arrests of African Americans are most often accomplished by police saturation at the street level. Gender is not mitigation for African Americans, and when arrested the poor are less often diverted from charging, conviction, and incarceration. In the United States, the faces of the poor are black[24] (despite notable advances by some groups within the African American population[25]), and women are the poorest.

The gang-related and drug-related activities in minority neighborhoods confirm stereotypes police have of African American involvement in criminal activity. Once arrested, African American women are adversely affected at each decision point in criminal justice processing. African American women are less likely to receive reduced bails than White females, who usually have bail set below what is provided for in bail guidelines.[26] Given the lack of financial resources available to them, African American women are not able to secure their release prior to adjudication.[27] In criminal justice processing, a favorable disposition is likely to result when the accused is released prior to trial. African Americans are usually detained before trial.[28]

Discretion exercised by prosecutors is largely unchecked in determining charges. In over-charging, however, prosecutors build in leverage to coax defendants to plead guilty. Prosecutorial decision making enhances the likelihood that nonviolent, property, and drug offenders are not diverted from carceral punishments. When charged with a violent crime, African American women are most often not pleaded down. African American women with drug-related charges are usually peripheral players such as users, lookouts, holders, or street-level merchants. Low-level drug-related offenders are subjected to prosecutorial punishments (that is, over-charging, multiple charging, or punitive sentence recommendation) to induce their cooperation in identifying persons higher up in the drug trade. In drug-related cases, African American defendants are less likely than White defendants to plea bargain.[29] What this means is "no plea, no reduction" in sentence type or length.

Sentencing

Who are these women being channeled into America's prisons at alarming rates? They are young, first-time, and low-level offenders. The women are parents who are usually supporting siblings as well as their own parents. They have, in most cases, been sexually assaulted. Although all women may become victims of sexual abuse and assault, known victims are young, low income, and single, separated, or divorced.[30]

Recent studies support earlier research that provided evidence that race and gender interact to produce bias in sentencing for African American women.[31] Steffensmeir, Kramer, and Strifel compared the sentences of Black and White women and found harsher treatment for Black offenders.[32] The average prison sentence for White defendants was three months less than that of Black defendants. Because traditional female stereotypes are not available to African American women, gender will not have a mitigating effect on the sentence imposed on them. For African American women, the impact that race and gender interaction has parallels the effect that race has for male offenders. In other words, race alone influences sentencing decisions, and thus for Black women gender is not a mitigating factor. Race not only affects the length of sentence but also appears to be more indicative of the type of sentence. This is demonstrated by Kramer and Steffensmeir's observation that Black defendants are sentenced to jail or prison while White defendants receive diversion or jail adjudications.[33] African American women are more frequently sentenced to prison than are White women. An examination of trial and adjudication processes provides evidence of this.

Farnworth and Teske discovered that "White females were about twice as likely as minority females to have assault charges at arrest changed to non-assault charges at final sentencing."[34] Farnworth and others reported that White women are more likely to receive reduced charges than non-White women.[35] A trial by jury that results in long-term imprisonment, however, is more characteristic of African Americans.[36]

Drug convictions are problematic. Under the federal system, incarceration sentences are 80 percent longer for trafficking offenders than for possession offenders. Although the number of women incarcerated for drug-related crimes has increased for White and African American women, careful attention should be given to the type of conviction offense. Trafficking and distribution are serious offenses while possession and sale are less serious offenses in the war on drugs. Most African Americans are engaged in less serious drug-related offenses that occur on the street. They are involved with crack cocaine, which is marketed on the street. Trafficking and distribution are not street-level offenses. However, the crack/powder cocaine anomaly under federal sentencing sends many street-level offenders to prison in states that have adopted the federal sentencing requirements. Powder cocaine is the drug of choice for Whites. Law enforcement practices and sentencing laws for powder cocaine require higher gram weights (a ratio of 100 to 1 for powder and crack) to trigger criminal justice processing. African Americans use and market crack cocaine and are more likely to be prosecuted for serious crack offenses.[37] Many women crack users pay for their drugs through prostitution. When drug involvement is coupled with the "traditional" female stereotypical crime of prostitution, women are not diverted from the criminal justice system. In her evaluation of the U.S. war on drugs, Fishman suggests that African American women "are the heart and core of the drug problem in America."[38]

Imprisonment

What should be obvious from the previous discussion is that current and future policies of incarceration will target drug law violators. While the rate of violent crime commission has not increased for African Americans, especially women, the rate of imprisonment for nonviolent offenses has risen. For African American women, drug law violations become a ticket to prison. And just as there was little or no leniency given to these women in presentencing procedures, prisons also offer no leniency. The Black woman stereotype is more entrenched and pervasive in prison society than in free society. In fact, African American women may be forced to live up to the mammy and matriarch stereotypes just to survive the demands of the staff and the demands of the prison system.[39] Acting to survive brings them into conflict with prison rules and earns them the label of "troublemaker." Closer inspection, however, reveals that behavior that is troublemaking inside prison is fostered by social institutions outside of prison.

American society's image of imprisoned African American women is no different from the image it has of African American women who have not been imprisoned. Because American society does not recognize the culture-specific gender roles created by African American women, those who deviate from the Black woman role are labeled troublemakers. The prevailing Eurocentric explanation for the similarity in experiences of African American women cites deviant behavior as an integral feature of African American culture. Poverty, low or no educational attainment, unemployment, and the unmarried female-headed household are identified as manifestations of this deviance. By defining these as social problems that are cultural artifacts of African Americans, the United States establishes institutional inequality (in its rejection of the gender roles created by African American women), and also perpetuates racial oppression (in equating socioeconomic status to race). This evokes behaviors from African Americans that are described as fatalistic and disorganized[40] (that is, deviant). In turn, Black culture is identified as pathological, but this is an ecological fallacy. The pathology may be descriptive of conditions within many African American communities, but it is not explanatory of the culture. After all, culture consists of folkways, values, beliefs, norms, and the language of a people. The cultural norms of a people determine behavioral expectations and manifest conduct. An Afrocentric explanation, in contrast to the Eurocentric view, rejects these negativistic and pathological characterizations of Black culture and Black women.

From an Afrocentric perspective, the personality attributes that bring Black women into conflict with prison rules are African American culturally normative mandates for survival in American society. For example, dominance is not the feminization of a masculine trait; rather it is an index of individual worth in the African American community. Specifically, the index consists of self-help, competence, confidence, and consciousness. African American women help themselves and perceive themselves as talented and worthwhile individuals. They meet challenges to their individual worth with resistance. The resistance confirms a negative stereotype of African American women advanced by the Eurocentric view of gender-role expectations.

It is this stereotype that permeates the U.S. prison system and leads to intensive surveillance of African American women. Control of this type ensures that any questionable behavior will be negatively labeled and responded to as disciplinary infractions. Confronted with such extraordinary prison restraint, Black women, not unexpectedly, resort to familiar cultural mandates for direction in responding to oppressive conditions. In prison, a mere accusation of wrongdoing is evidence of guilt and requires punishment. Separation from the general population of prisoners (segregation) is the punishment meted out to troublemakers. According to Fishman,[41] numerous disciplinary reports resulting in forfeiture of good time days "can lead to delayed release on parole." The manipulation of sentence length via disciplinary infractions means that women do hard time. All of this can be traced back to the Black woman stereotype. The stereotype has an adverse impact on length of time served and the nature of time served. It becomes apparent that the African American woman is imprisoned not only for "serious crimes," but also because of her racial status and its inherent sex role.

The more important implication of the Black female stereotype is that imprisonment is not the ultimate punishment; rather, the final, latent punishment is the degradation accompanying the label of "troublemaker." Within prison, African American women are singled out as more criminal and deserving of harsher treatment. Not only have they violated the American societal gender role stereotype (a stereotype withheld from African American women), they have also violated the prison stereotype and warrant being treated "little better than animals."[42] Such treatment is similar to that experienced by African Americans who are not in prison. For African American women, imprisonment does not begin with carceral facilities; it begins when society deems the criminal justice system an appropriate response to African American cultural mores and principles. Wider recognition of the cultural context of violence, oppression, drug abuse, and inequality engulfing many Black communities is necessary to counterbalance the devaluation of African American culture and people. In the absence of an Afrocentric or balanced view of African American women as cultural beings, their accelerated entry into the criminal justice system will continue unabated.

Implications of Imprisonment Practices

The effect of imprisonment on women of color can be measured in at least three areas: sexual assault, devaluation of cultural autonomy, and bastardization of dependent children. The extent of the problem of sexual assault in prison is not really known because of the reluctance of inmates to report[43] and the refusal of correction officials to respond to reports.[44] For

African American women, sexual assault in prison[45] is particularly difficult to deal with because the Black woman stereotype casts them as sexual Amazons. With the a priori label of sexual deviant, African American women who are assaulted by prison workers are usually dismissed as making false accusations or as soliciting the sexual liaison. Although the traditional response to inmate charges of sexual assault against prison workers is to punish the inmate, there is reason to believe that the type of punishment administered (administrative, disciplinary, or protective confinement) is race based. The negative stereotype of African American women's sexuality justifies attempts to punish and rehabilitate. Punishment is necessary as a deterrent to other women and is achieved with disciplinary confinement. Rehabilitation of the sexual deviant occurs with the passage of time and the provision of examples of genteel role models. Administrative confinement provides the appropriate environment for rehabilitation. In the case of either rehabilitation or punishment, manipulation of sentence length is a requisite and an outcome objective.

The devaluation of cultural autonomy is unique to the African American and Native American peoples in the United States. For these two groups, eradication of their culture was an integral part of the creation of an American cultural heritage. African American culture consists of values, beliefs, and ways of relating that have been shaped by the institution of slavery in the United States. Despite the history of oppression, African Americans have relied on traditions and norms that ensured their survival. The survival of African Americans is based on autonomous determination within the restrictive confines of social isolation and legalized repression. Autonomy of African American women is manifested in the way they speak (authoritatively), how they act (confidently), why they act (to become independent), and what they think about themselves (competent). Prisonization methodically erodes this autonomy. In so doing it strips African American women of survival tools needed for life beyond prison walls. Every attempt by the inmate to hold on to her autonomy is countered with prison discipline. Physical segregation is only one type of discipline to which the inmate is subjected. Isolation, fear, and helplessness are experienced by the inmate as she struggles to retain and reassert individual self-worth. This type of discipline exemplifies coercive power. In the case of

African American women inmates, however, it is malign coercion. Rules and practices designed to deculture are indeed malevolent because they (1) stigmatize culture-specific beliefs and values manifested in attitudes, (2) silence the culture-bearers, and (3) cast them out as naked babes to navigate the worlds of imprisonment and freedom. African American culture is a casualty of the imprisonment of African American women.

The criminal justice trend of simultaneously locking up successive generations of women is creating a generation of parentless children. The erroneous and negative stereotype of absentee fathers in the African American community has been replaced by one of absentee parent. In fact the existence of a prison record of a parent is sufficient for child protective services to make a finding of children in need of supervision. In the past, women who were imprisoned could expect to serve a definite period of time and return to the community to start life anew. The new sentencing laws, however, remove that reasonable expectation and will result in the necessity to terminate the parental rights of women who are sentenced to life without parole. Women who receive determinate sentences are still at risk of having parental rights terminated. Many African American women who enter prison pregnant are intravenous drug users and usually are infected with HIV or have AIDS.[46] Their infants are at risk of being born drug addicted or carriers of the HIV virus. Unfortunately for the inmate, giving birth to an impaired child is evidence of child abuse. The criminal justice response of criminalizing this type of childbirth charges the mother with a crime and takes away her child.

Decarceration of drug-involved offenders is the most obvious policy change to reduce the number of African American women in prison. However, indications are that more women will be incarcerated before the United States rethinks its sentencing policies. The venue for change, then, is the prison. Although prevention, diversion, and reintegration are necessary components of a successful regimen for returning women to society, this regimen will not succeed with African American women unless it is race-specific. Any program targeting African American women inmates must validate African American cultural values. Because the community is more important than the individual, family and community ties must be reestablished. Discipline that takes away visitation rights must be discontinued.

Excellence is valued in the African American community; consequently inmates must be encouraged to be self-sufficient. Correctional workers must be sensitized to these self-sufficient behavioral affectations and not see them as challenges to their authority. Finally, the prison culture must accommodate the rituals of womanhood taught by African American elders. The rituals are prosocial and allow the women to attend to spiritual, emotional, and intellectual needs. African American cultural values, beliefs, and traditions are a stark contradiction to a lifestyle of drugs, deviance, and violence. Involving women in culture-enriched, self-validating activities will make them resistant in drug-exposed environments and reverse the criminal justice policy of incarcerating women of color.

Conclusion

People of color in the United States have suffered from the effects of racism, discrimination, and neglect for many generations. As the next millennium approaches, population demographics indicate that people of color will be the numerical majority. The incarceration of a significant portion of a specific population is not unique in the history of mankind. What is unique, however, is that the warehousing of African Americans in U.S. prisons occurs at a time in history when slavery is unconstitutional, segregation is illegal, and the non-White population is the majority. A critical examination of race relations in the United States, as practiced by the criminal justice system, leads to the unmistakable conclusion that suppression, oppression, and maintenance of the status quo must be supported with all deliberate speed. Proof of this priority is evident in the speed at which fully functioning African American communities of the twentieth century have become the badlands of the twenty-first century. Many groups in the United States, including the Congressional Black Caucus, the National Black Police Association, and the Urban League have spoken out against the disparity in sentencing laws and urged revocation. Judges have acknowledged their powerlessness to impose individualized sentences for low-level offenders under the new sentencing laws. Organizations and leaders in minority communities have challenged race-based police operations. Professional and middle-class people of color have brought lawsuits to end racial bias in arrest, prosecution, and sentencing. These challenges to the criminal justice system have been met with statutory and judicial responses that have dismantled affirmative action and have cloaked legalized exclusion and differential treatment in the U.S. Constitution.

NOTES

1. Katie Cannon, *Katie's Cannon—Womanism and the Soul of the Black Community* (New York: The Continuum Publishing Company, 1995), 56.

2. National Women's Law Center, *Women in Prison* (Washington, D.C.: National Women's Law Center, 1998).

3. Bureau of Justice Statistics, *Correctional Populations in the United States, 1995* (Washington, D.C.: U.S. Department of Justice, 1997).

4. See, for example, Bureau of Justice Statistics, *Prison and Jail Inmates at Midyear 1996* (Washington, D.C.: U.S. Department of Justice, 1997); Bureau of Justice Statistics, *Special Report—Characteristics of Adults on Probation, 1995* (Washington, D.C.: U.S. Department of Justice, 1997); Bureau of Justice Statistics, *Compendium of Federal Justice Statistics, 1995* (Washington, D.C.: U.S. Department of Justice, 1998); Bureau of Justice Statistics, Special Report–Profile of Jail Inmates 1996 (Washington, D.C.: U.S. Department of Justice, 1998).

5. Bureau of Justice Statistics, *Census of State and Federal Correctional Facilities, 1995* (Washington, D.C.: Department of Justice, 1997).

6 . The index crimes are murder/manslaughter, aggravated assault, rape, robbery, larceny/theft, burglary, motor vehicle theft, and arson.

7. Bureau of Justice Statistics, *Sourcebook of Criminal Justice Statistics 1995* (Washington, D.C.: U.S. Department of Justice, 1996).

8. See, for example, Nicole Rafter and Elizabeth Stanko, "Introduction," in *Judge, Lawyer, Victim, Thief: Women, Gender Roles, and Criminal Justice,* ed. Nicole Rafter and Elizabeth Stanko (Boston, Mass.: Northeastern University Press, 1982). The authors proposed a typology consisting of five images of women. These images represented deviations from the "natural" role of women: women as the pawn of biology; women as impulsive and nonanalytical; women as passive and weak; women as impressionable and in need of protection; active women as masculine; and criminal women as purely evil.

9. Society's image of women as shallow in nature is represented by the Madonna/whore typology. See Clarice Feinman, *Women in the Criminal Justice System,* 2d ed. (New York: Praeger Publishers, 1986).

10. A different typology for African American women connotes society's perception that they are not deserving of consideration: Amazon, sinister sapphire, mammy, and seductress. See Vernetta Young, "Gender Expectations and Their Impact on Black Female Offenders and Victims," *Justice Quarterly* 3 (1986): 305-27.

11. Patricia Collins, "The Meaning of Motherhood in Black Culture," *SAGE: A Scholarly Journal on Black Women* 4 (1987): 3-10.

12. For more thorough discussions of racial disproportionality, see Coramae Mann, *Unequal Justice: A Question of Color* (Bloomington, Ind.: Indiana University Press, 1993); Marvin Free, *African Americans and the Criminal Justice System* (New York: Garland Press, 1996); Debra Binkley-Jackson, Vivian Carter, and Gary Rolison, "African American Women in Prison," in *Women Prisoners: A Forgotten Population*, ed. Beverly Fletcher, Lynda Shaver, and Dreama Moon (Westport, Conn.: Praeger Publishers, 1993), 65.

13. Marc Mauer and T. Huling, *Young Black Americans and the Criminal Justice System* (Washington, D.C.: The Sentencing Project, 1995).

14. Carolyn Temin, "Discriminatory Sentencing of Women Offenders: The Argument for ERA in a Nutshell," in *The Female Offenders*, ed. Laura Crites (Lexington, Mass.: D.C. Heath and Company, 1976).

15. Dorie Klein and June Kress, "Any Woman's Blues," *Crime and Social Justice* 5 (1976): 34-39.

16. Freda Adler, *Sisters in Crime: The Rise of the New Female Criminal* (New York: McGraw-Hill, 1975).

17. Vernetta Young, "Gender Expections."

18. See Joycelyn Pollock, *Prisons: Today and Tomorrow* (Gaithersburg, Md.: Aspen Publishers, 1997); Roslyn Muraskin and Ted Alleman, *It's a Crime: Women and Justice* (Englewood Cliffs, N.J.: Regents-Prentice Hall, 1993).

19. Laura Fishman, "Images of Crime and Punishment—The Black Bogeyman and White Self-Righteousness," in *Images of Color, Images of Crime: Readings*, ed. Coramae Mann and Marjorie Zatz (Los Angeles, Calif.: Roxbury Publishing, 1998).

20. Anne Edwards, *Early Reagan* (New York: William Morrow, 1987).

21. Joanne Belknap, *The Invisible Woman: Gender, Crime, and Justice* (Belmont, Calif.: Wadsworth Publishing, 1996), 74.

22. See William Chambliss, "Crime Control and Ethnic Minorities: Legitimizing Racial Oppression by Creating Moral Panics," in *Ethnicity, Race, and Crime: Perspectives Across Time and Place*, ed. Darnell Hawkins (Albany: State University of New York Press, 1995).

23. Laura Fishman, "Images of Crime and Punishment."

24. Jeffrey Reiman, *The Rich Get Richer and the Poor Get Prison—Ideology, Class, and Criminal Justice* (Boston, Mass.: Allyn & Bacon, 1998); Marc Mauer and T. Huling, *Young Black Americans and the Criminal Justice System*.

25. Reynolds Farley, "Racial Trends and Differences in the United States 30 Years After the Civil Rights Decade," *Social Science Research* 26 (1997): 235-62.

26. E. Patterson and Michael Lynch, "Bias in Formalized Bail Procedures," in *Race and Criminal Justice*, ed. Michael Lynch and E. Patterson (New York: Harrow and Heston, 1991), 36.

27. Joyce Brown and Jay Gaines, *Joyce Ann Brown: Justice Denied* (Chicago: Noble Press, 1990).

28. Cassia Spohn and Jerry Cederblom, "Race and Disparities in Sentencing: A Test of the Liberation Hypothesis," *Justice Quarterly* 8 (1991): 305-27.

29. Barbara Vincent and Paul Hofer, *The Consequences of Mandatory Minimum Prison Terms: A Summary of Recent Findings* (Washington, D.C.: Federal Judicial Center, 1994).

30. Marital sexual assault is a serious aspect of family violence and appears to be more common among couples living below the poverty line, particularly when men are unemployed. See Crime Victims Research and Treatment Center, "The National Women's Study" (Charleston, S.C.: Medical University of South Carolina, 1992).

31. See Dorie Klein and June Kress, "Any Woman's Blues"; L. Foley and Christine Rasche, "The Effect of Race on Sentence: Actual Time Served and Final Disposition," in *Theory and Research in Criminal Justice: Current Perspectives,* ed. John Conley (Cincinnati: Anderson Publishing, 1979); Candace Kruttschnitt, "Social Status and Sentences of Female Offenders," *Law and Society Review* 15 (1980-81): 247-65; Coramae Mann, "Race and Sentencing of Female Felons: A Field Study," *International Journal of Women Studies* 7 (1994): 160-72.

32. Darrell Steffensmeir, John Kramer, and Cathy Streifel, "Gender and Imprisonment Decisions," *Criminology* 31 (1993): 411-46.

33. John Kramer and Darrell Steffensmeir, "Race and Imprisonment Decisions," *Sociological Quarterly* 34 (1993): 357-76.

34. Margaret Farnworth and Raymond Teske, "Gender Differences in Felony Court Processing: Three Hypotheses of Disparity," *Women & Criminal Justice* 6 (1995): 38. See also Bureau of Justice Statistics, *Special Report-Lifetime Likelihood of Going to State or Federal Prison* (Washington, D.C.: U.S. Department of Justice, 1997).

35. Margaret Farnworth, Raymond Teske, and Gina Thurman, "Ethnic, Racial, and Minority Disparity in Felony Court Processing," in *Race and Criminal Justice,* ed. Michael Lynch and E. Patterson (New York: Harrow and Heston, 1991), 54.

36. See Spohn and Cederblom, "Race and Disparities in Sentencing"; Kathleen Daly, "Neither Conflict nor Labeling nor Paternalism Will Suffice: Interactions of Race, Ethnicity, Gender, and Family in Criminal Court Decisions," *Crime & Delinquency* 35 (1989): 136-68.

37. Mandatory minimum sentences are triggered for five (5) grams of crack and five hundred (500) grams of powder cocaine. Bureau of Justice Statistics, *Executive Summary-Felony Defendants in Large Urban Counties 1994* (Washington, D.C.: U.S. Department of Justice, 1998).

38. Laura Fishman, "Images of Crime and Punishment."

39. Brown and Gaines, *Joyce Ann Brown: Justice Denied.*

40. V. Demos, "Black Family Studies in the Journal of Marriage and the Family and the Issue of Distortion: A Trend Analysis," *Journal of Marriage and the Family* 52 (1990): 603-12.

41. Laura Fishman, "Images of Crime and Punishment."

42. See Regina Arnold, "Processes of Victimization and Criminalization of Black Women," *Social Justice* 17 (1990): 153–66; Patsy Sims, "Women in Southern Jails," in *The Female Offender,* ed. Laura Crites (Lexington, Mass.: D.C. Heath and Company, 1976), 137.

43. See Joycelyn Pollock, *Prison: Today and Tomorrow.*

44. Stop Prison Rape 1995. "Excerpts from Typical Prisoners' Letters on Rape." Available online at http://www.igc.apc.org/spr/docs/prison-letters.html

45. See Bureau of Justice Statistics, *Violence Against Women.*

46. The prevalence of HIV infection is greater among women inmates than among male inmates. Among women, a higher percentage of African Americans than either White or Hispanics test positive for HIV. See Bureau of Justice Statistics, *HIV in Prisons and Jails 1995* (Washington, D.C.: U.S. Department of Justice, 1997).

REFERENCES

Adler, Freda. *Sisters in Crime: The Rise of the New Female Criminal.* New York: McGraw-Hill, 1975.

Arnold, Regina. "Processes of Victimization and Criminalization of Black Women." *Social Justice* 17 (1990): 153–66.

Belknap, Joanne. *The Invisible Woman: Gender, Crime, and Justice.* Belmont, Calif.: Wadsworth Publishing, 1996.

Binkley-Jackson, Debra, Vivian Carter, and Gary Rolison. "African American Women in Prison." In *Women Prisoners: A Forgotten Population,* edited by Beverley Fletcher, Lynda Shaver, and Dreama Moon. Westport, Conn.: Praeger, 1993.

Brown, Joyce, and Jay Gaines. *Joyce Ann Brown: Justice Denied.* Chicago: Noble Press, 1990.

Bureau of Justice Statistics. *Census of State and Federal Correctional Facilities, 1995.* Washington, D.C.: U.S. Department of Justice, 1997.

————. *Compendium of Federal Justice Statistics, 1994.* Washington, D.C.: U.S. Department of Justice, 1997.

————. *Compendium of Federal Justice Statistics, 1995.* Washington, D.C.: U.S. Department of Justice, 1998.

————. *Correctional Populations in the United States, 1995.* Washington, D.C.: U.S. Department of Justice, 1997.

————. *Executive Summary—Felony Defendants in Large Urban Counties, 1994.* Washington, D.C.: U.S. Department of Justice, 1998.

————. *HIV in Prisons and Jails 1995.* Washington, D.C.: U.S. Department of Justice, 1997.

————. *National Crime Victimization Survey.* Washington, D.C.: U.S. Department of Justice, 1995.

————. *Prison and Jail Inmates at Midyear 1996.* Washington, D.C.: U.S. Department of Justice, 1997.

————. *Sourcebook of Criminal Justice Statistics 1995.* Washington, D.C.: U.S. Department of Justice, 1996.

————. *Special Report—Characteristics of Adults on Probation, 1995.* Washington, D.C.: U.S. Department of Justice, 1997.

————. *Special Report—Lifetime Likelihood of Going to State or Federal Prison.* Washington, D.C.: U.S. Department of Justice, 1997.

————. *Special Report—Profile of Jail Inmates 1996.* Washington, D.C.: U.S. Department of Justice, 1998.

————. *Violence against Women: A National Crime Victimization Survey Report.* Washington, D.C.: U.S. Department of Justice, 1994.

Cannon, Katie. *Katie's Cannon—Womanism and the Soul of the Black Community.* New York: The Continuum Publishing Company, 1995.

Chambliss, William. "Crime Control and Ethnic Minorities: Legitimizing Racial Oppression by Creating Moral Panics." In *Ethnicity, Race, and Crime: Perspectives Across Time and Place,* edited by Darnell Hawkins. Albany: State University of New York Press, 1995.

Collins, Patricia, "The Meaning of Motherhood in Black Culture." *SAGE: A Scholarly Journal for Black Women* 4 (1987): 3-10.

Crime Victims Research and Treatment Center, "The National Women's Study." Charleston, S.C.: Medical University of South Carolina, 1992.

Daly, Kathleen. "Neither Conflict nor Labeling nor Paternalism Will Suffice: Interactions of Race, Ethnicity, Gender, and Family in Criminal Court Decisions." *Crime & Delinquency* 35 (1989): 136-68.

Demos, V. "Black Family Studies in the Journal of Marriage and the Family and the Issue of Distortion: A Trend Analysis." *Journal of Marriage and the Family* 52 (1990): 603-12.

Edwards, Anne. *Early Reagan.* New York: William Morrow, 1987.

Farley, Reynolds. "Racial Trends and Differences in the United States 30 Years after the Civil Rights Decade." *Social Science Research* 26 (1997): 235-62.

Farnworth, Margaret, and Raymond Teske. "Gender Differences in Felony Court Processing: Three Hypotheses of Disparity." *Women & Criminal Justice* 6 (1995): 23-44.

Farnworth, Margaret, Raymond Teske, and Gina Thurman. "Ethnic, Racial, and Minority Disparity in Felony Court Processing." In *Race and Criminal Justice,* edited by Michael Lynch and E. Patterson. New York: Harrow and Heston, 1991.

Feinman, Clarice. *Women in the Criminal Justice System.* 2d ed. New York: Praeger, 1986.

Fishman, Laura. "Images of Crime and Punishment—The Black Bogeyman and White Self-righteousness." In *Images of Color, Images of Crime: Readings,* edited by Coramae Mann and Marjorie Zatz. Los Angeles, Calif.: Roxbury Publishing Co., 1998.

Foley, L., and Christine Rasche. "The Effect of Race on Sentence: Actual Time Served and Final Disposition." In *Theory and Research in Criminal Justice: Current Perspectives,* ed. John Conley. Cincinnati: Anderson Publishing, 1979.

Free, Marvin. *African Americans and the Criminal Justice System.* New York: Garland Press, 1996.

Klein, Dorie, and June Kress. "Any Woman's Blues." *Crime and Social Justice* 5 (1976): 34-49.

Kramer, John, and Darrell Steffensmeir. "Race and Imprisonment Decisions." *Sociological Quarterly* 34 (1993): 357-76.

Kruttschnitt, Candace. "Social Status and Sentences of Female Offenders." *Law and Society Review* 15 (1980-81): 247-65.

Mann, Coramae. "Race and Sentencing of Female Felons: A Field Study." *International Journal of Women's Studies* 7 (1993): 160-72.

————. *Unequal Justice: A Question of Color.* Bloomington, Ind.: Indiana University Press, 1993.

Mauer, Marc, and Huling, T. *Young Black Americans and the Criminal Justice System.* Washington, D.C.: The Sentencing Project, 1995.

Muraskin, Roslyn, and Alleman, Ted. *It's a Crime: Women and Justice.* Englewood Cliffs, N.J.: Regents-Prentice Hall, 1993.

National Women's Law Center. *Women in Prison.* Washington, D.C.: National Women's Law Center, 1998.

Patterson, E., and Michael Lynch. "Bias in Formalized Bail Procedures." In *Race and Criminal Justice,* edited by Michael Lynch and E. Patterson. New York, Harrow and Heston, 1991.

Pollock, Joycelyn. *Prisons: Today and Tomorrow.* Gaithersburg, Md.: Aspen Publishers, 1997.

Rafter, Nicole, and Elizabeth Stanko. "Introduction." In *Judge, Lawyer, Victim, Thief: Women, Gender Roles, and Criminal Justice,* edited by Nicole Rafter and Elizabeth Stanko. Boston, Mass.: Northeastern University Press, 1982.

Reiman, Jeffrey. *The Rich Get Richer and the Poor Get Prison—Ideology, Class, and Criminal Justice.* Boston, Mass.: Allyn & Bacon, 1998.

Sims, Patsy. "Women in Southern Jails," in *The Female Offender,* edited by Laura Crites. Lexington, Mass.: D.C. Heath and Company, 1976.

Spohn, Cassia, and Jerry Cederblom. "Race and Disparities in Sentencing: A Test of the Liberation Hypothesis." *Justice Quarterly* 8 (1991): 305-27.

Steffensmeier, Darrell, John Kramer, and Cathy Streifel. "Gender and Imprisonment Decisions." *Criminology* 31 (1993): 411-46.

Temin, Carolyn. "Discriminatory Sentencing of Women Offenders: The Argument for ERA in a Nutshell." In *The Female Offenders,* edited by Laura Crites. Lexington, Mass.: D.C. Heath and Company, 1976.

Vincent, Barbara, and Paul Hofer. *The Consequences of Mandatory Minimum Prison Terms: A Summary of Recent Findings.* Washington, D.C.: Federal Justice Center, 1994.

Young, Vernetta. "Gender Expectations and Their Impact on Black Female Offenders and Victims. *Justice Quarterly* 3 (1986): 305-27.

A Video Camera
Can Change Your Life

Margaret Shaw

Incident at Kingston

> *The video camera has become the new tribune of truth. Little escapes its steady gaze. From the beating of Rodney King in Los Angeles to the initiation rites of the Canadian Airborne Regiment, the video camera reveals behaviour once dismissed as hearsay, hyperbole or imagination. . . . We are reminded of the power of the video camera today as we contemplate its latest disclosure. A videotape of an incident at the Prison for Women in Ontario contradicts the interpretation of events by the Correctional Service of Canada. Indeed, it calls its credibility into question.*[1]

"Everybody is a star. The video camcorder is the ultimate toy for a narcissistic age," writes a journalist reviewing one of the latest versions on the market, one that can be operated continuously for twelve hours or more.[2] Advertised as a toy, as an essential tool for recording family life, the video camera has indeed become a powerful component of our lives. Far from merely providing an accurate record of reality, however, it has become a weapon, a source of contested interpretations, a protection against false accusation, a method of surveillance, a deterrent, and a form of social control. In few situations has it played a more complex role than during recent events in the women's federal prison system in Canada. There, a video recording intended to protect staff from false accusation became the vehicle for exposing those staff, shocking the public and resulting in a major public inquiry into the treatment of women prisoners. Yet these events in themselves helped to realign policies toward women's prisons, leading to the installation of video surveillance to protect the public and to deter and control those prisoners.

This chapter examines the role of the media and the power of the video camera to both bring about change (public inquiries) and minimize risk (monitor movements), and the complex way in which public attention, through the media, can briefly affect the internal working of the prison. It follows zigzags in the philosophies, intentions, policies, and practices that have taken place in the Canadian federal system since 1990, during what has been one of the first attempts to incorporate feminist ideals into the philosophy and practice of women's prisons.

Media Messages

Studies of the relationship between the media and crime have traditionally focused on the impact of media messages on public attitudes and on their construction and maintenance of dominant ideologies.[3] They have also focused on the early stages of the criminal justice system, on arrest, trial, and sentence.[4] It is commonly concluded that the media pay little attention to prisons and to the application of punishment and the progress of a sentence. Explanations for this lack of attention variously cite the "veiling" of punishment following the nineteenth-century development of the penitentiary;[5] the resulting focus on the declaration of punishment and the decline in interest in its process; the limited access to source material and heavy reliance on official accounts, a result of the tight official control exercised over information; and the apparently mundane nature of daily prison life, which does not constitute "news." Certainly some cultural media studies have paid attention to prisons in feature films, comedies, and documentaries,[6] but they are also exceptions compared to the relative cultural weight of courtroom and police dramas. Attempts by governments in some countries to open prisons up to the media seem to have been a relatively recent development since the end of the 1970s. For example, the governor of Holloway Prison, a women's prison in England, invited the BBC in to make a documentary in the 1980s.[7] For some writers, prison documentaries do allow the secret world of the prison to be unveiled briefly. As Mason puts it,

> [P]rison programs provide an opportunity for the audience to share the world of the criminal and be compelled to tread the slippery and vertiginous path between sympathy and vilification. The unruly mass at the gallows are now the voyeurs on the sofa.[8]

Nevertheless, as one United States study suggests, documentaries or news stories about prisons have tended to focus on celebrity prisoners, penal policy issues, disturbances, and escapes; on "news" rather than on everyday lives.[9]

Such studies are also rarely gendered. Little consideration has been given to the relationship between the media and women's prisons, although there have been some powerful examinations of the earlier criminal justice stages, particularly around women's violence.[10] There have also been some sensationalist and misguided accounts by women journalists focusing, as is usually the case, on women's violence.[11] The latter fall into the same tradition as commercial feature films about women in prison, with their "cherished misogynist stereotypes" that demonize women prisoners as monsters, lesbian villains, teenage predators, and "pathological killer beauties."[12] Television soap opera has also occasionally focused on women's prisons, as in the Australian program *Prisoner: Cell Block H.* Some recent documentaries about women's prisons have, nevertheless, presented a more realistic portrayal of daily life and the lives of women inmates than such television programs and feature films.[13]

When press attention has been focused on women's prisons, it has tended to do so for sensationalist news reasons. Holloway, the women's prison in England, has been described as a "voyeur's delight" by the media; one reporter wrote that "Holloway will always be a story because it's both prisons and women and there is something special and unusual in that."[14] As Chris Tchaikovsky has noted, media inquiries to women's prison groups usually ask for comments about the rise in female crime and violence, or girls' gangs, and she quotes one journalist's chilling comment that "a woman putting out another woman's eye was news, a woman putting out her own was not."[15] In the view of most critics, media accounts and representations of women's crimes or prisons act to reinforce the dominant value system, providing deviant images of unruly, violent, and disturbed women "against which the standard of normality can be set."[16] For the media, violence by women doubles the fascination.

Recent discussions of the relationship between the media and prisons suggest that it is in fact more complex and pluralistic than usually portrayed, that dominant ideology explanations and the notion of tight control over information are not sufficient.[17] In a study of sources of prison news in Canada, Doyle and Ericson concluded that prison officials are in fact unable to exert strict control over news. Pressure groups and prison activists, prisoners, staff and staff unions, and families of prisoners may all provide stories and information; correctional officials see themselves for the most part engaging in "damage control."[18] Such a combination of sources was certainly evident in the aftermath of the events at the Prison for Women (P4W) in April 1994, the maximum security prison for women in Kingston, Ontario.

A Feminist Blueprint

Built in 1934 along nineteenth-century penitentiary lines, the Prison for Women has long been the focus of attempts to bring about change in women's imprisonment in Canada.[19] The blueprint for the future of federally sentenced women, those serving sentences of two years or more,[20] was laid down by *Creating Choices,* the 1990 report of a government-appointed task force.[21] Women serving such sentences were only a small population of some 200 at that time, minute in comparison to the 14,000 federally sentenced men; the majority were held at P4W, the only federal women's prison.[22] The report set out the philosophy and design for a women-centered prison. It laid down five feminist principles emphasizing empowerment, meaningful and responsible choices, respect and dignity, a supportive environment, and the sharing of responsibility with the community. P4W was to close and five new facilities and a Healing Lodge were to be built.[23] They were to feature cottage-style housing, giving the women greater control over their daily living conditions, and were to be set in pleasant surroundings. There were to be facilities for mothers with babies or small children. There was to be strong staff support, eliminating the need for fences or static security measures. On the grounds that women do not represent the security risks posed by men, only one cottage in a facility was to have "enhanced security" for the handful of women who could not cope with the communal living conditions. Programming was to be women-centered and holistic, recognizing the particular and interconnected needs of women in conflict with the law and their extensive histories of abuse at the hands of men. Staff were to be carefully selected and receive specific training in gender and cultural issues, and no male staff were to occupy "front-line" positions.[24] The most innovative recommendation, in response to the overrepresentation of Aboriginal women in the federal population, was for a Healing Lodge to be built and run on Aboriginal principles.

Overall, *Creating Choices* can be seen as an attempt to incorporate a liberal-welfare feminist philosophy into federal women's corrections, one that denied the harsh realities of prison life, constructed women as victims, and allowed for the incorporation of feminist discourse into correctional policies. Nevertheless, at the time of its publication it was widely praised.[25] With the acceptance of the recommendations, plans for the new facilities were developed, although not without considerable problems, as the blueprint was reshaped to meet government, correctional, and public sensibilities.[26]

The Events of April 1994

> As the prison authorities tell it, the riot squad was sent into the isolation unit to remove women inmates after four days of intermittent violence. The women were running amok—throwing urine, screaming obscenities, setting fires, breaking up beds. The videotape shows several women stripped naked, shackled and marched from their cells by men in riot gear. The manacled women were forced onto the floor face down, their clothes sliced off with a knife. The inmates did not resist.[27]

In April 1994 a group of six women prisoners was involved in a fight with staff members. Locked in segregation cells, they continued to resist their conditions over a four-day period, demanding access to legal services, phone calls, and day-to-day supplies such as blankets, sanitary napkins, and clothes. They were noisy, set fire to toilet paper, and threw what they could to attract attention; staff response was to withdraw more facilities, including running water in the toilets. An all-male emergency response team from a nearby male prison was brought in to strip-search the six women and two others who had not taken part in the initial event but were already in segregation, bringing with them a video camera to record the procedure. At the time of the strip-search no riot was in progress, some women were asleep, and most offered little resistance. Subsequently, six women were involuntarily and illegally transferred to Kingston Penitentiary, a maximum security for men, until a court ordered them back to P4W. Overall, they were kept in isolation for up to nine months and were further punished by the internal discipline board on their return to the general prison population.[28]

An internal board of investigation of the incident concluded that appropriate procedures had been followed during the whole event, including the strip-searching. It made no mention of the fact that the women had been strip-searched by men. The initial fight was construed as a planned attack and an escape attempt by a group of violent women. Fifteen pages of the report itemizing the violent crimes for which the women had been convicted and reports of their institutional behavior set out the "justification" for the handling of the affair.[29] A photograph appended to the report, but not specifically identified with the women in question, showed examples of methods by which contraband drugs had been brought into the prison, emphasizing staff concerns about security. There was no discussion in the report of the context and history of the eighteen months that preceded the initial fight, of precipitating factors, of the contribution of the staff and management, or of the high turnover of staff and declining morale as the prison's closure approached.[30] The only issues in the report were the propensities and control of violent women.

Among other things, the report recommended the separate housing of "violent" women, the introduction of male front-line workers, a review of inmate privileges and a review of the role of the prison psychologists (who had been instrumental in developing feminist therapeutic programming). On the recommendation of the report, an additional ten-cell segregation area was built at P4W, a prison due to be closed in two years, and plans were made to double the enhanced security accommodation in the new regional prisons. "Violent disruptive women," as the report referred to them, required "a separate secure environment" and "intensive therapeutic programming" in order for them to "take responsibility for their actions."[31] In spite of the fact that its existence was known to a number of people, there was no mention in the report, as it emerged into public hands the following January, of the videotape.[32]

Media Responses

For the local media in Kingston, a town that has ten correctional institutions in its vicinity, access to the inside of institutions is not easy. Although the local newspaper, the *Whig Standard,* is regarded as "the leading media outlet in terms of corrections news in Canada,"[33] they feel discriminated against by the correctional authorities because their reporters are constantly denied access inside prisons while others are let in: "We worked for eight months on [one story]. We were never allowed into the Prison for Women. We were never allowed to talk to anyone in there."[34]

Unlike many male prisoners, women cannot rely on the network of wives identified in Doyle and Ericson to raise their cases with the media. They tend to be more isolated both by virtue of their much greater distance from home communities than men and by the absence of partners outside prison. Nevertheless, between April 1994 and February 1995 a series of "leaks" hinted at infringement of the rights of the women. Lawyers representing women prisoners, journalists, and prison activists including the local Elizabeth Fry Society and its national organization, the Canadian Association of Elizabeth Fry Societies (CAEFS), all reported concerns and pressed the prison authorities for information. Still the Correctional Service of Canada (CSC) denied that the event had been inappropriately handled or that women had been strip-searched by men, suggesting only that they would have preferred an all-female riot squad. A report in the *Globe and Mail* quoted the view of the Correctional Service of Canada that the riot squad had been necessary to maintain the safety of staff and the institution, and concluded, "Staff members still bristling over the April 22 incident in which one female guard was stabbed with a needle and another severely kicked, say the inmates got what they deserved."[35] A letter from the deputy commissioner in the *Kitchener Record* in December 1994 responded to criticism by CAEFS. It argued that a strong and effective staff response had foiled the plans of the inmates and that staff were to be commended for their efforts.[36] Even when the existence of the videotape became known to journalists, there were still public denials by CSC that it showed women being strip-searched by men.[37] The correctional investigator, a government-appointed prison watchdog, undertook his own investigation and in a report submitted to the Solicitor General in February 1995 concluded that there had been serious breaches of prison regulations and inmate rights in the handling of the events. He recommended that CSC offer compensation packages to the women.

All this relatively low-key press attention was changed dramatically by the presentation of the videotape of the strip-search on prime time television in February 1995.[38] The Correctional Service had failed in its attempt to get a court injunction to stop its broadcast. The tape showed very graphically the women being slowly and systematically stripped and shackled by men in full riot gear with helmets, masks, sticks, and plexiglas shields. Some of the women were asleep as the team arrived, some forced face down on the ground while their clothes were cut off. No riot was in progress. The response from the press was swift and largely condemnatory. Under a headline "Men Use Force in Shocking Riot Video; Guards Strip Women Cons" *The Ottawa Citizen* showed a still from the video and gave a detailed account of it contents.[39] Other papers that day had similar responses: "Terror Behind Bars";[40] "Inmates Stripped, Female Prisoners Subjected to Humiliation and Degradation";[41] "Women Stripped in Cells by Men, Video Shows";[42] "Prison Videos Shocking View."[43] Reflecting on the video the following week, Robert Everett-Green argued in "Bringing Home Prison's Brutal Reality" that the main point of the strip-search seemed "to have been to demonstrate total physical domination," "to prove that authorities have the power to look." "We saw a curious instance of how one government department's idea of routine practice may be another department's idea of actionable conduct."[44] Not all papers were so condemnatory. In an article in the *Toronto Sun,* "They Whine and We Pay," a columnist expressed outrage at the notion that the women should be compensated, suggesting the women's concerns about "being stared at" by the male team had more to do with their sexual orientation than the "beastly behavior of the men."[45] Its editorial "Video Truths" offered "Congratulations to the all-male emergency response team that so professionally put down the April riot at Kingston's infamous Prison for Women." An accompanying cartoon personifies all the misogynist stereotypes about women prisoners. It shows a heavily set, glowering woman sitting in her cell. A hand extends toward her with a tiny little girl's dress suspended from a hanger. The caption reads: "Now dear, slip this on, and go out and tell them what those animals did."

Nevertheless, the overwhelming initial press and public response was to condemn the actions of CSC and their attempts to cover up and justify what had taken place:

> Yesterday, Solicitor General Herbert Gray tabled a report from the federal correctional investigator which concluded that the incident featured "excessive use of force" which was "degrading and dehumanizing" to the inmates. The more we learn about this, the greater the doubts. From the time critics began to raise questions about the Prison for Women—the use of force, the solitary confinement, the length of isolation—the Correctional Service has denied, delayed and equivocated. More and more this looks like abuse of authority.[46]

Within days the Solicitor General announced the setting up of an independent inquiry, to be conducted by Madame Justice Louise Arbour, then a judge in the Ontario Court of Appeal. Over the subsequent year the lengthy process of hearings and uncovering evidence about the incident took place, followed by a series of roundtable discussions about the future course of federal imprisonment for women in Canada. Her inquiry brought together both CSC staff and administrators, the women prisoners involved in the event, the correctional investigator, and CAEFS who were granted "standing" throughout the inquiry.[47]

The Arbour Report

In her report made public in April 1996, Madame Justice Arbour underlined the importance of the videotape in raising public concern about the internal life of the prison:

> The incidents which gave rise to this inquiry could have gone largely unnoticed. Until the public viewing of a videotape which shed light on

part of these events, and the release of a special report by the Correctional Investigator in the winter of 1995, the Correctional Service of Canada had essentially closed the book on these events.[48]

Her report confirmed that the inmates had been accurate in their accounts of the events and that their grievances and rights had been systematically ignored by the correctional system. It also concluded that contrary to its mission statement to act with "openness," "integrity," and "accountability," the approach of the Correctional Service of Canada during the course of the events themselves, and in the course of the public inquiry, was "to deny error, defend against criticism, and to react without proper investigation of the truth."[49] There was no institutional acknowledgement of responsibility or accountability. There was no acknowledgement that other versions of the "truth" were accurate.

> The deplorable defensive culture that manifested itself during this inquiry has old, established roots within the Correctional Service, and there is nothing to suggest that it emerged at the initiative of the present Commissioner or his senior staff. They are, it would seem, simply entrenched in it.[50]

In her long list of recommendations, Madame Justice Arbour argued for the central importance of establishing a "culture of rights" within CSC, including far greater attention to the use of segregation throughout CSC, the establishment of the position of deputy commissioner for women, and the continuation of the women-centered philosophy and policies set out in *Creating Choices*. Thus the video camera had performed the crucial function of enabling events inside prison to be viewed from the outside and by a nation. It has changed the lives of those women prisoners and staff and the rules and procedures under which the federal correctional system must now work.

Razor Wire and Video Security

Local reactions to the siting of the new regional prisons and a generally increasing discussion of fear of crime in the media resulted in changes to the initial plans.[51] The April 1994 events and a spectacular murder trial involving the kidnapping, sexual assault, and torture of two school girls by a young married couple added to the reconstruction of women offenders as violent criminals rather than victims.[52] An article in one local newspaper entitled "There Are Women Inmates Who Are Indeed Violent" suggested that staff should be equipped with weapons to protect themselves from such women.[53] At two sites, Edmonton and Kitchener, local citizens negotiated with CSC for the erection of security fencing around the new prisons. The first of the new regional facilities began to open in November 1995. By the spring of 1996, however, there were already problems. At the Edmonton facility a rigorous policy of strip-searching women in the "enhanced unit" had been instituted.[54] There followed a number of slashings; a suicide, later to be reclassified as murder; an attack on a member of staff; and "escapes" by seven women who walked out of the institution.[55] Public reaction to the Edmonton escapes was strong; the government was accused of not placing public security at the "top of the agenda."[56] CSC now decided to increase the height of that fencing to 2.5 meters, and to add razor wire, an improved alarm system, and video camera surveillance in all the new prisons. Thus the video camera was now to be used for controlling movement, to deter escapes, and above all to protect the public from women who were being recast as tough customers who were violent and dangerous. In September 1996, further disturbances took place in the "enhanced unit" in Truro prison.[57] There followed another change of policy: Women classified as maximum security would be excluded from the new prisons and be accommodated in men's maximum security facilities in each region. In the light of both *Creating Choices* and the Arbour Report this was an extraordinary decision. The mother and baby units were also put "on hold" and a new mental health policy for women "experiencing psychological and behavioral problems" was initiated.

Taken together, these changes amounted to a major realignment of the policies laid down in 1990 or even as they stood in April 1994. The new regional prisons were now to be restricted to women without "behavioral problems" and those who were classified as medium or minimum security. In this process many Aboriginal women, who are overrepresented among those classified as maximum security, found themselves excluded not only from the new regional prisons but also from the Healing Lodge that was specifically built to respond to their very different cultural needs and experiences.

Video Power and Advocacy

The videotape was, as the Arbour Report suggests, the catalyst that tipped the balance. Without those graphic visual images of women being stripped naked and shackled by men in riot gear, coupled with the exposure of the denials and attempts by CSC to cover up the events, there would probably have been little widespread press condemnation or public concern, even after the publication of the report by the correctional investigator. The videotape brought actual events inside a women's prison into people's living rooms. The government's response was to establish an inquiry that retained a high profile.

The importance of the visual images can be seen in the press and in the public reaction to another public inquiry relating to federally sentenced women, but one for which no video "event" pertains. The Ratushny Inquiry was established to review the self-defense provisions in the Criminal Code. It included a reexamination of all cases of women sentenced for killing an abusive spouse. It was the outcome of a long campaign by CAEFS and other women's groups to seek redress for such women and an issue that has received extensive sympathetic media coverage in Canada in the recent past.[58] In spite of considerable press coverage and proactive press activity by CAEFS, Judge Ratushny's report[59] has never received the amount of attention accorded to Justice Arbour, nor such favorable attention. Nor was the government's initial response to the recommendations of Judge Ratushny's report as immediate as it was to those of the Arbour report.[60]

The videotape and the Arbour Inquiry also publicly demonstrated the credibility not only of women prisoners, but also of CAEFS, defense lawyers, and others who had questioned official accounts. Their versions of events were shown to be more accurate than those of correctional staff. Even in the course of the inquiry the approach of the correctional service was to "deny error, defend against criticism, and to react without proper investigation of the truth."[61] The clear demonstration that official statements or viewpoints are unreliable and intended to conceal, although not unusual in the current Canadian context, went beyond acceptable limits even in relation to the prison.[62] The videotape subsequently generated a series of thoughtful TV follow-up programs and magazine articles about women prisoners, some involving women prisoners and staff who had been involved in the P4W events, as well as Kim Pate, the executive director of CAEFS.

But other conditions amplified the power of those video images. These include the now long-term awareness and sensitivity of the press, public, and government to issues of violence and abuse against women in Canada, and the long-term advocacy of CAEFS, which has achieved a higher profile in Canada than is usual in relation to prison pressure groups. Gender seems to have made a difference beyond the traditional prurient media interest in the unusual — a women's prison and violent women. As Rock has noted, since the 1980s the women's movement in Canada has focused on the body and the right of women to have control over their own bodies.[63] Violence against women — in terms of sexual assault and abuse whether by strangers or intimates, has been the central and unifying focus. And for the government, violence has become "politically laden."[64] It is difficult to imagine a video of a strip-search in a men's penitentiary having the same effect, even if the searchers were women. Nor would news of a fight between six male inmates and guards have raised much concern beyond the local press in the vicinity of the institution. A member of the John Howard Society, a voluntary organization working with men's prisons, reports that prison events have to be seen to be "outrageous" to be newsworthy.[65]

CAEFS has also achieved a level of visibility and power in terms of both public acceptance as an authority on women's corrections (or for some, notoriety as a "special interest group") and government sensitivity to its actions and views, which it never had fifteen or twenty years ago. In 1982 it was described in a government magazine as an organization engaged in counseling, court assistance, prison visiting, and rehabilitation work for women.[66] Since that time and up to the present, through its central role in the task force that produced *Creating Choices*, it has continued to campaign for women's rights both nationally and internationally.[67] Apart from its participation in the Arbour Inquiry, CAEFS was more recently involved in a successful bid by women inmates at P4W to prevent their transfer to the men's maximum security penitentiary in Kingston.[68] Nevertheless, neither media constructions nor correctional policies are static. Within weeks of the conclusion of the Arbour Inquiry, the death of a woman at the Edmonton prison and a suicide at P4W were again presented by CSC in terms of the propensities of individual women. Kim Pate expressed her "despair and anger" that she was "left without even a fleeting sense that things might actually change as a result" of the Inquiry.[69] Release of the reports on the Edmonton and Truro incidents took many months. As Carlen and Tchaikovsky have urged,

> It is essential to keep open to public view the inner workings of the whole carceral machinery, so that its endemic secrecy can be held in check, and its chronic tendency for periodic reversion from progressive to retrogressive practices constantly monitored.[70]

But it is hard.

Conclusion

The role of the media in relation to prisons is thus a complex one, relying on a variety of sources inside and outside the institution. The media is now less likely to privilege official accounts of events over others than in the past, and there is now more expectation of accountability by government institutions. The media is both essential to, and the bane of, advocacy groups who must select their media contacts with great care in any proactive attempt to raise public awareness or publicize a problem. But the media, whether print, radio, or television, popular or more "serious," is still primarily interested in "outrageous" events, celebrity prisoners, or related newsworthy issues, not in day-to-day events or experiences. It reacts rather differently to events in women's and men's prisons. In the case of women's federal imprisonment in Canada, gender has had an impact beyond the prurient. With the changing public sensitivities to violence against women, and the increasing visibility of advocacy groups such as CAEFS, an outrageous event that is witnessed by the public can be a catalyst for exposure and some change. As one of the new wardens has put it following the Arbour Inquiry, "[W]omen's corrections serve as a lightning rod for the public scrutiny of the Correctional Service of Canada."[71]

But just as concerns about prison security and public perceptions of safety in the 1990s have placed British prisons under much greater media scrutiny than before,[72] so too have security and public safety come to dominate media and public concerns about women at *some* of the new regional prisons, although not all. The local context and public attitudes are also important mediators of media responses.[73] The media can work to raise issues of fairness, rights, and accountability but can also work to generate opposition and fear of the violent, unknown, stereotyped female offender, and in this the video camera plays a watchful role in minimizing risk as a protector and observer. It offers safety and security to a public who does not want to know too much about what goes on inside, only about what goes on at the perimeter. Those images, however, are not for public viewing but are part of the closed, controlling world of women's prisons. "Perfect technology, perfectly simple."[74]

NOTES

1. Editorial, *Globe and Mail,* 22 February 1995. The *Globe and Mail* was at the time the only newspaper that claimed national status in Canada and was available in all provinces. Its editorials and columns were thus more widely read and "authoritative" than locally based newspapers.

2. Cecily Ross, "Everybody Is a Star," *Globe and Mail,* 18 September 1998.

3. See, for example, David Kidd-Hewitt and Richard Osborne, eds., *Crime and the Media: The Post-modern Spectacle* (London: Pluto Press, 1995); Bronwyn Naylor, "Women's Crime and Media Coverage: Making Explanations," in *Gender and Crime,* ed. R. Emerson Dobash, Russell P. Dobash, and Leslie Noaks (Cardiff: University of Wales Press, 1995).

4. See Paul Mason, "Prime Time Punishment: The British Prison and Punishment," in *Crime and the Media: The Post-modern Spectacle,* eds. David Kidd-Hewitt and Richard Osborne (London: Pluto Press, 1995); Margaret Shaw, "Conceptualizing Violence by Women," in *Gender and Crime,* ed. R. Emerson Dobash, Russell P. Dobash, and Leslie Noaks (Cardiff: University of Wales Press, 1995); Aaron Doyle and Richard Ericson, "Breaking into Prison: News Sources and Correctional Institutions," *Canadian Journal of Criminology* 38, no. 2 (1996): 155–90.

5. A reference to the loss of the public spectacle of execution and punishment discussed in work by Michel Foucault, *Discipline and Punish* (Middlesex: Peregrine Books, 1977) and David Garland, *Punishment and Modern Society* (Chicago: University of Chicago Press, 1990).

6. See Karlene Faith, *Unruly Women: The Politics of Confinement and Resistance* (Vancouver: Press Gang Publishers, 1993); Karlene Faith, "Media, Myths and Masculinization: Images of Women in Prison," in *In Conflict with the Law: Women in the Canadian Justice System,* ed. Ellen Adelberg and Claudia Currie (Vancouver: Press Gang Publishers, 1993); Mason, "Prime Time Punishment."

7. Paul Rock, *Reconstructing a Women's Prison: The Holloway Redevelopment Project 1968–88* (Oxford: Clarendon Press, 1996), 307.

8. Mason, "Prime Time Punishment," 203.

9. Jacobs and Brooks (1983) cited in Doyle and Ericson, "Breaking into Prison."

10. See, for example, Alison Young, *Femininity in Dissent* (London: Routledge, 1990); Helen Birch, ed., *Moving Targets: Women, Murder and Representation* (London: Virago Press, 1993); Bronwyn Naylor, "Women's Crime and Media Coverage: Making Explanations," in *Gender and Crime,* ed. R. Emerson Dobash, Russell P. Dobash, and Leslie Noaks (Cardiff: University of Wales Press, 1995); Maggie Wykes, "Passion, Marriage and Murder: Analysing the Press Discourse," in *Crime and the Media: The Post-modern Spectacle,* ed. R. Emerson Dobash, Russell P. Dobash, and Leslie Noaks (London: Pluto Press, 1995).

11. Patricia Pearson, *When She Was Bad: Violent Women and the Myth of Innocence* (Toronto: Random House, 1997); Lisa Priest, *Women Who Killed* (Toronto: McClelland and Stewart, 1992).

12. Faith, *Unruly Women,* 256; Christine Holmlund, "A Decade of Deadly Dolls: Hollywood and the Woman Killer," in *Moving Targets: Women, Murder and Representation,* ed. Helen Birch (London: Virago Press, 1993).

13. For example, recent Canadian documentaries include "P4W" (Holly Dale and Janis Cole, 1981); "Castle/No Princesses" (1986); "To Heal the Spirit" (Why Not Productions, 1991); "A Year Whose Days are Long" (Juliet Belmas,1992); "Getting Out" (Why Not Productions, 1992); "Twice Condemned" (Marie Cadieux, NFB 1994); "When Women Kill" (Barbara Doran, NFB 1994). Examples in the United States include "Through the Wire" (Nina Rosenblum, 1989); "Drug Mules" (Mervaz Ozeri, 1992); "We Are Not Who You Think We Are" (Video/Action Fund, 1993). And in the United Kingdom, "Locking Up Women" (Anne Webber, 1992). In England an international film festival on women's prisons was organized by the National Association for the Care and Resettlement of Offenders in 1993. See also Faith, *Unruly Women.*

14. Rock, *Reconstructing a Women's Prison,* 287.

15. Chris Tchaikovsky, "Without Fear or Favour: The Role of the Independent Advocacy Group," in *Imprisoning Women: Recognizing Difference,* ed. Stephanie Hayman (London: Institute for the Study and Treatment of Delinquency, 1998), 35.

16. Faith, *Unruly Women,* 270. See also Naylor, "Women's Crime and Media Coverage"; Wykes, "Passion, Marriage and Murder."

17. Richard Ericson, Patricia Baranek, and Janet Chan, *Representing Order: Crime, Law, and Justice in the News Media* (Toronto: University of Toronto Press, 1991); Aaron

Doyle and Richard Ericson, "Breaking into Prison: News Sources and Correctional Institutions," *Canadian Journal of Criminology* 38, no. 2 (1996): 155–90.

18. Doyle and Ericson, "Breaking into Prison," 165.

19. Sheelagh Cooper, "The Evolution of the Federal Women's Prison," in *In Conflict with the Law: Women in the Canadian Justice System,* ed. Ellen Adelberg and Claudia Currie (Vancouver: Press Gang Publishers, 1993); Margaret Shaw, "Reforming Federal Women's Imprisonment," in *In Conflict with the Law: Women in the Canadian Justice System,* ed. Ellen Adelberg and Claudia Currie (Vancouver: Press Gang Publishers, 1993).

20. Those sentenced to under two years are the responsibility of each province and serve their sentences in provincial prisons.

21. The task force was unusual for a number of reasons. It was composed of a balance of government officials and voluntary organizations and individuals. The latter included Aboriginal women and organizations, in recognition of their heavy overrepresentation in the prison population. Two federally sentenced women were also members, and many of the nongovernment members worked from a feminist perspective.

22. Under exchange of service agreements, some women could serve their federal sentences in provincial prisons. A further 200 federally sentenced women were on conditional release in the community, bringing the total population to around 400. The much larger provincial population consisted at that time of some 800 women serving very short sentences, usually under two weeks, but over 9,000 a year would be sentenced to prison. Of the federally sentenced women in prison, 25 percent were Aboriginal, although they represented only 2 percent of the Canadian population as a whole.

23. Subsequently, the plan was changed to four new facilities and a Healing Lodge. British Columbia was excluded from the plan because a new federal-provincial institution had recently been built.

24. Staff training was to "emphasize counselling, communications and negotiation skills and . . . training focused on sexism, sexual orientation, racism, Aboriginal traditions, spirituality, as well as issues relating to power and class" (The Task Force on Federally Sentenced Women, *Creating Choices* [1990], 140). Only female staff were to undertake front-line work, both to act as role models and, primarily, because of the high proportion of women in the prison population who had experienced physical and sexual abuse.

25. See Kathleen Kendall, "Review Essay: The Discipline and Control of Women," *Journal of Human Justice* 6, no. 1 (1994): 111–19; Kelly Hannah-Moffat, "Feminist Fortresses: Women Centered Prisons?" *Prison Journal* 75, no. 2 (1995): 135–64; Kelly Hannah-Moffat, "Prisons that Empower: Neo-Liberal Governance in Canadian Women's Prisons," *British Journal of Criminology* (forthcoming); Margaret Shaw, "Issues of Power and Control: Women in Prison and Their Defenders," *British Journal of Criminology* 32, no. 4 (1992): 438–52; and Margaret Shaw, "Is There a Feminist Future for Women's Prisons?" in *Prisons 2000: An International Perspective on the Current State and Future of Imprisonment,* ed. Roger Matthews and Peter Francis (New York: St Martin's Press, 1996) for detailed discussion of these issues.

26. Hannah-Moffat, "Feminist Fortresses"; Shaw, "Is There a Feminist Future for Women's Prisons?"

27. Editorial, *Globe and Mail,* 22 February 1995.

28. See Karlene Faith, "Aboriginal Women's Healing Lodge: Challenge to Penal Correctionalism?" *The Journal of Human Justice* 6, no. 2 (Spring/Autumn 1995): 79–104; Kim Pate, "CSC and the 2 Percent Solution," *Journal of Prisoners on Prisons* 6, no. 2 (1995): 41–61; Louise Arbour, "Commission of Inquiry into Certain Events at the Prison for Women in Kingston" (Ottawa: Public Works and Government Services Canada, 1996).

29. Three other women in the segregation cells were also involved in the strip-searching.

30. See Pate, "CSC and the 2 Percent Solution"; Margaret Shaw, "'Knowledge without Acknowledgment': Violent Women, the Prison and the Cottage," *Howard Journal of Criminal Justice* 38, no. 3 (1999): 252–66.

31. "Report: Board of Investigation—Major Disturbance and Other Related Incidents—Prison for Women from Friday April 22 to Tuesday April 26, 1994." Correctional Service of Canada (1995), 58.

32. *Contact,* an inmate cable television show in Kingston, was reported to have been shut down briefly after it aired, and tried to sell video footage of the strip search at P4W (reported in Doyle and Ericson, "Breaking into Prison," 173).

33. Ibid., 164.

34. Ibid., 179.

35. Henry Hess, "Women Stripped in Kingston Cells by Men, Video Shows," *Globe and Mail,* 16 December 1994.

36. *Kitchener Record,* 16 December 1994.

37. CBC, *As it Happens,* November 1994.

38. The video was shown on Canadian Broadcasting Corporation's *Fifth Estate,* a high-profile investigative current affairs program.

39. *The Ottawa Citizen,* 21 February 1995.

40. *Winnipeg Free Press,* 21 February 1995.

41. *Winnipeg Sun,* 21 February 1995.

42. *Globe and Mail,* 21 February 1995.

43. *Prince George Citizen,* 21 February 1995.

44. Robert Everett-Green, "Bringing Home Prison's Brutal Reality," *Globe and Mail,* 28 February 1995.

45. "They Whine and We Pay," *Toronto Sun,* 22 February 1995.

46. Editorial, *Globe and Mail,* 22 February 1995.

47. Pate, "CSC and the 2 Percent Solution."

48. Arbour, "Commission of Inquiry," xi.

49. Ibid., 173.

50. Ibid., 174.

51. Much of this press reporting and public debate highlighted exceptional cases involving young offenders, as well as sex offenders and parole releases. Tougher policies and legislative changes were usually urged in response to these events.

52. Shaw, "Knowledge without Acknowledgment."

53. *Kitchener Record,* 4 November 1994.

54. Pate, "CSC and the 2 Percent Solution."

55. The three escapees were not noticed by staff for three hours, and a fourth turned herself in before staff realized she was missing.

56. *Globe and Mail,* 16 April 1996.

57. Those incidents were subsequently seen to have been instigated by staff reactions to earlier minor events, and one woman received an apology and settlement after her lawyer's intervention.

58. See Elizabeth Comack, "Feminist Engagement with the Law: The Legal Recognition of the Battered Women Syndrome," *The C.R.I.A.W. Papers No. 31* (Ottawa: Canadian Research Institute for the Advancement of Women, 1993); Sheila Noonan, "Strategies of Survival: Moving Beyond the Battered Woman Syndrome," in *In Conflict with the Law: Women in the Canadian Justice System,* ed. Ellen Adelberg and Claudia Currie (Vancouver: Press Gang Publishers, 1993).

59. Lynn Ratushny, *Final Report of the Self-Defence Review* (Ottawa: Public Works and Government Services Canada, 1997).

60. A landmark Supreme Court of Canada decision (*R. v. Lavallee,* 1990) agreed that the context of a relationship was to be taken into account in such cases, not just the immediate objective facts. Established by the Department of Justice at the urging of CAEFS and other critics, there were long delays before any government response to Judge Ratushny's report, and few of her recommendations relating to the retrial or release of individual women were accepted. In the case of the Arbour Report, the commissioner of corrections immediately resigned, a Task Force to Review Segregation was set up, and a deputy commissioner for women was appointed.

61. Arbour, "Commission of Inquiry," 173.

62. One previous example, in 1995, was a videotape of the torture of a Somalian prisoner by soldiers in the Canadian Airborne Regiment, which caused a major public outcry and government action.

63. Paul Rock, *A View From the Shadows* (Oxford: Clarendon Press, 1986), 213.

64. Ibid., 381.

65. Doyle and Ericson, "Breaking into Prison," 175.

66. Rock, *A View From the Shadows,* 22.

67. Much of the credit for this increased visibility and voice has been due to the energies of Executive Directors Bonny Diamond, who co-chaired the task force, and Kim Pate, the current executive director, who was appointed in 1990.

68. The case against CSC was brought by four women to the Ontario Court of Justice (Beaudry et al. Court File No. 10982/97, Ontario Court of Justice [General Division] between Beaudry et al. [Applicants] and The Commissioner of Corrections, The Warden of Prison for Women, the Warden of Kingston Peniteniary [Respondents], 1997). Following a ruling against CSC in the Ontario Court of Appeal, plans for the transfer of maximum security women to a newly designated women's unit in Kingston Penitentiary were dropped.

69. Pate, "CSC and the 2 Percent Solution," 41.

70. Pat Carlen and Chris Tchaikovsky, "Women's Imprisonment in England at the End of the Twentieth Century: Legitimacy, Realities and Utopias," in *Prisons 2000: An International Perspective on the Current State and Future of Imprisonment,* ed. Roger Matthews and Peter Francis (New York: St. Martin's Press, 1996), 211.

71. Marie-Andrée Drouin, "Rethinking Women's Imprisonment: A Canadian Perspective," in *Imprisoning Women: Recognizing Difference,* ed. Stephanie Hayman (London: Institute for the Study and Treatment of Delinquency, 1998), 19.

72. Mason, "Prime Time Punishment."

73. In Quebec, for example, there has been little opposition to the new women's prison, and when three women escaped over the fence in 1998 there was very minimal press and public response.

74. A television advertisement for a JVC camcorder, 1998.

REFERENCES

Arbour, Louise. "Commission of Inquiry into Certain Events at the Prison for Women in Kingston." Ottawa: Public Works and Government Services Canada, 1996.

Beaudry et al. Court File No. 10982/97 Ontario Court of Justice (General Division) between Beaudry et al. (Applicants) and The Commissioner of Corrections, The Warden of Prison for Women, the Warden of Kingston Peniteniary (Respondents), 1997.

Birch, H., ed. *Moving Targets: Women, Murder and Representation.* London: Virago Press, 1993.

Carlen, Pat, and Chris Tchaikovsky. "Women's Imprisonment in England at the End of the Twentieth Century: Legitimacy, Realities and Utopias." In *Prisons 2000: An International Perspective on the Current State and Future of Imprisonment,* edited by Roger Matthews and Peter Francis. New York: St. Martin's Press, 1996.

Comack, Elizabeth. "Feminist Engagement with the Law: The Legal Recognition of the Battered Women Syndrome." *The C.R.I.A.W. Papers No. 31.* Ottawa: Canadian Research Institute for the Advancement of Women, 1993.

Cooper, Sheelagh. "The Evolution of the Federal Women's Prison." In *In Conflict with the Law: Women in the Canadian Justice System,* edited by Ellen Adelberg and Claudia Currie. Vancouver: Press Gang Publishers, 1993.

Correctional Services Canada. *Creating Choices: The Report of the Task Force on Federally Sentenced Women.* Ottawa: Correctional Services of Canada, 1990.

Doyle, Aaron, and Richard Ericson. "Breaking into Prison: News Sources and Correctional Institutions." *Canadian Journal of Criminology* 38, no. 2 (1996): 155-90.

Drouin, Marie-Andrée. "Rethinking Women's Imprisonment: A Canadian Perspective." In *Imprisoning Women: Recognizing Difference,* edited by Stephanie Hayman. London: Institute for the Study and Treatment of Delinquency, 1998.

Ericson, Richard, Patricia Baranek, and Janet Chan. *Representing Order: Crime, Law, and Justice in the News Media.* Toronto: University of Toronto Press, 1991.

Faith, Karlene. "Aboriginal Women's Healing Lodge: Challenge to Penal Correctionalism?" *The Journal of Human Justice* 6, no. 2 (Spring/Autumn 1995): 79-104.

———. "Media, Myths and Masculinization: Images of Women in Prison." In *In Conflict with the Law: Women in the Canadian Justice System,* edited by Ellen Adelberg and Claudia Currie. Vancouver: Press Gang Publishers, 1993.

———. *Unruly Women: The Politics of Confinement and Resistance.* Vancouver: Press Gang Publishers, 1993.

Foucault, Michel. *Discipline and Punish: The Birth of the Prison.* Middlesex: Peregrine Books, 1977.

Garland, David. *Punishment and Modern Society.* Chicago: University of Chicago Press, 1990.

Hannah-Moffat, Kelly. "Feminist Fortresses: Women Centered Prisons?" *The Prison Journal* 75, no. 2 (1995): 135-64.

———. "Prisons that Empower: Neo-Liberal Governance in Canadian Women's Prisons." *British Journal of Criminology.* Forthcoming.

Holmlund, Christine. "A Decade of Deadly Dolls: Hollywood and the Woman Killer." In *Moving Targets: Women Murder and Representation,* edited by Helen Birch. London: Virago Press, 1993.

Kendall, Kathleen. "Review Essay. The Discipline and Control of Women: A Review of Adelberg & Currie." *Journal of Human Justice* 6, no. 1 (1994): 111-19.

Kidd-Hewitt, David, and Richard Osborne, eds. *Crime and the Media: The Post-modern Spectacle.* London: Pluto Press, 1995.

Mason, Paul. "Prime Time Punishment: The British Prison and Punishment." In *Crime and the Media: The Post-modern Spectacle,* edited by David Kidd-Hewitt and Richard Osborne. London: Pluto Press, 1995.

Naylor, Bronwyn. "Women's Crime and Media Coverage: Making Explanations." In *Gender and Crime,* edited by R. Emerson Dobash, Russell P. Dobash, and Leslie Noaks. Cardiff: University of Wales Press, 1995.

Noonan, Sheila. "Strategies of Survival: Moving Beyond the Battered Woman Syndrome." In *In Conflict with the Law: Women in the Canadian Justice System,* edited by Ellen Adelberg and Claudia Currie. Vancouver: Press Gang Publishers, 1993.

Pate, Kim. "CSC and the 2 Percent Solution." *Journal of Prisoners on Prisons* 6, no. 2 (1995): 41-61.

Pearson, Patricia. *When She Was Bad: Violent Women and the Myth of Innocence.* Toronto: Random House, 1997.

Priest, Lisa. *Women Who Killed.* Toronto: McClelland and Stewart, 1992.

Ratushny, Lynn. *Final Report of the Self-Defence Review.* Ottawa: Public Works and Government Services Canada, 1997.

Rock, Paul. *Reconstructing a Women's Prison: The Holloway Redevelopment Project 1968-88.* Oxford: Clarendon Press, 1996.

———. *A View From the Shadows.* Oxford: Clarendon Press, 1986.

Shaw, Margaret. "Conceptualizing Violence by Women." In *Gender and Crime,* edited by R. Emerson Dobash, Russell P. Dobash, and Leslie Noaks. Cardiff: University of Wales Press, 1995.

———. "Is There a Feminist Future for Women's Prisons?" In *Prisons 2000: An International Perspective on the Current State and Future of Imprisonment,* edited by Roger Matthews and Peter Francis. London and New York: Macmillan Press Ltd., 1996.

———. "Issues of Power and Control: Women in Prison and their Defenders." *British Journal of Criminology* 32, no. 4 (1992): 438-52.

———. "'Knowledge without Acknowledgment': Violent Women, the Prison and the Cottage." *Howard Journal of Criminal Justice* 38, no. 3 (1998): 252-66.

———. "Reforming Federal Women's Imprisonment." In *In Conflict with the Law: Women in the Canadian Justice System,* edited by Ellen Adelberg and Claudia Currie. Vancouver: Press Gang Publishers, 1993.

Tchaikovsky, Chris. "Without Fear or Favour: The Role of the Independent Advocacy Group." In *Imprisoning Women: Recognizing Difference,* edited by Stephanie Hayman. London: Institute for the Study and Treatment of Delinquency, 1998.

Wykes, Maggie. "Passion, Marriage and Murder: Analysing the Press Discourse." In *Gender and Crime,* edited by R. Emerson Dobash, Russell P. Dobash, and Leslie Noaks. Cardiff: University of Wales Press, 1995.

Young, Alison. *Femininity in Dissent.* London: Routledge, 1990.

Neglect or Punishment?
Failing to Meet the Needs of Women Post-Release

Susanne Davies and Sandy Cook

> *From a situation of imposed infantile dependence, rules and regulations covering every aspect of your life; what time you get up, how to make your bed, what time you eat breakfast, what time you're allowed out to exercise, being locked in your cell—a person is then let out and expected to cope immediately.*[1]

THESE ARE THE WORDS of a woman reflecting upon the difficulty of adjusting to life after imprisonment. Her sentiments capture the despair and frustration that many women feel when the certainty of the prison and its controlled routine is replaced by freedom and the expectation that they be self-reliant and law abiding even though they are usually poorly placed to secure even the most basic necessities of life.

The fact that many women soon return to prison attests to the difficulty of this transition. Indeed, for some, it proves fatal. In recent years, in the Australian state of Victoria, ex-prisoners, community workers, and prison activists have identified the death of women shortly after leaving prison as a matter of urgent concern.[2] The problems of recidivism and post-release mortality have less to do with the character and actions of individual women than with the intolerance and neglect shown toward women prisoners, their particular circumstances, and their needs. The failure of many women to return successfully to a life outside of prison raises questions about the adequacy of existing post-release services and, even more fundamentally, about the effectiveness of imprisonment. Do prisons, for example, provide either the environment or support necessary to acknowledge or address the specific circumstances and problems that so often underlie women's offending? In this chapter, the post-release experiences of women prisoners are explored and are situated on a continuum of control and neglect that ensures women's disempowerment, be they inside or outside of prison.

One Woman's Story

Beth was born in Melbourne in the mid-1960s.[3] At the age of fourteen, she began to use heroin and was made a ward of the state on the grounds that she was "uncontrollable." Her early life had been difficult. Her relationship with her father had been "tense"; he had not wanted a daughter and preferred his sons to her. Beth was placed in a juvenile detention center, but soon escaped to St Kilda, a Melbourne suburb well known for its bohemian culture, rife drug trade, and street prostitution.

By eighteen, Beth had been convicted of various offenses, had served a year of probation, and was on her way to prison. Possession and use of a drug of dependence and loitering for the purpose of prostitution were the charges that would be most frequently brought against her over the next ten years. Added to these was a mixture of other charges ranging from evading payment of a taxi fare and various driving offenses to theft, burglary, handling stolen goods, and various forms of deception. Although Beth was convicted of numerous offenses, 156 in all, none were particularly serious. Nevertheless, she served sixteen terms of imprisonment. The longest sentence she ever received was twelve months; however, the frequency of her convictions meant that for more than a decade she was rarely free for more than a month or two at a time.

Beth also got into trouble when she was in custody. She escaped twice and, during her earlier sentences especially, was found guilty of breaching prison rules, particularly those pertaining to drugs. Loss of privileges and sometimes transfer within or between prisons resulted. While in custody, she served time at every institution used to house women prisoners in Victoria. At a men's prison, where a small number of women were located after a fire at Fairlea Women's Prison, she tried to hang herself. She was just nineteen.

Life inside for Beth was difficult but it was little better on the outside. During her longest period of freedom she established a relationship with a man and had a child. Her partner abused her and drank heavily, however, and their daughter was soon removed by the authorities to foster care. When Beth returned to prison soon after, she was reported to be more motivated than ever before and was hoping to start "a new life with [her] daughter." Her urine samples were returning negative and she was said to be "working hard to further her education and personal development." She was released on parole, but with accommodation problems, mounting bills, unhelpful contact with an old associate, and the unavailability of the social worker responsible for assisting her she soon returned to working the streets. From there it was straight back to prison.

Beth was paroled on at least three occasions, but each time she soon found herself back in prison, having breached the conditions of her release. After her second failed attempt, it was noted that the decision of the authorities to place her daughter in permanent care had "contribut[ed] to her sense of loss and failure." She said she had become "extremely depressed and had contemplated suicide," knowing that she had failed meet her parole conditions again.

At twenty-seven, Beth returned to prison pregnant. It was noted that she looked considerably healthier than on previous receptions and that she had expressed her desire to raise her second child herself. Over the years her behavior when in prison had improved. She was granted parole and upon her request it was brought forward by two weeks. An earlier release, she had written, would mean that she no longer had to spend five days a week working behind a sewing machine in the prison which, in her seventh month of pregnancy, she found tiring and hard to cope with. More important, she needed time to prepare for the birth of her child. She had not yet been able to organize accommodation and needed to buy nappies, clothing, and furniture for her baby. An earlier release would provide her with time to attend to such matters and would also mean that she might gain an additional, albeit meager, Social Security payment to help make ends meet.

Less than two weeks after her release, Beth gave birth to a son. He was born with a heroin addiction. She discharged herself from the hospital, leaving him there, and was soon being searched for. An anonymous man made phone calls to various government agencies asserting that Beth had used heroin while she was pregnant, that she was back working on the streets, and would soon escape to Queensland. She was found soon after and when asked to account for what had happened she reported that she had been unable to secure permanent accommodation and that her de facto husband had gone to Tasmania, leaving her to cope alone. She said she had panicked and had avoided seeing anyone of authority "for fear of having her child removed when it was born."

Having breached parole for a third time, Beth was again returned to prison. Her child was placed in care, and she was told that if she was ever to regain custody of him she would have to meet a series of onerous conditions. She undertook counseling for her drug use and for the other personal issues that had dogged her during her life. She completed a drug program and, as part of it, a parenting program. She wrote a letter requesting that her re-parole be considered. She reported that her son had been visiting her for an hour a week for a month and a half, but that given the distance he had to be brought to see her, these visits had been reduced to once a fortnight. She offered to continue urine testing post-release and to live with her son in a residential program upon leaving prison. "I am willing to do anything to get my son back," she wrote.

Beth's request for re-parole was denied and she stayed in prison for a further four months. During that time she was visited by housing support workers so that accommodation and support could be arranged for her outside prior to her release. She established a strong rapport with them and spoke of her fear of getting out. She was anxious and distressed about how she was going to cope. The workers had no available houses on their list, and although they continued to visit her until her release they had to refer her to another accommodation agency. Workers from that agency were to collect her from the prison on the morning of her release but, as had happened so often before, she had arranged for friends to pick her up.

This was to be the last time Beth would leave prison. Years before, a prison officer had written, "no doubt she will be seen in the system again, unless she O.D's [*sic*]." Others concurred. The only point of disagreement was whether it would be sooner or later. By the time it finally happened, Beth had been in and out of prison more times than expected. She had tried many times to sort out her life, but every time she had tried the hurdles had become higher and her reasons for having to jump them had become greater. Every time she tried and was unsuccessful her sense of failure and loss increased. On the day of her final release Beth went to St Kilda, shopping with a friend she was planning to live with. They bought groceries and she bought heroin. She had promised not to use that day, but when they returned home late in the afternoon Beth shot up. She quickly lapsed into unconsciousness and was dead by the time the ambulance arrived.

Shared Experiences

Beth's story is not unusual. She is one of more than eighty women who died shortly after being released from Victorian prisons between 1987 and 1997. It is likely that the number of deaths is even higher, but identifying such cases is difficult. More often than not women are hard to trace once they are outside of prison. That is one reason why so little research has been done into the post-release experiences of women prisoners. Women sometimes make themselves deliberately difficult to find. Some move substantial distances to start a new life away from old friends and old lifestyles. They make minimal contact with authorities and support services, preferring to make their own way unassisted and free of supervision. Others maintain contact to varying degrees, but even then it is sometimes not long before they once again become immersed in the lifestyle they know best; one that may at best be unhappy and difficult, and at worst, fraught with problems and dangers.

The workers at Flat Out, a Melbourne post-release accommodation service for women and their children, have long experience in dealing with what they refer to as "post-release trauma."[4] This trauma is manifested in women's anxiety and distress in the days and weeks prior to their release and it can sometimes last for up to a year afterward. Like Beth, women prisoners often express fear about their impending return to the outside world. They are anxious about whether or not they will be able to cope and their fears often dramatically affect their likelihood of achieving a successful transition. Significantly, this trauma is not merely an emotional response to changing circumstances; it is also inextricably related to a recognition of the myriad of personal and practical problems that have to be confronted upon release. This is how Leah, a New South Wales woman, described her experience of release:

> Getting out of jail after a long sentence is scary. You've got this security for so long. The only thing you have to worry about is yourself and surviving. Stealing a celery stick off the kitchen officer was your biggest problem of the day. Then you find yourself on the street with money to think about and decisions to make. I was happy of course to be getting out, but prison had become my life. I'd had six months out in five years and I was really scared of leaving the life I knew and being insecure. After three and a half years, going out to virtually no support was terrifying.[5]

Leah's term of imprisonment was longer than the sentences usually served by women; however, fears such as hers are not uncommon among women leaving prison. Whether they have served long or short sentences, by the time they get to the prison gates few women are prepared adequately for release. Pat Carlen has argued that four "penal ideologies subvert education and pre-release schemes for women in prison." The first she identifies as the "numbers game," which is expressed in the argument that because there are fewer women in prison than men, it is uneconomical to provide them with as many facilities and opportunities as men. A second obstacle, Carlen argues, is the ideology that prisons are for punishment. A third ideology is "being realistic," which is manifested in claims that "prisoners do not want to change" and that they "should not be educated above their station" or "led to believe that life either can or will be better upon release." Finally, she argues that the belief that women are essentially emotional beings, "dependent upon personal relationships to give their lives meaning," is a further ideology that operates to undermine the interests of women prisoners.[6]

Inadequate pre-release schemes and a lack of information in prison about what women can expect on the outside, what assistance is available to them, and how they might access it often paves the way for future problems. Of the eighteen prisoners interviewed by Helen Carnaby for a recent study of the post-release housing and welfare needs of Victorian women prisoners, 78 percent reported that they had not had any information about post-release accommodation made available to them by the prison. Only 40 percent of the women knew about housing agencies and other community services, and what little information they had was gained through conversations with other women.[7] Because of limited resources and the weight of demand, the community housing workers who visit women in prison are generally unable to meet all requests for assistance. Their activities are also constrained by the particularities of the prison regime and by a lack of appropriate facilities in which to interview women. Although it is important for women to establish a trusting relationship while in prison with the workers who are available to assist them after release, time and privacy are limited inside. As one woman commented to Carnaby: "I cannot speak through a pane of glass and I have to yell and everybody hears my personal problems; plus, how can you get to know a person by talking through glass?"[8]

Having accommodation prior to release has been identified as one of the key factors in determining whether or not a woman will successfully survive outside. Most women, even those sentenced to short terms, lose their accommodation once they are imprisoned. Of the eighteen women prisoners interviewed by Carnaby, 77 percent needed to arrange accomodation post-release and all thought they would have trouble doing so.[9] Without the references needed to secure private rental and lacking economic resources, their options are few. With the assistance of housing workers, a small number manage to obtain cheap public housing. Others are put on waiting lists and, in the meantime, are placed in emergency accommodation in refuges, shelters, and hostels.[10] Some return to their parents' home or find space on the floor of a friend's house, often someone they've met in prison. When their presence becomes a burden or the atmosphere intolerable or when their money runs out they usually end up living on the streets. That's what happened to Courtney:

> At one stage I was sleeping in the Fitzroy Park. I slept there for two
> weeks on a bench. And I had the Aboriginals each night. They would
> set up a 44 gallon drum and keep the fire going and someone would sit
> there each night, to make sure I was OK, while I slept. They were fan-

tastic to me, because I had nowhere—I didn't want to stay at Staffa House anymore. That's how bad it had become. I just felt like "If I don't get away from this place I'm going to become claustrophobic—I'm not going to want to leave here ever." So I left and I went to the park and at night time I would lay on the bench and you know one of the Aboriginal guys would sit by me and make sure I was OK, no one [would] come near me, so I could get some sleep and then I'd get up in the morning and I used to get the train to Sunshine, because there was a place in Sunshine where you can have a shower and wash your hair and all that sort of stuff.[11]

For most women, accommodation post-release means more than just having a roof over their head. Of the women interviewed by Carnaby, 77 percent wanted to live independently.[12] After living in such close quarters with other people during their imprisonment, they wanted to be able to establish a home for just themselves, their children, and sometimes their partner. For many, having a home far removed from old associates and localities is an important first step in distancing themselves from their former lives as offenders and prisoners. For most women, however, finding accommodation that is secure and affordable, adequately sized, and suitably located proves difficult, if not impossible. Returning to the familial home is sometimes the only option available to women after release, but often relationships are strained as a consequence of imprisonment and can quickly disintegrate, as Wendy's experiences illustrate:

My mum and dad came and picked me up and it was all wonderful for the first two hours, hugs and kisses and all the rest. They got me home and then I felt like I didn't belong. I felt like I was an outsider. . . . My family talked, or more argued, about my time in jail. I was trying to reach them and trying to explain. I stayed with my dad initially and a couple of nights he almost put me through the wall, the fights got that bad. It was just the fact that I went to jail, and he had to come in and see me. The last time Dad and I had a fight, I just got my gear and left and moved up to Mum's one-bedroom flat and I just slept on the sofa bed for the next 12 months, which didn't do much for my need for

privacy, or Mum's. . . . I walked a lot, to get out of the flat on my own.
I always felt closed in, like my mother always wanted to know where I
was, what I was doing, who I was with, if I was going to be home.[13]

In Victoria, correctional authorities recognize that many women will
return to a violent partner upon release.[14] Feelings of guilt and fear,
together with concern for the welfare of their children, no doubt contribute to this. Numerous studies have indicated that the vast majority of
women who enter prison have previously experienced physical and/or sexual abuse. Those who return to a violent partner after leaving prison often
find themselves trapped, even if alternative accommodation is arranged. As
one Victorian woman recounted: "Flat Out did get me a house after I had
my baby, but the father would not let me leave him as he was very abusive
and held drugs over my head."[15] Another inmate interviewed by Carnaby
spoke of her difficulty in maintaining accommodation for herself and her
children because of her former partner's domineering and violent behavior:

When I left my husband I had to find accommodation for myself, four
kids and a dog. As the children were young the real estate agents did
not want to rent their properties to me and when I did find something
my violent ex-husband would call around and cause problems. The
landlord did not like that.[16]

The paramount goal of women prisoners who are mothers most often
is to reestablish relationships with their children post-release. Although
some prisons may permit women to have babies and young children in residence with them, this possibility is only infrequently pursued because
many women feel that prisons do not provide a suitable environment in
which to raise children. For the vast majority of mothers, imprisonment
therefore entails separation from their children. Indeed, some, like Beth,
have already had children removed from their care prior to imprisonment.
Whether children are cared for by partners, grandparents, other relatives,
friends, or foster parents, the contact they have with their imprisoned
mother is limited to visits. The duration and frequency of these may vary
according to any one of a number of factors. The distance between the
prison and the children's place of residence and the willingness of the care-

givers to bring children for visits and the rules governing particular prisons can all affect how often a mother sees her child.[17] In Victorian prisons, for example, visits from children are regarded as a privilege rather than as a right and can be withdrawn as a penalty for breaches of prison regulations. Having little direct contact with their children and no sure way of knowing how they are faring, most mothers remain deeply concerned over the welfare of their children while they are in custody.

Being reunited with children and attempting to build a new life with them after release can prove difficult, especially for those women who have previously lost custody. The reflections of Kathy, a former Victorian inmate whose parents cared for her daughter during her period of imprisonment, provide an insight into the bureaucratic, practical, and emotional hurdles that mothers leaving prison often have to jump if they are to reestablish their family.

> The pressure starts to build once women are released. The system we have now has set up women with problems especially single mothers to fail as mothers. Firstly, there is the pressure of being away from your children and all the associated problems. Then there is the proving of yourself to Office of Corrections, Community Services of Victoria, the court system in order to regain custody, as well as maintaining yourself financially and setting up a home again, in many cases starting from scratch! Then, when and if you regain custody, there is more pressure dealing with your children's problems, anger and confusion at your absence. All this with virtually no support and a Social Security allowance that just isn't enough.[18]

Securing an adequate level of income presents a major obstacle for women post-release regardless of whether or not they have children. When women leave prison in Victoria, for example, they receive any money they may have accrued while working in prison, which is usually only a small sum, and are eligible to receive a special benefit that is equivalent to two weeks of Social Security payment. The following fortnight they can expect to receive only half of a regular payment. When women are released on the weekend, the Social Security offices and banks that they need to call upon to claim and cash their benefit are closed and they have to wait until the next working day. Problems relating to identification, coupled with the discriminatory attitudes of some bank and Social Security staff can also make obtaining an immediate payment difficult.[19]

This money represents the largest sum that women leaving prison are likely to have in the near future and it is rarely enough to cover reestablishment costs. Bond and rent in advance, food, and clothing are just a few of the essentials that have to be paid for. Those women seeking to overcome a drug addiction might also need to purchase methadone. And then there is also the need for women to replace necessary items that they may once have owned but lost during their imprisonment.[20] When Victorian women leave prison, their possessions are given to them in a plastic garbage bag; for most, it contains all that they own. As one former New South Wales prisoner observed:

> When a judge sentences you to a period of imprisonment, he/she also effectively sentences you to lose all or most of your possessions, and all or most of your friends. What happens is this. Your friends "look after" your possessions for you while you're in jail. They forget about you coming back and wanting your goods again. They decide to use your things, sometimes breaking them or even giving them away to other people. They justify this in their minds somehow. Then they hear that you're out and realise that you will probably want your things back. They're often embarrassed about what they've done with them, and so they'd rather not see you to explain it, or they put it off for a long time. Either way they avoid you and the explanation you're going to want. So you lose both ways.[21]

For most women who leave prison, even the easiest things can prove difficult. Many feel disoriented and marked, as Cara did:

> I really felt like an outsider. I also felt I had "criminal" tattooed on my forehead, for the whole world to see. And I was very self-conscious. I had no confidence in myself at all. The whole thing was just horrible, even crossing the road was difficult.[22]

Shopping, catching public transport, speaking with people, even simply being in public are acts that many women find hard to negotiate after release.

Seeking and securing employment, of course, is even harder. Most women prisoners have had little education and lack the skills needed to secure employment.[23] Although women are less likely than men to have been employed prior to their imprisonment, while they are in prison they are generally afforded fewer opportunities for educational and vocational training than their male counterparts. Upon release, even those with skills have to contend with their status as ex-prisoners. Some women try to keep their past hidden by inventing work histories or other explanations about why they have not been recently employed. Those on parole, however, often have little choice but to inform employers of their past. As Elizabeth recalled:

> I received no help from Probation and Parole only the restriction of being forced to tell any future employer I'd just served two years for misappropriation. Can a member of the public really understand what it's like to try for a position of bookkeeper—know you've got the job and then have to blow it all by saying you're on parole for what crime?[24]

Women who are paroled from prison often report that the conditions they have to meet are needlessly onerous and indeed hinder them from attending to their most immediate needs. In addition to having to meet regularly with their parole officer, women may be required to undertake programs of various sorts or to engage in some form of community work. Leah, who like many women prisoners had been sexually abused as a child and had later turned to drugs, found that while she was in prison and on parole she had not had the opportunity to receive effective counseling in relation to either of these issues. She is not unusual in asserting that punishment and control rather than positive support and care informed her treatment. Like many women, she found her parole officer often to be more concerned with bureaucratic matters than her welfare, and when she did display interest it was rarely positive:

> The first parole officer I had wouldn't believe that I wasn't using. She used to tell the woman I lived with that I was probably using and that she should lock up her jewellery. I was doing nothing wrong. I was going to work and doing everything right. One day, after the parole officer hassled me to admit I was using, I finally said, "Well, as a matter of fact, I do feel like using." Then she looked really happy.[25]

Many women consider parole to be simply an extension of their imprisonment, but in some ways its conditions are even more difficult to comply with. There are numerous problems and demands that have to be confronted outside of prison and there is always the opportunity to escape or to simply give up. One women described her failure to meet her parole conditions in this way:

> Parole was like a mini jail. I was working, attending group therapy, doing community work, and seeing my parole officer. I didn't have a spare moment. I lasted six months and went back to my friends at St Kilda.[26]

For some women, the resumption of old habits occurs sooner rather than later, as was the case for this woman:

> I remember when I went to jail the first time I was going in for a month or two months and when you got out they would give you a $56 social security cheque or something like that, and basically it wasn't enough to do anything with bar go and score. And then it was just back on the street, you know, surviving from there, because getting out with $50 and having to think about buying clothes and accommodation and getting a job — $50 was not enough. So the other outlet was just to go and score.[27]

Despite prohibitionist policies aimed at creating "drug-free" prisons, it is clear that even during incarceration most women are never far removed from drugs. In Victoria, most women who enter prison have an existing drug dependency and are faced with the prospect of immediate withdrawal. Similarly, women on methadone are withdrawn rapidly from this treatment if sentenced to longer than three months imprisonment. Strip-searching and urinalysis constitute the main mechanisms used to control illicit drug use in Victoria's women's prisons. In 1996 it was revealed that during 1994 and 1995, 13,752 strip-searches had been conducted at Fairlea Women's Prison, which at that time had a daily population of only around 100 inmates.[28]

Strip-searching has long been identified by prisoners, activists, and researchers as a highly intrusive and humiliating experience for women, especially for those who have prior histories of sexual abuse.[29] In addition to this, however, such practices fail to stem the flow of drugs into prisons and together with a lack of adequate drug treatment programs create an environment that is in fact conducive to illicit drug-taking and risky behavior. Of the women prisoners interviewed for a 1994 study into the drug use of Victorian women prisoners, for example, 41 percent reported that they had shared needles in prison and 68 percent stated that they had taken "pills," smoked dope, or used other drugs while incarcerated.[30]

In prison, prescription drugs also often take the place of illicit drugs. Some women use them as a replacement when other substances on which they are dependent are unavailable. Some use them to ward off the effects of withdrawal, while others, who may never have had a drug dependency, begin using prescription drugs as a means of alleviating stress.[31] At Fairlea Women's Prison in late 1995, 365 doses of prescription drugs were being dispensed daily to the eighty-seven women imprisoned there. Tranquilizers and psychotropic drugs were the most frequently dispensed.[32] Such extensive use of prescription drugs stands in stark contrast to the policy of "drug-free" prisons. In Victoria as elsewhere, the overprescribing of drugs in women's prisons has been linked to the perception that women prisoners are emotionally unstable and particularly difficult to manage. Their use has frequently been identified as another form of control exercised over the lives of women prisoners.[33]

By the time most women are released from prison, their susceptibility to drug use has not diminished. In some cases it has merely been intensified. It is therefore not surprising that drug overdose, usually involving heroin in combination with prescription drugs, is the most common cause of death among women who leave prison. This is particularly so for the numerous women who die within thirty hours of being released. For most of those who survive, however, every day remains a struggle until such time as they can establish some degree of power over their lives. After imprisonment, gaining any semblance of dignity and control can be almost impossible. Courtney's experiences illustrate how hard it can be:

> I had my daughter in '84 and I didn't use for three years. And then
> when I started three years later within six months I'd lost my house, my

car, my savings and I lost her and I was in jail. And then it was just a downhill spiral, there was nothing for me at all. And I was just so completely depressed that I could not talk—if someone tried to talk to me I would just get so emotionally overwrought that I just couldn't stop crying and the crying would go [on] for hours and hours and hours. And it got to the stage that with all . . . the crying and the using I was sleeping sometimes from like ten o'clock in the morning till like ten o'clock at night till ten o'clock the next night and it was really really bad. And then I started using pills. Started using roies and serapax and valium and basically before I woke up—when I woke up I would have to take 25 rohipnol, 25 serapax to be able to get up, out of bed.[34]

A Continuum of Control and Neglect

Women's post-release experiences can best be understood as composing one stage on a continuum of control and neglect. As prisoner profiles have long shown, women who go to prison are among society's most disadvantaged. They tend to come from backgrounds of poverty, have low levels of education, few skills to equip them for employment, and many are single mothers. The vast majority have prior histories of sexual and physical abuse and most have been or are drug dependent. All but a small minority of women are sentenced to short periods of imprisonment for minor offenses.

While women are in prison, their lives are disrupted and they are further disempowered. Margaret, a former prisoner, describes the process:

When one enters jail a process of dispossession and disempowerment occurs. You are separated from family, lovers and friends. You are separated from all your possessions. . . . you are in a state of shock with total loss of privacy and dignity. . . . The plan is to crush the inmate's spirit. Eventually most prisoners lose the ability to initiate action. This is at odds with the expectation that prisoners will manifest the initiative to recreate their lives after release. You are nobody and your needs are immaterial.[35]

Within prisons, the problems and circumstances that have often contributed to women's offending are rarely dealt with; indeed, they are often exacerbated. Rather than being assisted or supported, women in prison are punished and then spat out into a world that once again neglects them. If they return to prison, it is usually seen as their fault. After all, they must have been "bad" women to have ended up in prison in the first place.

In 1991, Bev Fabb, then the Uniting Church chaplain for women prisoners in Victoria, conducted a small survey of women's post-release experiences. She interviewed twelve women; of these only three had not returned to prison. These three women had a number of things in common. All had left prison with adequate identification and had secured their initial and subsequent Social Security payments without difficulty. All had managed to secure accommodation, had made no contact with other ex-prisoners, and had at least one or two people on whom they could rely for support. In addition, they were all well integrated into local community services.

This list may not represent all of the requirements that all women need to successfully reestablish themselves after imprisonment; however, it does highlight how simple things can make a difference. Unfortunately, though, most women who leave prison today still have difficulty securing even these. Because the number of imprisoned women is increasing dramatically and, at the same time, welfare and community services are being cut back, it seems likely that in the future even more women will find themselves trapped in this cycle of control and neglect; one that renders them suspect and vulnerable. As Mary Eaton has observed, the woman who leaves prison

> is a prisoner and she brings this knowledge, this identity out into the world. The prison experience will affect her response to the outside world, the prison record will affect the response of others to her. When she comes out she brings something of the prison with her. . . . As Fran [a former prisoner] put it: "You can never leave prison, because prison never leaves you."[36]

NOTES

1. Quoted in Fitzroy Legal Service, "Women and Imprisonment: Submission to the Social Development Committee into Community Violence," (Fitzroy, Victoria: Fitzroy Legal Service, 1988), 36.

2. For a fuller discussion of this specific issue see Susanne Davies and Sandy Cook, "Women, Imprisonment and Post-Release Mortality." *Just Policy* no. 14 (1998): 15-21.

3. This case study has been compiled through reference to official records and interviews with community workers who knew Beth. A psuedonym has been used in order to preserve her anonymity. All quotes included in this case study have been derived from documents written either by Beth or workers who knew her.

4. Special thanks to Helen Carnaby of Flat Out for introducing this term to us and allowing us to make use of it in this chapter. Her knowledge, together with that of her coworkers Karen Taylor and Dallas Taylor, has been invaluable to us in learning about women's post-release experiences.

5. Leah, quoted in Blanche Hampton, *Prisons and Women* (Kensington: New South Wales University Press, 1993), 171.

6. Pat Carlen, *Alternatives to Women's Imprisonment* (Buckingham: Open University Press, 1990), 36–38.

7. Helen Carnaby, *Road to Nowhere: A Report of Women's Housing and Support Needs When Leaving Prison* (Collingwood: Flat Out, 1998), 49.

8. A 43-year-old ex-prisoner quoted in Helen Carnaby, *Road to Nowhere,* 50.

9. Ibid., 58.

10. For a discussion of the accommodation difficulties confronted by women ex-prisoners in England see Pat Carlen, *Alternatives to Women's Imprisonment,* 40–70.

11. Interview with "Courtney" (pseudonym), a former inmate of a Victorian women's prison, September 1998.

12. Carnaby, *Road to Nowhere,* 59.

13. Wendy, quoted in Blanche Hampton, *Prisons and Women,* 180–81.

14. Department of Justice, *The Victorian Prison Service in 1995* (Melbourne: Department of Justice, 1996), 48.

15. Quoted in Carnaby, *Road to Nowhere,* 65.

16. Ibid.

17. For a personal account of the difficulties associated with maintaining mother-child relationships during imprisonment see Kathy, "Women and Children in Custody," in *Women and Imprisonment,* ed. Women and Imprisonment Group (Fitzroy, Victoria: Fitzroy Legal Service, 1995), 100–102.

18. Kathy, "Women and Children in Custody," 103.

19. Carnaby, *Road to Nowhere,* 70–71.

20. Elaine Genders and Elaine Player, "Women in Prison: The Treatment, the Control and the Experience," in *Gender, Crime, and Justice,* ed. Pat Carlen and Anne Worrall (Milton Keynes: Open University Press, 1987), 169–70.

21. Blanche, quoted in Blanche Hampton, *Prisons and Women,* 161–62.

22. Cara, quoted in Mary Eaton, *Women after Prison* (Buckingham: Open University Press, 1993), 57.

23. Ibid., 71.

24. Elizabeth, quoted in Blanche Hampton, *Prisons and Women,* 170.

25. Leah, quoted in ibid., 173.

26. Quoted in Bev Fabb, "Post Release: Female Prisoners' Experience," in *Women and Imprisonment,* ed. Women and Imprisonment Group (Melbourne: Fitzroy Legal Service, 1995), 121.

27. Thirty-eight-year-old ex-prisoner quoted in Carnaby, *Road to Nowhere,* 71.

28. Davies and Cook, "Women, Imprisonment and Post-Release Mortality," 19.

29. Amanda George, "Sexual Assault by the State," *Alternative Law Journal* 18, no. 1 (1993), 31–33; Stella Simmering and Ruby Diamond, "Strip Searching and Urine Testing: Women in Prison," in *Legalizing Justice for All Women: National Conference on Sexual Assault and the Law,* comp. by Melanie Heenan (Melbourne: Project for Action Against Sexual Assault, 1996), 277–81.

30. Barbara Denton, *Prisons, Drugs and Women: Voices from Below* (Canberra: Government Publishing Service, 1994), 45.

31. Ibid., 51.

32. Davies and Cook, "Women, Imprisonment and Post-Release Mortality," 19.

33. Carol Major, "Women in Prison: A Cycle of Punishment and Sedation," *Connexions* (May/June 1993): 3–7; Francine Pinnuck, "The Medication of Women in Prison: A Cause for Concern," *Just Policy* no. 12 (1998): 13–19.

34. Interview with "Courtney," September 1998.

35. Margaret, quoted in Carnaby, *Road to Nowhere,* 12.

36. Eaton, *Women after Prison,* 56.

REFERENCES

Carlen, Pat. *Alternatives to Women's Imprisonment.* Buckingham: Open University Press, 1990.

Carnaby, Helen. *Road to Nowhere: A Report on Women's Housing and Support Needs When Leaving Prison.* Collingwood: Flat Out Inc., 1998.

Davies, Susanne, and Sandy Cook. "Women, Imprisonment and Post-Release Mortality," *Just Policy* no. 14 (1998): 15–21.

Denton, Barbara. *Prisons, Drugs and Women: Voices from Below.* Canberra: Government Publishing Service, 1994.

Department of Justice. *The Victorian Prison Service in 1995.* Melbourne: Department of Justice, 1996.

Eaton, Mary. *Women after Prison.* Buckingham: Open University Press, 1993.

Fabb, Bev. "Post Release: Female Prisoners' Experiences." In *Women and Imprisonment,* edited by Women and Imprisonment Group. Melbourne: Fitzroy Legal Service, 1995.

Fitzroy Legal Service. "Women and Imprisonment: Submission to the Social Development Committee into Community Violence." Melbourne: Fitzroy Legal Service, 1988.

Genders, Elaine, and Elaine Player. "Women in Prison: The Treatment, the Control and the Experience." In *Gender, Crime and Justice,* edited by Pat Carlen and Anne Worrall. Milton Keynes: Open University Press, 1987.

George, Amanda. "Sexual Assault by the State." *Alternative Law Journal* 18, no. 1 (1993): 31-33.

Hampton, Blanche. *Prison and Women.* Kensington: New South Wales University Press, 1993.

Kathy. "Women and Children in Custody." In *Women and Imprisonment,* edited by Women and Imprisonment Group. Melbourne: Fitzroy Legal Service, 1995.

Major, Carol. "Women in Prison: A Cycle of Punishment and Sedation." *Connexions* (May/June 1993): 3-7.

Pinnuck, Francine. "The Medication of Women in Prison: A Cause for Concern." *Just Policy* no. 12 (1998): 13-19.

Simmering, Stella, and Ruby Diamond. "Strip Searching and Urine Testing: Women in Prison." In *Legalizing Justice for All Women: National Conference on Sexual Assault and the Law,* compiled by Melanie Heenan. Melbourne: Project for Action Against Sexual Assault, 1996: 277-81.

Diminishing Opportunities
Researching Women's Imprisonment

Cherry Grimwade

Introduction

SINCE THE LATE 1970S, feminist criminological research and literature has focused attention on women's offending, their treatment by criminal justice systems, and on women's experiences and understandings of these. While the gap in our understanding of women's experiences of imprisonment seems to be narrowing, there has, however, been very little attention paid to the considerable difficulties associated with undertaking research in this field. The difficulties associated with researching women's imprisonment, both in Australia and overseas, are often not explicitly raised in the literature, being either glossed over in methodological discussions or hidden away in footnotes and appendices. In fact, it is rare to find in-depth descriptions and discussions of the methodological problems, ethical pitfalls, political battles, and personal dilemmas involved in actually carrying out such research. A reason for this absence may well be that dominant research paradigms have traditionally viewed descriptions of difficulties in the field as "unscientific" and "subjective" accounts that are inappropriate, trivial, or secondary to the research itself.[1] An even more immediate reason may be that in today's politically volatile climate it might be considered dangerous to commit accounts of the difficulties associated with research to hard copy because their public expression may potentially jeopardize existing or future research.[2]

Alternative inquiry paradigms, particularly those informed by feminism, argue that the difficulties associated with particular qualitative and quantitative research methodologies are integral to and inform the process of research.[3] Indeed, feminist criminologists have argued that these difficulties have profound implications for the way research into women's imprisonment is designed and implemented and its research findings disseminated.[4] For these reasons, it is important to begin to collectively identify and examine some of the difficulties and dilemmas faced worldwide by researchers in this field.

This chapter has two aims. The first is to identify and examine some of the persistent methodological and practical problems that have previously been identified by Australian and international independent academic and community-based researchers undertaking research into women's imprisonment. The second is to focus attention on the new difficulties facing researchers in Australia today as a result of the changing social, economic, and political climate of economic rationalism and privatization. Australia is used in this discussion as an example of recent international trends. In Australia, as in other Western nations, opportunities to research women's imprisonment have been dramatically limited and constrained by the changing culture and resources of universities and funding bodies and the power and policies of governments and private institutions. In particular, the context of economic rationalism in Australia has limited the funding for both community and academic research into women's imprisonment and has challenged the independence of research by limiting who can research, the issues that can be canvassed, and the manner in which findings can be disseminated. Similarly, the privatization of prisons has had serious implications for researchers; it is becoming increasingly difficult to gain approval to undertake research and to gain access to prison facilities and to information. While this chapter is by no means exhaustive, it attempts to identify recurring issues and recent trends in relation to researching women's imprisonment and, moreover, offers an initial insight into how these factors may affect the nature and direction of independent research in the future.

The Difficulties of Negotiating Access and Gaining Trust

In comparison to men, women constitute a significantly smaller proportion of the general prison population, both in Australia and overseas.[5] Therefore, one of the inevitable difficulties of undertaking research into women's imprisonment is that access is more constrained and is limited by the fact that there are fewer women in prison and that there are fewer correctional facilities for women than there are for men. Because men make up a much larger proportion of the prison population and are more visible, the perception is that male prisoners are much more in need of research than their female counterparts. Undertaking research in order to redress the dearth of knowledge and understanding of issues relating to women's imprisonment means confronting and challenging the strong patriarchal and positivistic tradition in the fields of criminology and corrections. This tradition has viewed women's experiences, understandings, politics, writing, and research as peripheral to "real" issues. Consequently, difficulties associated with research into women's imprisonment are exacerbated by the institutionalized ideologies that have directly contributed to the marginalized and neglected status of women prisoners.

One of the major obstacles to research that is frequently discussed in the literature concerns the process of negotiating access. As researchers both in Australia and overseas have highlighted, this involves dealing with the formal access procedures of government agencies, correctional authorities, or corporate representatives that are intended to determine whether research is acceptable in terms of its methodological design, political ideology, rationale, significance, and ethics. A key challenge facing most researchers is the necessity to mediate through the needs, resources, roles, and agendas of these agencies and authorities to obtain the access necessary to carry out research. As gatekeepers, these agencies tend to be protective of their institutions and practices and are often unwilling to approve particular research unless certain conditions are met. As British criminologist Alison Liebling notes, gaining approval to conduct research into male and female youth suicide at juvenile institutions in England and Wales involved submitting detailed application forms to the British Home Office and subsequently engaging in lengthy negotiations. As she describes it, this process was "time-consuming, difficult," and entailed an "anxiety of uncertainty" because the research proposal was subjected to intensive scrutiny. She notes that this process culminated in "several serious constraints" being imposed on the research, including that the fieldwork be restricted to four young-offender institutions chosen by the Home Office.[6]

The difficulties involved in negotiating access to prisons and prisoners have also been discussed by researchers in Australia. Patricia Easteal, for example, had to obtain permission from the relevant state government departments in Victoria, Queensland, and New South Wales before her research into overseas-born women in prisons could be conducted.[7] Easteal found that the process of negotiating access and the degree of cooperation she was given varied from state to state and from prison to prison. Not surprisingly, she characterizes this process as "a struggle through a bureaucratic maze" of approval procedures, communication difficulties, and frustration engendered by the inertia of prison administration.[8] Australian project worker Helen Carnaby also encountered difficulties gaining access from government authorities to undertake her community-based needs study into women leaving prison in Victoria. As Carnaby notes, the process involved time-consuming negotiations with two separate government departments over the study design. Access was finally granted after several modifications were made to the research methodology.[9]

These accounts reveal how the process of negotiating access can raise very thorny and complex questions concerning the independence of research. On the one hand, researchers require the approval and cooperation of correctional authorities and prison management in order to carry out research. However, these authorities are often highly suspicious of, or averse to, research that examines their institutions and practices. Research that closely relates to the needs, goals, and agendas of particular government correctional authorities may be more likely to be approved than research that questions or is critical of current correctional policies and practices. Furthermore, because of the traditional approach to research adopted by most correctional authorities, research paradigms based on quantitative methods, such as surveys and statistical analyses, may be seen as more legitimate and acceptable than research paradigms that adopt qualitative methods, such as participant observation, in-depth interviews, or case studies.[10] Gaining the approval of correctional authorities may mean that constraints and limitations are placed on the research and that the original research design and methodology may have to be revised or reoriented to meet the demands of correctional authorities.

Even when approval has been granted and the researcher is finally through the prison gates, numerous difficulties are associated with gaining the trust of prison staff and women prisoners. Their trust is crucial to effectively carry out research, but it can be difficult to earn. For those entering prison as an "outsider," practical problems may stem from a lack of familiarity with the prison regime in terms of its organizational structure, layout, security regulations, shift patterns, rules, and patterns of behavior. Outsiders usually also have to contend with suspicion, curiosity, and hostility and may be viewed as intruding on the daily organization and management of the prison.[11] The initial period of being new to a prison may involve a difficult period of testing out by both prison staff and prisoners. Liebling, for example, describes how she had to prove herself able to cope with the daily routine of prison life. She found that "staff were impressed by long working hours, early starts, participation, good listening and low pay" and "did not like early finishes, any exclusive concern for the inmates, women in trousers, being left out, criticism, strangers with keys, demanding non-strangers without keys and strangers going to lunch with the governor grades."[12] Similarly, Australian researcher Barbara Denton found that gaining the acceptance of staff and prisoners in order to carry out research into women's participation in the illicit drug economy in Victoria meant being aware of how demeanor and dress signified particular roles and statuses within the prison.[13]

The Difficulties of the Research Role

Research in any prison involves an understanding of its culture, including its hierarchical organization of power and control, rules of behavior, and codes of secrecy. It also involves being acutely aware of how prison management, prison staff, and prisoners may view the researcher's role, both in relation to the actual research and within the prison. Being an outsider, however, may confound understanding and interpretation of the researcher's role and position. This is aptly highlighted by Lorraine Gelsthorpe's discussion of the problems she experienced while undertaking research into the humane containment of prisoners in the United Kingdom.[14] For Gelsthorpe, being an outside researcher meant being seen as a government "spy" or as a "trainee governor, representative of the board of visitors or magistrate spending a day in prison."[15] Even "the term 'researcher' created some confusion in that it was often taken to mean 'psychological tester.'"[16] The problem of misidentification and confusion may necessitate continual explanations and justification of the research and of the researcher's role.

The researcher's role almost invariably entails significant ethical and personal considerations. Indeed, accounts of research frequently touch on the difficulties associated with deep personal involvement, role conflicts, and levels of immersion. Although these dilemmas vary depending on the nature of the research, the method of data collection, and the context of the prison setting, they reveal the complexities and moral ambivalences that confront researchers in the field. As U.S. writer Beth Richie's experience illustrates, her role as a researcher and prison advocate caused concern when she found herself involved in particular cases. She explains: "[T]he nature of the data collection process that enabled me to use myself and my experiences to be close to the women I interviewed also posed a series of dilemmas for my role as researcher."[17] Ritchie experienced ethical conflicts between her two roles and faced difficulties in remaining detached from women's life stories and custodial outcomes.

Similarly, Liebling's list of "don'ts" summarizes her dilemmas: "[D]on't get involved, don't take sides, express opinion, breach confidences or react to very much at all."[18] For Liebling, the aftereffect of long communications and informal contact with inmates meant that she became personally affected by their actions and had an increased desire to intervene in situations in which particular inmates were experiencing depression or feelings of hopelessness.[19] Likewise, Australian researcher Margaret D'Arcy describes how her personal reaction to the horror of the stories of women prisoners and the way in which women described their lives often interrupted her ability to effectively carry out research.[20] These accounts highlight the way in which women's experiences of imprisonment often confront and conflict with the personal values and perspectives of those conducting research in ways that may be emotionally difficult and distressing.

Even more important, the research process may also have a significant impact on the lives and experiences of women in prison. For women inmates, expressing feelings and opinions or recounting particular experiences may be personally disturbing, emotionally harrowing, and/or dangerous given the disciplined nature of prison settings. A key challenge for the researcher, then, is to be aware of and understand the sensitivities and risks that are involved. Invariably a number of ethical issues such as privacy, confidentiality, individual rights and obligations, minimization of harm, and the safety of individuals are raised throughout the research process. In fact, even when they are aware of these issues, researchers frequently describe how the prison setting heightens potential ethical difficulties. For example, a common problem repeatedly discussed in both the Australian and international literature concerns the general lack of privacy in the prison setting. Researchers frequently speak of the difficulties that were involved in trying to find a suitable place in the prison that afforded a level of privacy and quietness conducive to effective research and to the confidentiality and safety of participants.[21] This ethical dilemma may be further exacerbated if, as Helen Carnaby experienced, there is uncertainty as to the placement of security devices in the prison, and hence a possibility that conversations can be overheard.[22] Although the major safeguard against the invasion of privacy is the assurance of confidentiality, this may be very difficult to guarantee given the reality of the prison setting.

Unofficial and Official Information: Whose Truth?

A majority of the Australian and international research on women's imprisonment has been based on methodological triangulation,[23] that is, the use of a range of quantitative and qualitative research methods that includes interviewing, surveying via questionnaires, participant observation, statistical analyses of documentary material, or the compilation of case studies. Triangulation has been frequently described as an approach that improves validity and reliability, provides a depth of meaning to data, and allows for multiple perspectives to be examined.[24] Although this approach does have numerous advantages, it also poses several methodological and practical difficulties. There may be practical difficulties in obtaining official documents and, as Liebling highlights, this material may be incomplete, incorrect, or contain contradictory information.[25] As Gelsthorpe argues, official documents and information need to be used carefully because they are not "objective" accounts but socially constructed discourses that are the result of particular social and political processes. She warns that although these documents may generate useful data, an uncritical acceptance of and reliance on this information may mean that the researcher's perceptions and ideas of women prisoners are colored or biased.[26] Using this information to inform the research may involve painstaking and time-consuming validity checks to ensure the reliability of data.

"Official" information may also contradict actual events, practices, or information gained from prison management, staff, and/or women prisoners themselves. There may be problems interpreting information and continually having to verify or nullify particular assertions. In addition, Gelsthorpe warns that "informants may consciously and unconsciously distort or conceal information from the interviewer,"[27] especially if information is going to be used in some "official" way. Deciphering the question of truth is a vexed one, given that prisons involve an array of actors who occupy different social, economic, and political positions and who in turn may have very different perspectives, opinions, and experiences of the prison. Information may vary between prison staff and women prisoners and may not, as Liebling highlights, be consistent with particular actions or real events.[28] In fact, Easteal even goes so far as to warn researchers not to entirely trust versions about the prison system offered by women prisoners and to be aware of the "potential game of conning the researcher."[29] Although this statement does highlight the dilemmas involved, it fails to address the reasons why women inmates may not be inclined to be truthful in some situations. The power differentials that operate within prison are such that women inmates may not always be willing to divulge certain "truths" about their experiences of imprisonment or be frank about particular events or practices within the prison because it may have dangerous or uncertain consequences.[30] The context of imprisonment promotes a certain degree of game-playing by a number of actors, including correctional management, prison staff, and inmates. Therefore, the vexed question of "truth" is often less about the honesty and sincerity of individuals and more about imprisonment and its effects. Nevertheless, the problem of validity and reliability does create innumerable problems for researchers.

The Australian Experience—The Land of Opportunity?

Over the last decade, Australian and international researchers undertaking research into women's imprisonment have faced a number of complex

practical and methodological difficulties. Some of these are of course peculiar to the social, economic, and political context of the prison setting;
however, others are pertinent to the nature of research. Today, Australian
and international researchers also face a new set of difficulties as a result of
worldwide economic, social, and political developments brought about by
economic rationalism and mass privatization. This section examines some
of the new difficulties faced by Australian researchers in particular and
serves as an example of the recent trends taking place in research today.

Australia, like other Western countries, has undergone significant
social, economic, and political change in the last decade. The liberal ideology of economic rationalism has led to major economic reforms that rely
on the policies of privatization, corporatization, and contractualization.
Economic rationalism has led to a modern reinvention of government,
whereby the notion of the contract pervades the economic and political
landscape.[31] One of the key characteristics of this change in Australia has
been the massive restructuring of the public sector and the sale of government enterprises and assets. The promise of "greater efficiency, higher economic growth and increased employment opportunities for the economy as
a whole"[32] have coincided with extensive cutbacks to community-based
services, education, and health and the downsizing of both private and
public sectors.[33] The emergence of the modern contract state has also had
serious implications for the concept and mechanisms of government
accountability and notions of public interest.[34]

One of the key instruments of economic reform in Australia has been
the move toward privatization. Although in Australia the involvement of
commercial interests in the criminal justice system is not new, the move
toward the privatization of prisons has been a relatively recent phenomenon. A striking feature of the Australian experience of private prisons has
been the unprecedented speed at which they have been introduced. Australia was the second country to establish privately run prisons and today it
has the highest proportion of its prisoners housed in private prisons in the
world. Furthermore, the Metropolitan Women's Correctional Centre in
Victoria was the first private women's prison to be established outside the
United States.[35] The introduction of private prisons in Australia has been
met with considerable criticism and debate. Concerns have been raised by

academics, researchers, and prison activists about the social, legal, ethical, and practical consequences of private involvement in correctional institutions and questions have been asked about how, when, and by whom private prisons will be evaluated.[36] As prison activists Catherine Gow and Donna Williamson explain, the magnitude of concern has been such that prison activism and community education is now focused on publicly exposing and debating issues relating to the management of private prisons rather than on the plight of those incarcerated within them.[37] In fact, the manner in which these drastic changes to penal policy have taken place have been characterized by former Australian Law Reform Commissioner George Zdenkowski as both "arrogant and breathtaking."[38] In effect, privatization of prisons has been introduced with little public debate or community input or the establishment of effective regulatory mechanisms.[39]

An Era of Diminishing Resources—The Problem of Funding

One of the most significant obstacles for independent research into women's imprisonment, and social science research in general, concerns the issue of funding. As a consequence of economic and political change, the last decade in Australia has been characterized as "an era of diminishing resources."[40] In the past, funding for research could be obtained through state and federal government departments and agencies. Now, however, the level of government activity and funding for social science research has been dramatically reduced. In fact, the situation was recently described in the Australian Research Council's[41] review of research into social science funding as "unparalleled in the last two decades in the lack of support of federal government departments outside the education sector for social science research and researchers outside or within their departments."[42] In addition to cuts to direct funding, government activities such as "in-house" research and the outsourcing of research to universities and private consultants have also decreased significantly over the last few years.[43]

The effect of government cuts to the operating grants and funds of universities has also had a significant effect on the availability of resources for research. The recent 1998 federal budget reductions to university operating grants have further exacerbated the need for universities to compete in the marketplace for funds. Job losses, department closures, crowded lecture theaters and cuts to research are now becoming commonplace across universities in Australia.[44] The possibility of further budget cuts to university research over the next three years will mean that the issue of resources for research will become increasingly important.[45] Given that traditional sources of research funds are fast becoming extinct, there is now an increased reliance on alternative funding bodies. The Australian Research Council (ARC) remains the predominant funding body for social science research in Australia. However, in 1995 only 16 percent of ARC funding went to social science research. Competition for research grants was extremely high and with a "lower than 20 per cent success rate" a large majority of research projects went unfunded by the ARC.[46] Similarly, in 1996–1997 the Criminology Research Council funded only five new research grants and one research consultancy.[47] In the same year, a budget reduction of one-third meant that the Australian Institute of Criminology withdrew three research positions and outsourced particular services.[48]

Whereas once researchers could expect to rely on government, university, or alternative funding bodies, the onerous task of fighting for scarce resources is now fast becoming the norm. With respect to researching women's imprisonment, this problem is further exacerbated by the fact that government departments and funding bodies tend to fund research that meets strict government policy directives, uses specific inquiry paradigms,[49] or raises further revenue and funds.[50] Universities and research institutions may exclude support and funding for research on topics that they may consider to be sensitive, unpopular, unimportant, or detrimental to their interests. In today's political and economic climate, universities and funding bodies may also be reluctant to support research that may be critical of government practices and policies, especially if their survival depends on government revenue. The perception that one is aligned with, or supportive of, research that is critical of government practices and policies may have very serious financial ramifications.

It has always been difficult to secure funding for research into women's imprisonment; however, in an era of diminishing resources finding funding is now increasingly arduous for a number of significant reasons. First, because the number of women imprisoned is small compared to the number of imprisoned men, women are often invisible within prison systems. Second, the ideology of sexism that pervades governments and correctional institutions operates in such a way that women's experiences of imprisonment and their specific needs and concerns are not taken seriously. Consequently, issues relating to the correctional treatment of women rarely appear on the social and political agenda. In a context of drastic government cutbacks, it is viewed as much more financially viable to research issues relating to the much larger male prison population and to extrapolate findings to include women rather than to examine issues specific to women's imprisonment. Trying to secure government funding for research into women's imprisonment is usually met with the question: "But why not men?" In today's context of economic pragmatism, research into women's imprisonment is viewed as an unnecessary waste of money and resources. Furthermore, in a climate of considerable public debate and community criticism over the privatization of women's prisons, independent research into women's imprisonment is looked upon as extremely suspicious and politically volatile.

Conflict of Interest: The Fate of Independent Research

Securing funding and approval for research into imprisonment is now also complicated by the fact that in the context of privatization there is an increasing number of "interested parties." These include politicians, government correctional authorities, private contractors, and prison management. All of these parties operate according to very different political, economic, and social agendas and inevitably draw conflicting opinions and conclusions about the significance and need for research. The potential for conflict between interested parties is a problem that Australian prison researcher Paul Moyle encountered with regard to his research at Borallon, a private prison for men in Queensland. [51] For Moyle, obtaining financial assistance and approval to conduct research involved dealing with two distinct organizations: the Queensland Corrective Services Commission (QCSC) and the Corrections Corporation of Australia (CCAust), the private contractor. [52] Both of these organizations had very different roles and agendas and gaining approval to conduct research at Borallon involved practical difficulties and legislative restrictions. Moyle's experience in Queensland in the early 1990s highlighted the unresolved issue of whether the decision to approve independent research in a private prison should lie with a public authority or the private contractor, or both.[53]

Given the array of parties now involved and the difficulties involved in securing funding and approval for prison research it is becoming increasingly hard to claim the "independence" of any research. Moyle and others have argued that it is important to maintain independence from correctional authorities and private corporations in order to effectively evaluate the privately contracted management of prisons.[54] However, this may be extremely difficult because researchers need the cooperation and approval of those whose programs are being evaluated and government correctional departments and private companies are highly suspicious of "independent" researchers. In fact, as Moyle notes, in an environment in which companies are competing for market shares in the criminal justice system "academics are seen to be meddling, perhaps even hindering, the economic expansion of companies."[55] Furthermore, because the emphasis in evaluating private prisons tends to be directed toward economic cost-benefit analyses,[56] there may be a reluctance to support qualitative evaluations that focus on the social implications of private women's prisons and on private prisons in general. It is not surprising, then, to find that to date there has been no Australian research that has examined the management of women's private prisons in relation to the quality of confinement, managerial and staff attitudes, the perceptions and morale of women prisoners, and rehabilitative outcomes.

Research into women's prisons, whether they be privately or publicly managed facilities, has become a highly sensitive and politically volatile issue. Now that there are profits at stake it has become very dangerous to criticize prisons or the private corporations that manage them. The result of speaking publicly about prison policies and practices was demonstrated clearly in Victoria in 1993 when former Equal Opportunity Commissioner Moira Rayner sought to prevent the Office of Corrections from moving female prisoners into prisons designed for men. Despite her position of authority, the ramifications of her decision to raise the issue publicly were that the state premier denounced public confidence in her and systematically abolished her position.[57] Similarly, community lawyers and prison activists in Victoria have been threatened with writs of legal defamation for speaking publicly about issues relating to the private management of the Melbourne Women's Correctional Centre. Prison companies have used threats of legal action on the grounds that public debate and criticism may potentially damage their commercial reputation.[58] Threats of legal action have also been leveled at media agencies to the extent that they are now "overly cautious in their reporting of even minor incidents."[59] The media are a valuable source of information for researchers. When the media do not report on incidents occurring in prison because of a "context of fear," constraints and limits are placed on research itself. Private corporations have also attempted to hinder the publication of research findings and to prevent academics who have been engaged in such research from speaking publicly about this period of involvement with correctional authorities.[60]

Moyle argues that because of the danger that private corporations will take legal action it is now "difficult to know where to draw the line in terms of direct engagement in public discussion about the advantages and disadvantages of private sector involvement" in prisons.[61] Now more than ever, community lawyers, prison activists, researchers, and academics are faced with the threat of legal action if critical issues are canvassed in the public arena. This poses significant concerns about the independent nature and direction of research into women's imprisonment and involves questions concerning public accountability and the ownership of knowledge.

Commercial Confidentiality and the Problem of Access

Traditionally, a crucial means of gaining access to information from government correctional departments and agencies for research was under Freedom of Information (FOI) provisions. Freedom of Information laws are in place in all jurisdictions in Australia[62] and are designed to give the public access to information relating to the operation and practices of government departments and agencies. Since their establishment, FOI laws have been viewed as one of the central mechanisms of accountability in Australia; "a prerequisite to the proper functioning of a democratic society."[63] Over the years, government-provided correctional services have been, albeit reluctantly, subject to this public accountability mechanism. However, with the introduction of privatization, researchers are now finding it increasingly difficult to access information relating to the management and service provision of private prisons because recourse to this information has been severely constrained. Under the new system of contractualization, FOI legislation is problematic because it is not clear how exemptions can be interpreted, given the diverse arrangements between governments and private agencies.[64] Commercial confidentiality agreements between governments and private contractors mean that the release of information via FOI legislation can be opposed if it can be demonstrated that "the disclosure will breach the trust between parties" or if it will "adversely affect the commercial interests of the contractor."[65] This was highlighted in 1991 when CCAust refused to give Moyle access to information relating to the contract between it and the Queensland Corrective Services Commission (QCSC) and to policy documents relating to Borallon prison on the grounds of commercial confidentiality. Extensive nondisclosure clauses in the contract between QCSC and CCAust in effect meant that neither party would discuss contractual obligations relating to the prison. As Moyle stated, not having access to particular tender documents, contractual agreements, and financial and policy information held by both parties meant that it was impossible to undertake a comprehensive evaluation of the first privately contracted men's prison in Australia.[66]

Similarly, in 1996, FOI requests made by the Federation of Community Legal Centres in Victoria to access tender documents and contracts relating to the tendering and contracting out of services to Australia's first private women's prison were denied on the basis of commercial confidentiality.[67] In response, the Coburg-Brunswick Community Legal Service took the matter to the Administrative Appeals Tribunal (AAT). Two and a half years later, with the state government still reserving the right to maintain the secrecy of these documents, the AAT appeal process has only just been heard. At the time of this writing, the appeal case had just concluded after running for only two days. The appeal was represented by one community lawyer who stood against sixteen lawyers for the state government and three private prison companies. It remains to be seen whether these documents will eventually be made public. Indeed, the outcome of this case will have serious implications for notions of public accountability and will affect the future of independent research into women's imprisonment.

As this article highlights, there has to date been a number of unsuccessful attempts to gain information relating to the management and organization of private prisons in Victoria and Queensland. Access to
information has been severely restricted and now only limited information
is available regarding the operations, rules, and procedures of privately managed prisons. In effect, information previously in the public domain such as
prison operating manuals, monitoring reports, and general information
relating to prison operations is now bound by commercial confidentiality
and is inaccessible. Furthermore, it is now becoming increasingly common
to encounter delays in response to FOI requests, increased charges for using
FOI legislation,[68] and lengthy and expensive legal actions. Although other
traditional forms of public accountability in Australia are slowly being
eroded,[69] FOI legislation nevertheless remains one of the few avenues left
through which researchers, community lawyers, and prison activists can
access vital information. However, the commercial-in-confidence shield
now being deployed by governments and private companies seriously
threatens access to information via this avenue. The ability to access information regarding the management and operation of women's prisons and
the services and procedures implemented in them is of fundamental concern for researchers. It is very difficult to understand the context of women's
imprisonment, and to locate women's experiences of imprisonment within
this context when researchers do not have access to this information. Without this information it is almost impossible to conduct effective, independent, and comprehensive research. The present situation, characterized by
profits, secrecy, and little government accountability, has significant implications for the future development of correctional policies and practices for
women in private and public prisons.

The Future of Research into Women's Imprisonment?

Researching women's imprisonment has traditionally involved complex
and persistent practical and methodological problems. Feminist researchers
have had to walk a tightrope of theoretical, political, moral, and personal
dilemmas in order to begin to provide some knowledge and understanding
of women's experiences of imprisonment. Now researchers must face a new
set of difficulties that are more complex than ever before. In the context of

economic rationalism and privatization, only limited funds are made available for research into women's imprisonment and access to vital information has been severely curtailed. Indeed, the very political, social, and economic factors that have led to the private management of prisons in Australia and overseas are creating a climate in which opportunities to research women's imprisonment are steadily diminishing. What we see happening in Australia exemplifies the recent international trends in women's imprisonment research. Indeed, if the prevailing economic, social, and political climate persists, opportunities to research women's imprisonment in Australia and overseas will be even more limited and constrained than in the era of public prisons. Under such circumstances, the nature and direction of independent research into women's imprisonment will be even more severely threatened. As a consequence, it is highly probable that the issue of women's imprisonment will continue to be denied and forgotten, and the experiences of those incarcerated behind prison walls will rarely be heard.

NOTES

1. There has been much discussion and debate in research methods literature about the limitations of traditional research paradigms and how they have systematically suppressed discussions on the grounds that such discussions are "nonscientific." See, in particular, Egon Guba and Yvonna Lincoln, "Competing Paradigms in Qualitative Research," in *Handbook of Qualitative Research,* ed. Norman Denzin and Yvonna Lincoln (Thousand Oaks, Calif.: Sage Publications, 1994), 105–17; Maurice Punch, "Politics and Ethics in Qualitative Research," in *Handbook of Qualitative Research,* ed. Norman Denzin and Yvonna Lincoln (Thousand Oaks, Calif.: Sage Publications, 1994), 83–97; and Claire Renzetti and Raymond Lee, *Researching Sensitive Topics* (Newbury Park, Calif.: Sage Publications, 1993).

2. In private communications with a number of Australian and international researchers they have disclosed that they have been reluctant to speak publicly, or to put accounts of the difficulties they encountered in fieldwork to print, because this may risk future research being denied funding or approval by correctional authorities.

3. In particular, see Sandra Harding, *Feminism and Methodology* (Bloomington, Ind.: Indiana University Press, 1987); Chris Weedon, *Feminist Practice and Poststructuralist Theory* (Oxford: Basil Blackwell, 1987); and Liz Stanley, *Feminist Praxis* (New York: Routledge & Kegan Paul, 1990).

4. Lorraine Gelsthorpe and Allison Morris, eds., *Feminist Perspectives in Criminology* (Milton Keynes: Open University Press, 1990); Pat Carlen, "Women, Crime, Feminism and Realism," *Social Justice* 7, no. 4 (1996): 106–23.

5. Linda Hancock, "Economic Pragmatism and the Ideology of Sexism: Prison Policy and Women," *Women's Studies International Forum* 9, no. 1 (1986): 101–107.

6. Alison Liebling, *Suicides in Prison* (London: Routledge, 1992), 123.

7. Patricia Easteal, *The Forgotten Few: Overseas-Born Women in Australian Prisons* (Canberra: Australian Government Publishing Service, 1992).

8. Ibid., 12.

9. Helen Carnaby, *Road to Nowhere: A Report on Women's Housing and Support Needs When Leaving Prison* (Melbourne: Flat Out Inc., 1998).

10. For example, a number of feminist theorists have generated vigorous discussion about the choice of appropriate methods in feminist inquiry and have challenged the traditional assumption that quantitative research methods are somehow more "scientific," "objective," and "vigorous" than qualitative research methods. Despite this, correctional authorities continue to uphold the view that quantitative research methods are a more legitimate source of data collection or theory construction. See Lorraine Gelsthorpe, *Sexism and the Female Offender* (Aldershot: Gower Publishing, 1989); Ann Aungles, *The Prison and the Home: A Study of the Relationship Between Domesticity and Penalty* (Sydney: Institute of Criminology, 1994).

11. Tony Maden, *Women, Prisons, and Psychiatry* (Oxford: Butterworth-Heineman, 1996).

12. Liebling, *Suicides in Prison,* 119.

13. Barbara Denton, "Women's Business: Working in the Drug Economy" (Ph.D. diss., La Trobe University, Melbourne, 1998), 39.

14. Lorraine Gelsthorpe, "Feminist Methodologies in Criminology: A New Approach or Old Wines in New Bottles?" in *Feminist Perspectives in Criminology,* ed. Lorraine Gelsthorpe and Allison Morris (Milton Keynes: Open University Press, 1990), 89–107.

15. Ibid., 96.

16. Ibid.

17. Beth Ritchie, *The Gender Entrapment of Battered Black Women* (New York: Routledge, 1996), 26.

18. Liebling, *Suicides in Prison,* 118.

19. Ibid., 121.

20. Margaret D'Arcy, "Women in Prison: Women's Explanations of Offending Behaviour and Implications for Policy" (M.A. thesis, La Trobe University, Melbourne, 1995).

21. See, in particular, Gelsthorpe, "Feminist Methodologies in Criminology," 89–107; Liebling, *Suicides in Prison; Carnaby, Road to Nowhere;* Di Gursansky et al., *Who's Minding the Kids?: Developing Coordinated Services for Children Whose Mothers Are Imprisoned* (Australia: University of South Australia Social Policy Research Group, 1998).

22. Carnaby, *Road to Nowhere,* 40.

23. Norman Denzin, *Sociological Methods: A Sourcebook* (London: McGraw-Hill, 1978).

24. See Gelsthorpe, *Sexism and the Female Offender;* Liebling, *Suicides in Prison;*

Aungles, *The Prison and the Home*; Allison Morris and Chris Wilkinson, "Responding to Female Prisoners' Needs," *Prison Journal* 75, no. 3 (1995): 295–306; Beverley Fletcher, Lynda Shaver, and Dreama Moon, *Women Prisoners: A Forgotten Population* (Westport, Conn.: Praeger, 1996).

25. Liebling, *Suicides in Prison*, 115.

26. Gelsthorpe, *Sexism and the Female Offender*, 43.

27. Ibid.

28. Liebling, *Suicides in Prison*, 124.

29. Easteal, *The Forgotten Few*, 13.

30. For example, women inmates may feel that their situation in the prison may be compromised if they are critical of particular prison practices, prison staff, or other inmates.

31. John Alford and Deidre O'Neill, eds., *The Contract State: Public Management and the Kennett Government* (Victoria: Deakin University Press, 1994).

32. Frederick Hilmer, Mark Rayner, and Geoffrey Taperell, *National Competition Policy Review* (Canberra: Australian Government Publishing Service, 1993), 1.

33. Patricia Ranald and Richard Thorowgood, *Review of Competitive Neutrality Policies and Local Government Policies of Government under National Competition Policy* (Sydney: University of New South Wales, 1997), 10.

34. John Alford and Deidre O'Neill, "The New Legislative Order," in *The Contract State: Public Management and the Kennett Government*, ed. John Alford and Deidre O'Neill (Victoria: Deakin University Press, 1994), 22–45; Arie Frieberg, "Commercial Confidentiality, Criminal Justice and the Public Interest," *Current Issues in Criminal Justice* 9, no. 2 (1997): 125–52.

35. Catherine Gow and Donna Williamson, "From Penal Colony to Corporate Colony: Australia's Prison Experience" (paper presented at the Critical Resistance Conference, San Francisco, University of California, 1998).

36. Paul Moyle, "Private Sector Involvement in Criminal Justice: Explorations of Recent Developments," *Socio-Legal Bulletin* 9 (1993): 41–42; Janet Chan, "The Privatisation of Punishment: A Review of Key Issues," *Australian Journal of Social Issues* 27, no. 4 (1992): 223–47; Amanda George, "Private Prison: The Punished, The Profiteers, and the Grand Prix of State Approval," *The Australian Feminist Law Journal* 4 (1994): 153–78; Paul Moyle, ed., *Private Prisons and Police: Recent Australian Trends* (Leichhardt, New South Wales: Pluto Press, 1994).

37. Gow and Williamson, "From Penal Colony to Corporate Colony," 10.

38. George Zdenkowski, foreword to *Private Prisons and Police: Recent Australian Trends*, ed. Paul Moyle (Leichardt, New South Wales: Pluto Press, 1994), 11.

39. Paul Moyle, "Privatisation of Prisons and Police: Recent Trends in Australasian Developments," in *Private Prisons and Police: Recent Australian Trends*, ed. Paul Moyle (Leichhardt, New South Wales: Pluto Press, 1994), 15–23.

40. Australian Research Council, *Challenges for the Social Sciences in Australia*, vol. 1. (Canberra: Australian Government Publishing Service, 1998), 25.

41. The Australian Research Council (ARC) is a constituent council of the National Board of Employment, Education, and Training (NBEET). The ARC provides advice to the Federal Minister for Employment, Education Training and Youth Affairs on national research priorities and the coordination of research policy and makes recommendations on the allocation of resources for research.

42. Australian Research Council, *Challenges for the Social Sciences*, 25.

43. Ibid.

44. Christopher Richards, "Education Cuts to Slice Staff by 10%," *Age*, 12 May 1998, 6.

45. Sandra McKay, "Research Bears the Brunt of Job Cuts," *Age*, 30 May 1998, 9.

46. Australian Research Council, *Challenges for the Social Sciences*, 334.

47. Criminology Research Council, *Annual Report 1996-97* (Canberra: Australian Government Publishing Service, 1998).

48. Australian Institute of Criminology, *1997 Annual Report* (Canberra: Australian Institute of Criminology, 1997).

49. Government departments and funding bodies tend to be attracted to traditional positivistic inquiry paradigms, which use quantitative methods to verify or nullify particular hypotheses. In contrast, alternative inquiry paradigms such as those offered by feminist researchers tend to be critical of traditional positivistic ontological, epistemological, and methodological approaches to understanding crime and imprisonment. However, because of the conventional view of research adopted by government departments and funding bodies, these alternative paradigms are not seen as legitimate and "scientific" forms of inquiry.

50. Australian Research Council, *Challenges for the Social Sciences*, 25.

51. Paul Moyle, a research fellow at the University of Western Australia, is the only academic to date to publish discussions that explicitly examine the difficulties of conducting research in a private prison in Australia.

52. Paul Moyle, "Practical and Legislative Restrictions to Access to Information for Private Prison Research in Queensland," *Socio-Legal Bulletin* 7 (1993): 24–30.

53. Richard Harding, *Private Prisons and Public Accountability* (Buckingham, England: Open University Press, 1997), 113.

54. See, in particular, Moyle, *Private Prisons and Police: Recent Australian Trends*; David Shichor, *Punishment for Profit: Private Prisons/Public Concerns* (Thousand Oaks, Calif.: Sage Publications, 1995); Adrian James et al., *Privatising Prisons: Rhetoric and Reality* (Thousand Oaks, Calif.: Sage Publications, 1997).

55. Moyle, "Privatisation of Prisons and Police," 17.

56. Richard Harding, *Private Prisons and Public Accountability*, 114.

57. Moira Rayner, *Rooting Democracy* (St Leonards, New South Wales: Allen and Unwin, 1997).

58. Gow and Williamson, "From Penal Colony to Corporate Colony," 10.

59. Ibid.

60. Moyle, "Privatisation of Prisons and Police," 16.

61. Ibid., 17.

62. Freedom of Information Act, 1982 (Commonwealth); Freedom of Information Act, 1982 (Victoria); Freedom of Information Act, 1989 (New South Wales); Freedom of Information Act, 1989 (Australia Capital Territory); Freedom of Information Act, 1991 (South Australia); Freedom of Information Act, 1991 (Tasmania); Freedom of Information Act, 1992 (Queensland); Freedom of Information Act, 1992 (Western Australia).

63. Australian Law Reform Commission, *Freedom of Information: A Discussion Paper,* no. 59 (Sydney, New South Wales: Australian Law Reform Commission, 1995), 6.

64. Freiberg, "Commercial Confidentiality," 133.

65. Ibid., 130.

66. Moyle, "Practical and Legislative Restrictions," 26, note 17.

67. Shelley Burchfield, "Private Prisons," *The Australian Rationalist* 37 (March 1994): 26-36.

68. O'Neill and Alford, "The New Legislative Order," 22-45.

69. Freiberg, "Commercial Confidentiality," 147.

REFERENCES

Alford, John, and Deidre O'Neill, eds. *The Contract State: Public Management and the Kennett Government.* Victoria: Deakin University Press, 1994.

———. "The New Legislative Order." In *The Contract State: Public Management and the Kennett Government,* edited by John Alford and Deidre O'Neill. Victoria: Deakin University Press, 1994.

Aungles, Ann. *The Prison and the Home: A Study of the Relationship Between Domesticity and Penalty.* Sydney: Institute of Criminology, 1994.

Australian Institute of Criminology. *1997 Annual Report.* Canberra: Australian Institute of Criminology, 1997.

Australian Law Reform Commission. *Freedom of Information: A Discussion Paper.* No. 59. Sydney: Australian Law Reform Commission, 1995.

Australian Research Council. *Challenges for the Social Sciences in Australia.* Vol. 1. Australia: Australian Government Publishing Service, 1998.

Burchfield, Shelley. "Private Prisons." *The Australian Rationalist* 37 (1994).

Carlen, Pat. "Women, Crime, Feminism and Realism." *Social Justice* 7, no. 4 (1996).

Carnaby, Helen. *Road to Nowhere: A Report on Women's Housing and Support Needs When Leaving Prison.* Melbourne: Flat Out Inc., 1998.

Chan, Janet. "The Privatisation of Punishment: A Review of Key Issues." *Australian Journal of Social Issues* 27, no. 4 (1992).

Criminology Research Council. *Annual Report 1996-97.* Canberra: Australian Government Publishing Service, 1997.

D'Arcy, Margaret. "Women in Prison: Women's Explanations of Offending Behaviour and Implications for Policy." Masters thesis, La Trobe University, Melbourne, 1995.

Denton, Barbara. "Women's Business: Working in the Drug Economy." Ph.D. diss., La Trobe University, Melbourne, 1998.

Denzin, Norman. *Sociological Methods: A Sourcebook.* London: McGraw-Hill, 1978.

Denzin, Norman, and Yvonna Lincoln. *Handbook of Qualitative Research.* Thousand Oaks, Calif.: Sage Publications, 1994.

Easteal, Patricia. *The Forgotten Few: Overseas-Born Women in Australian Prisons.* Canberra: Australian Government Publishing Service, 1992.

Fletcher, Beverley, Lynda Shaver, and Dreama Moon. *Women Prisoners: A Forgotten Population.* Westport. Conn.: Praeger Press, 1996.

Freiberg, Arie. "Commercial Confidentiality, Criminal Justice and the Public Interest." *Current Issues in Criminal Justice* 9, no. 2 (1997).

Gelsthorpe, Lorraine. "Feminist Methodologies in Criminology: A New Approach or Old Wine in New Bottles?" In *Feminist Perspectives in Criminology,* edited by Lorraine Gelsthorpe and Allison Morris. Milton Keynes: Open University Press, 1990.

———. *Sexism and the Female Offender.* Aldershot, England: Gower Publishing, 1989.

Gelsthorpe, Lorraine, and Allison Morris, eds. *Feminist Perspectives in Criminology.* Milton Keynes: Open University Press, 1990.

George, Amanda. "Private Prison: The Punished, The Profiteers, and the Grand Prix of State Approval." *The Australian Feminist Law Journal* 4 (1994).

Gow, Catherine, and Donna Williamson. "From Penal Colony to Corporate Colony: Australia's Prison Experience." Paper presented at Critical Resistance Conference, San Francisco, California, September 1998.

Guba, Egon, and Yvonna Lincoln. "Competing Paradigms in Qualitative Research." In *Handbook of Qualitative Research,* edited by Norman Denizen and Yvonna Lincoln. Thousand Oaks, Calif.: Sage Publications, 1994.

Gursansky, Di, Judy Harvey, B. McGrath, and Bev O'Brien. *Who's Minding the Kids?: Developing Coordinated Services for Children Whose Mothers are Imprisoned.* Australia: University of South Australia Social Policy Research Group, 1998.

Hancock, Linda. "Economic Pragmatism and the Ideology of Sexism: Prison Policy and Women." *Women's Studies International Forum* 9, no. 1 (1986).

Harding, Richard. *Private Prisons and Public Accountability.* Buckingham, England: Open University Press, 1997.

Harding, Sandra. *Feminism and Methodology.* Bloomington, Ind.: Indiana University Press, 1987.

Hilmer, Frederick, Mark Rayner, and Geoffrey Taperell. *National Competition Policy Review.* Canberra: Australian Government Publishing Service, 1993.

James, Adrian, Keith Bottomley, Alison Liebling, and Emma Clare. *Privatising Prisons: Rhetoric and Reality.* London: Sage Publications, 1997.

Liebling, Alison. *Suicides in Prison.* London: Routledge, 1992.

Maden, Tony. *Women, Prisons, and Psychiatry.* Oxford: Butterworth-Heineman, 1996.

Morris, Allison, and Chris Wilkinson. "Responding to Female Prisoners' Needs." *Prison Journal* 75, no. 3 (1995).

Moyle, Paul. "Practical and Legislative Restrictions to Access to Information for Private Prison Research in Queensland." *Socio-Legal Bulletin* 7 (1993).

———. "Private Sector Involvement in Criminal Justice: Explorations of Recent Developments." *Socio-Legal Bulletin* 9 (1993).

———. "Privatisation of Prisons and Police: Recent Trends in Australasian Developments." In *Private Prisons and Police: Recent Australian Trends,* edited by Paul Moyle. Leichhardt, New South Wales: Pluto Press, 1994.

Moyle, Paul, ed. *Private Prisons and Police: Recent Australian Trends.* Leichhardt, New South Wales: Pluto Press, 1994.

Punch, Maurice. "Politics and Ethics in Qualitative Research." *In Handbook of Qualitative Research,* edited by Norman Denzin and Yvonna Lincoln. Thousand Oaks, Calif.: Sage Publications, 1994.

Ranald, Patricia, and Richard Thorowgood. *Review of Competitive Neutrality Policies and Local Government Policies of Government Under National Competition Policy.* Sydney: Public Sector Research Centre, University of New South Wales, 1997.

Raynor, Moira. *Rooting Democracy.* St Leonards: Allen and Unwin, 1997.

Renzetti, Claire, and Raymond Lee. *Researching Sensitive Topics.* Newbury Park, Calif.: Sage Publications, 1993.

Ritchie, Beth. *The Gender Entrapment of Battered Black Women.* New York: Routledge, 1996.

Shichor, David. *Punishment for Profit: Private Prisons/Public Concerns.* Thousand Oaks, Calif.: Sage Publications, 1995.

Stanley, Liz. *Feminist Praxis.* New York: Routledge & Kegan Paul, 1990.

Weedon, Chris. *Feminist Practice and Poststructuralist Theory.* Oxford: Basil Blackwell, 1987.

Zdenkowski, George. Foreword to *Private Prisons and Police: Recent Australian Trends,* edited by Paul Moyle. Leichhardt, New South Wales: Pluto Press, 1994.

CONTRIBUTORS

Helen Barnacle was once a heroin addict and experienced nearly eight years of imprisonment as a result of drug-related charges. Her baby daughter spent four of those years with her in prison. Since her release, Helen has qualified as a psychologist and has worked as the Drug Program Director of a community agency in Melbourne. She is currently writing her autobiography and developing drama/music workshops around issues relating to drug and alcohol use for long-term drug users and school children. She also performs with Somebody's Daughter Theatre Company which is composed of women who have experienced drug addiction and imprisonment.

Marcia Bunney obtained her A.A. degree while incarcerated at the California Institution for Women. To set forth for others both her own feelings and those of women similarly situated, she has published articles and essays in such diverse media as the *San Jose Mercury News* (Silver Pen Award, 1990), the *Sonoma County Free Press,* the *California Prisoner,* National Lawyers Guild/Prison Law Project *Legal Journal,* and *Frontiers of Justice, Volume 2: Coddling or Common Sense?* (Brunswick, Maine: Biddle Publishing Co., 1998).

Stephanie R. Bush-Baskette is Assistant Professor of Criminology and Criminal Justice at Florida State University. She is currently completing research for her dissertation that investigates the impact of the war on drugs on Black females. Prior to entering graduate school she practiced law, was elected to the New Jersey State Legislature for three terms, and was appointed to the Governor's Cabinet as Commissioner of the New Jersey Department of Community Affairs. Her research interests include the impact of public policies, girls in the juvenile justice system, and the effects of race, gender, and class in the administration of justice.

Pat Carlen is Professor of Sociology at Bath University and before that was Professor of Criminology and Founder of the Department of Criminology at Keele University. She has published fourteen books on the relationships between criminal and social justice, the latest being *Sledgehammer: Women's Imprisonment at the Millennium* (Macmillan 1998) and *Crime Unlimited? Questions for the 21st Century* (edited with Rod Morgan [Macmillan]). In 1997 she was recipient of the American Society of Criminology's Sellin-Glueck award for international contributions to criminology.

Sandy Cook is a senior lecturer in the School of Law and Legal Studies at La Trobe University. Her research and teaching are in the areas of violence against women, disability issues, and criminal justice. She is an associate editor of *Violence Against Women* and is on the editorial board of *Inclusive Education.* Prior to academic life, she worked as a teacher in prisons and youth training centers and the women's prison in Victoria.

Susanne Davies is the Director of the Women's Studies Program and a lecturer in the School of Law and Legal Studies at La Trobe University. Her teaching, research, and publication interests span sociolegal history, critical criminology, feminist epistemology, and sexuality studies. She was a founding member of the editorial board of the *Australian Feminist Law Journal* for five years and a founding member of the Australian Feminist Law Foundation.

Karlene Faith received her Ph.D. in the History of Consciousness at the University of California (Santa Cruz). A prisoners' rights educator and activist since the 1960s, she has done research in numerous women's prisons in California and in Canada, her home country. Her publications include *Unruly Women: The Politics of Confinement and Resistance* (Press Gang, 1993). Since 1989 she has been on the faculty of the School of Criminology, Simon Fraser University.

Amanda George has been a community lawyer and prison activist since the early 1980s. She is involved in an accommodation service for women leaving prison and has written on the issues of women in prison and prison privatization. In 1996 she was awarded the Australian Avon Spirit of Achievement Award for her work in domestic violence and women's prisons issues.

Evelyn Gilbert received a Ph.D. in criminology from Florida State University, with a specialization in homicide and women in law enforcement. Her current research interests include ethnoracial minorities in the criminal justice system, violence among the elderly, and criminal justice education.

Cherry Grimwade is a doctoral candidate in the School of Law and Legal Studies at La Trobe University in Melbourne. Her postgraduate research examines coronial investigations and inquests into women's deaths in custody in Victoria between 1980 and 1998. Over the past two years, Cherry has worked on three research projects that have focused on representations of sexed crime in the media, an evaluation of an innovative management program in a juvenile correctional institution, and post-release mortality of women prisoners in Victoria.

Venezia Kingi has a postgraduate degree in psychology from Victoria University of Wellington. She is currently working on a doctoral thesis in criminology that examines the problems encountered by mothers in prison. Venezia has lectured and tutored in criminology at the Institute of Criminology at Victoria University and has recently been involved in a research project relating to the decision making processes of juries.

Elizabeth Morgan is a certified plastic and reconstructive surgeon in private practice in Washington, D.C. She has done biomedical research at Oxford University and is currently a lecturer at the American University, Washington, D.C. She has published scientific chapters and articles, is the author of four popular books on surgery, and was the *Cosmopolitan* medical columnist from 1973 to 1980. From 1986 to 1989, Elizabeth was jailed for civil contempt three times, the third time for twenty-five months, for refusing District of Columbia Family Court orders that she continue to send her daughter on unsupervised visits with her father/abuser. The U.S. Congress, based on its special oversight of Washington, D.C., passed legislation that set Dr. Morgan free from jail in 1989 and passed further legislation that allowed her daughter to return to the United States from New Zealand in 1997, free from forced visits with her father/abuser.

Allison Morris is Professor in criminology and the Director of the Institute of Criminology at the University of Wellington. Her special research interests lie in the fields of juvenile justice and the treatment of females in the criminal justice system. She has published extensively in these areas and her most recent publications include *Women, Crime, and Criminal Justice* (1987), *Women and the Penal System* (1988), and *Feminist Perspectives in Criminology* (1990).

Barbara Owen is a prison sociologist with particular interests in the subculture of women's prisons, new forms of in-prison drug treatment, and prison ethnography. Her recent monograph is *In the Mix: Struggle and Survival in a Women's Prison*. Currently a Professor in the Criminology Department, California State University-Fresno, she has also conducted research in the evaluation of prison drug treatment programs, the gender-specific needs of girls and young women in the juvenile justice system, and two comprehensive surveys of the adult and youth prison populations in California.

Monika Platek is an Associate Professor in the Law Faculty, Warsaw University, Poland. She teaches comparative law, criminology, and feminist jurisprudence. At Warsaw University, Monika co-founded Poland's first and only interdisciplinary Gender Studies program. Monika has researched and taught in Washington, Chicago, Oslo, and Paris. She is Chairperson of the Polish Association of Legal Education and was involved in introducing Poland's first community legal center. Monika has two daughters, Maria (12 years old) and Natalia (11 years old), and she hopes through her work to provide them with an environment that is just and friendly toward women.

Carol Ransley is a postgraduate student in the School of Law and Legal Studies at La Trobe University in Australia and is currently employed as the Refugee Youth Policy Officer at Ethnic Youth Issues Network in Melbourne. A long-time Burma advocate, she recently returned from two years in Thailand where she worked extensively with Burmese women migrant workers, refugees, and political activists living in Thailand.

Lauren Shanahan was born and raised in Melbourne. She was a heroin addict for twenty years and, because of the lifestyle it necessitated, she was imprisoned five times between 1989 and 1997. At present, she is living in a Buddhist Center in rural Victoria and is rediscovering that life does indeed have meaning.

Margaret Shaw is a research consultant and sociologist who teaches in the Department of Sociology and Anthropology at Concordia University, Montreal, Canada. Prior to moving to Canada in 1986 she worked as a research and policy advisor in the Home Office Research and Planning Unit and conducted a number of projects on sentencing, delinquency, crime prevention, and prisons. Over the past ten years, she has undertaken extensive research relating to women's imprisonment and has published extensively in this area. Her current work includes research on classification and risk management in women's prisons and on restorative justice. She is a board member of the Canadian Association of Elizabeth Fry Societies and the Quebec Elizabeth Fry Society.

INDEX